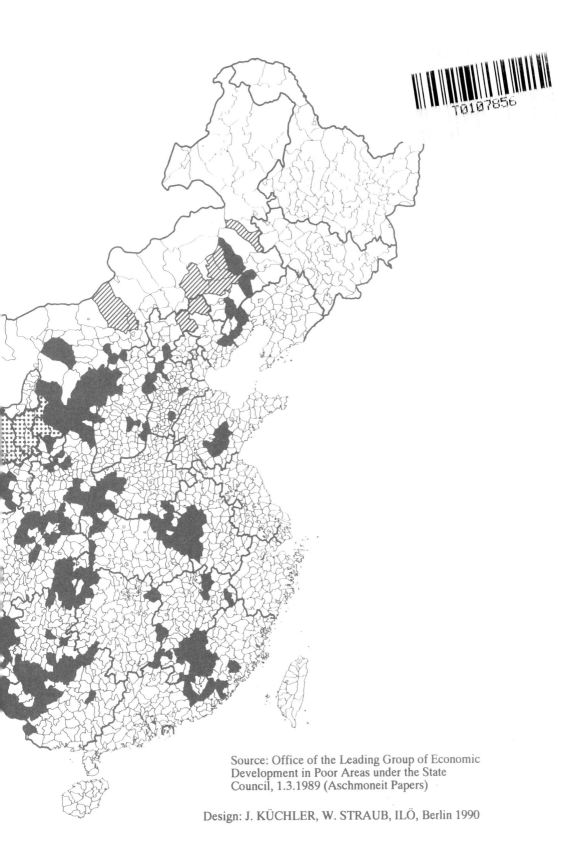

Source: Office of the Leading Group of Economic
Development in Poor Areas under the State
Council, 1.3.1989 (Aschmoneit Papers)

Design: J. KÜCHLER, W. STRAUB, ILÖ, Berlin 1990

REMAKING PEASANT CHINA

REMAKING PEASANT CHINA

Problems of rural development and institutions
at the start of the 1990s

Edited by
Jørgen Delman, Clemens Stubbe Østergaard,
and Flemming Christiansen

AARHUS UNIVERSITY PRESS

AARHUS UNIVERSITY PRESS
Aarhus University
DK-8000 Aarhus C, Denmark

Preface

The November 1989 European Conference on Agricultural and Rural Development in China (ECARDC) and the revised papers which constitute this volume, reflect the contributions of many individuals and some organizations. Our hope, in proposing a conference, was to bring together scholars from all over Europe whose work was relevant to understanding China's rural development. Our aim was not only to provide a forum for discussing questions of mutual interest, but to create a lasting network between individuals sitting in a variety of European research institutions. On the strength of such a network we further wanted to link up with scholars in America, Asia and Australia working on the cutting edge of research in this field. To that end, we began by inviting Dwight Perkins and Vivienne Shue to take part in the first conference. The meeting itself took place in the agreeable surroundings of the Sandbjerg Manor House, set amid Danish farmland.

We want to thank the discussants for the care with which they took apart the papers; we also want to thank Liu Yu'an of Shandong University and Elizabeth Croll, Stephan Feuchtwang, Jan-Erik Gustafsson, Sheila Hillier, George Waardenburg and Dwight M. Perkins for their particular contributions to the success of the gathering.

Conferences not only need ideas and people, but also organisations willing to support them. We were fortunate to have the backing of the Danish Social Science Research Council, the Daloon Foundation and the Aarhus University Research Foundation. The Institute of Political Science and the East Asian Institute at Aarhus University also supported us. Ivy Mortensen contributed a lot to the succes of our meeting by keeping the many strands together and holding the lines open to our participants. So did Anette Riber. During the conference itself we were thankful for the never-failing help of Anette Aarestrup, Lars Buhl and Henrik Westerby. The index has been prepared by Anette Aarestrup.

The Danish SSRC and the Aarhus University Research Foundation have kindly supported the production of the book. At the Aarhus University Press, Tønnes Bekker-Nielsen has exerted himself to speed this book through publication, yet at the same time give it an appealing format. The scoop of having a splendid map-version of the Life Quality Index of China we owe first to Walter Aschmoneit, second to the good offices of the Institut für Landschaftsökonomie, Technische Universität Berlin, of Professor J. Küchler and cartographer Wolfgang Straub. To all we wish to express our gratitude.

We are gratified to find that the ECARDC network has indeed been established and that we can look forward to increasing cooperation with an even larger circle of the scholars sharing our interest.

October 1990

Jørgen Delman
Flemming Christiansen
Clemens Stubbe Østergaard

Contents

The Framework of Resource Development: Land and Water

Appendix

Tables and Figures

Introduction

Clemens Stubbe Østergaard

Recently, after a good Chinese banquet, I asked two leading Chinese intellectuals their opinion on the main problem facing Chinas countryside. One fell asleep, the other fell silent. Funnily enough, when I had asked students on Tiananmen in May 1989 where the peasants were, their answer was: They are all asleep. Though generally China's intellectuals could not care less where the rice comes from, after the Mao-era a lot of serious research *has* gone into agricultural development. This may in part be a spin-off from sending intellectuals to the countryside in previous years, and it has certainly been stimulated by the creation of important research institutes.

In Europe too, over the last few years, China's agricultural and rural development has attracted increasing attention from researchers. A number of European organisations have built up quite extensive programmes of cooperation with China in the field of agriculture. There may be many reasons for the increased interest, such as a growing recognition that agricultural and rural development is—after all—the basis for all Chinese development, the mass of information and statistics now flowing from China, the improved possibilities for academic exchange with Chinese researchers, the chances of field work in China, and finally the recognition by the Chinese government that China's agriculture can benefit from technical assistance from outside. The establishment of The European Conference on Agricultural and Rural Development in China (ECARDC) is an expression of the need of European researchers to meet, discuss and share information and experiences among themselves and with European development assistance agencies, as well as concerned Chinese researchers. An important intention has been to establish a forum which will be cross-disciplinary and which will also attempt to bring together more technically oriented research with social-science based research and work in the humanities.

The present volume is a first result of these endeavours. Claude Aubert opens with a tour d'horizon of the basic problems in agriculture at the start of the decade of the 1990s. Whether they should be termed crisis or stagnation, he views them from the side of the peasants, while Jørgen Delman's work on projections sets us squarely in the chairs of the policy-makers and lets us see the problems as they perceive them. Projections are, as the author states, "catalogues of policy options which represent the anticipated convergence of reformist developmental goals and policies with growth potentials and potential structural adjustment to future needs."

Having raised the problems and the goals, we turn in Vivienne Shue's article to the state, the agent of change (whose agent?), that is to carry out policy. Future state-society relations may develop in distinctly different directions, she shows on the basis of case studies. The contrasting paths of two counties is a reminder of the care that should be taken in generalizing statements about China. One of the most incisive ways in which state policy impinges on the household is in the one-child campaign. As Delia Davin makes clear, there are momentous medium-term consequences for gender relations in the present modified version employed in rural China.

The state has certainly been expanding its share in alleviating rural poverty and increasing social security. Johannes Küchler describes in particular the new regional development strategies of the state towards the areas of persistent rural poverty which in the 1980s have emerged from hiding. The wide question of rural social security is treated by Athar Hussain who shows how policies in a number of fields, including the organisation of the economy, interact to affect the final outcome: the individuals and the household's security from deprivation. Standards of social welfare vary enormously, and in coastal provinces rural industry has become a new source of finance.

This is a point which is underscored in Ole Odgaards subsequent analysis of the individual enterprises and their impact on distribution of income locally. The paper gives particular emphasis to the way enterprise revenues are redistributed by local government, yielding some unexpected results. At this point in the volume we again come close to the changes affecting the household level. Between 1979 and 1985 one out of every five peasants has 'relocated himself, taken a new vocation, or changed his social status' (Parish, 1985). Flemming Christiansen looks at the bureaucratically imposed barriers to mobility, the wealth of labour opportunities, and the increased social inequality in a period of accelerated social change.

From the household level we finally move to analysis of the crucial factors land and water. Both are extremely scarce resources, and the need for using them efficiently is an issue, which attracts continuous attention from both national and local leadership.

In his article, Eduard B. Vermeer traces, from a historical point of view, how food-deficient Fujian Province has attempted over time, to make up for lack of food for its people by reclaiming so-called 'waste' land in the mountains or on coastal flat lands to grow grain or to grow other crops, e.g. tea and tree crops, which might be exchanged for grain in the external market. Various initiatives and institutional forms are examined. Dr. Vermeer concludes, on a somewhat positive note, that a growing concern for both economic results and environmental costs will be evident in local land reclamation efforts, despite an anticipated further reclamation of hill-slopes in Fujian's hinterlands and the well-known serious effects of such over-zealous interventions, like for example soil erosion.

The final article in the volume describes the impact of the rural reforms of the early 1980s on central policies on irrigation management at the collective level. In the article, Thiagarajan Manoharan examines legal, institutional, financial and investment aspects from a policy point of view. The author finds that, although various efforts to enhance the decision-making and fund generating capacity of local governments and various types of water user bodies are evident, the communist party intends to remain in firm control in this important field, which is not only the 'life-blood' of China's agriculture, but one of the basic institutional building blocks of rural society as well. In a series of conclusions, Dr. Manoharan posits: 1) that reforms appear not to have spurred an expansion of the effectively irrigated area; 2) that irrigation facilities are in general need of repair, regular maintenance and upgrading; 3) that authorities at the grassroot level have been able to increase the amount of locally generated funds to cover the expenses of the operation of irrigation facilities, but that the lack of state investment in infrastructural projects remains a constraint; 4) that new forms of contracts have been introduced to increase management efficiency, but that upgrading of local technical staff will have to match such management innovations to make them effective; 5) that until viable formats for cooperation between water user bodies and the local bureaucracy have been found, democratic influence on irrigation management will remain difficult.

Dr. Manoharan based his research on a variety of original materials, which are difficult to access. The editors have found that the bibliography at the end of the article might be useful for those professionally interested in the subject, and therefore it was included in its entirety although not all works are quoted in the revised version of the article.

Some central themes

Three themes are repeatedly taken up by the authors: What is the actual and the proper role of the state in rural development? What are the effects of current development on China's social goals? How are rural-urban relations and the environment affected by rural developments? In addition, I shall discuss the impact of the countryside on post-Tiananmen politics, as well as the indications of a conservatively influenced change in agricultural policy.

The role of the state

It has been argued that the problems in agriculture in the 1970s were not really rooted in the question of incentives at the micro-level, i.e. family vs. collective farming. Rather they had to do with macro-issues of government planning and administrative strategies around agricultural investment, pricing, loans and so on. Decollectivisation merely offered itself as the cheapest solution, and "living off policy" obviated the need to find money for loan funds or raise rural prices. In this way short term gains were possible, primarily based on freedom from cadre interference in cultivation decisions, without fundamentally disturbing the urban bias of development.(Parish, 1985).

This agenda still seems in evidence. Aubert points to the role of State grain marketing organisations in keeping down prices to peasants in order not to affect the standard of living in urban bases important to the Party. The implicit choice of urban interests is revealed in the State budget's niggardly investments in agriculture, even after the potential of decollectivisation exhausted itself by 1984. Government expenditures on agriculture as a percentage of total expenditures decreased from 13.7 in 1979 to 8.1 percent in 1988. Over the same period, State capital construction funds invested in agriculture declined from 11.9 percent of total construction funds to just 2.9 per cent. The rural areas are still funding 1/3 of the state's investment in the state's own industry.

At the level of local government, the picture has changed with reforms. Shue concludes that the Mao-era produced counties turned inwards economically, and with a cellularized or parcelized pattern of political authority. "Small, but complete", they led to rural social adaptations such as increased reliance on connections and localism, both of them delegitimizing the regime further. With reforms, so much motion was introduced that it became impossible for the undifferentiated "thin" state to ride it out: the new physical mobility and the multiform restructuring of society into new socio-economic groupings necessitated a thickened, more complex organisation. In both of the cases investigated by Shue, the state has obtained a bigger role, that is the state has surprisingly been strengthened under decentralising and depoliticizing reforms. But in one case it has become more responsive to social demands, in the other local government has become a competitive economic actor pursuing its own ends. And those ends would seem to have an urban bias.

The problem of rural bureaucracies is also raised by Delman who points to their 'colonial relationship' with farmers. This perpetuates an immature, risk-averting type of farming. Davin points to the increased power that the system of planned birth gives to local officials. Furthermore, it is a generally recognized problem that the state remains active in areas where it should have withdrawn, Christiansen shows this to be the case in the field of recruitment of labour, and Odgaard identifies local government that remains in place and with the kind of strength found by Shue. The rise of an interdependence between local government and private entrepreneurs will not necessarily change this, but the strength will be used differently. None of these developments are irreversible, it may be noted. The autonomy of society, such as it is, has been granted, not grabbed.

The effects of development on China's social goals

Generally, social goals like education, welfare, health, and sex equality, will suffer with declining rural support for social services. Services offered by cadre-dominated collective organisations may of course be useless, or even harmful to agricultural production. But, as Parish has noted, in the general enthusiasm for agricultural reforms there has been a tendency to forget progress made earlier. In a cooler comparative, historical perspective, past experiments with collective organisation may well be judged relatively or partially successful. Hussain points out that the responsibility system cut the ground from underneath social solidarity founded on collective cultivation. This has threatened the demise of the *wubao* system of guaranteed income for households lacking labour due to sickness, deaths or old age. The move towards family farming must be accompanied either by the growth of tax-financed social insurance or private insurance to cover the new risks. Ironically, it is not just the poorest who have become less safe, the richest households may, as Vermeer notes, also feel less safe because of local jealousy. The policy of letting state grants go to the top five per cent of peasants is not helping matters.

Health care has suffered, at least temporarily. Wholesale rejection of the Cultural Revolution period has led to the death of the systems responsible for extension of primary medical care to the villages, such as cooperative health insurance, barefoot doctors and transferred medical personnel from the cities. There may also be an element of wilful neglect on the part of a city-based leadership. Reappearance of parasitical and infectious diseases, Hussain notes, indicates a 'weakening of the social immune system' established by health campaigns. They now have to be paid for, and lack of public finance precludes this.

Results reached in the area of gender equality are threatened by many separate developments. But Davin convincingly shows that the gender-modified one-child policy will lead to girls generally growing up under less privileged conditions than boys. Some solace may be found in the consideration that in the many families where a girl is the only child, more resources will be spent on her education and upbringing than earlier.

Take out the map at the back of this book and look at it. The overall picture, as developed by Küchler, is a sombre one. Though the successes of rural reform have reduced the number of rural absolute poor, the problem still touches a third of Chinas counties or those characterised by mountains or minorities, boundaries or base-areas of the revolution. Many of the problems raised in this section can be solved in richer counties, where it is possible to establish insurance systems. But in the poorest counties, with extreme natural disadvantages, this solution is out of reach and they must depend on outside help.

Occupational diversification in the countryside, as shown by Christiansen, naturally leads to increased social inequality. As labour insurance is also lacking in rural industry, the lay-offs of recent years will have rising social problems. Paradoxically, the increased mobility of peasants may mean fewer state funds for the rural areas. Since the present regime is set on maintaining urban living standards, increased migration will mean that more state investment will go to the cities.

Rural urban conflicts and environmental problems

The rural-urban conflict has been touched on already. Since peasants are difficult to mobilise politically, short of a revolution, it makes political sense to 'pander to the urban base areas', in Aubert's words. The 1988 budget allocating 32 billion to urban residents and four billion to the peasants is but one expression of this. The dilemma is of course that looking after the interests of the urbanites sets limit to the extension of market forces in the countryside. Has the urban-rural divide begun to crumble, as implied by Christiansen? It might be more safe to speak of an extension of the economic sphere of the cities, drawing in land, capital and temporary labour power from surrounding counties.

Environmental problems can also be passed on to the peri-urban communities. Küchler notes the extent of environmental problems, not least in the poorer areas. Large-scale deforestation and grassland desertification have been going on throughout the reform-decade, and the water table in North China has continued to drop. Helping poor areas thus becomes helping the national economy as a whole. The environmental arena is an unpredictable political factor too. A sudden worsening of conditions in this field could lead renewed to calls for central planning and neo-authoritarian leadership. It might at the very least increase the role of local government in enforcement. In the event of a crisis, the marketization of Chinese agriculture could be halted because of the difficulties of making eco-farming systems competitive in the short run.

Towards a civil society?

Drawing on careful analysis, Aubert sees the only hope for the rural areas as lying in genuine peasant autonomy, with proper peasant organisations. Awareness of the need to promote voluntary cooperation is shared by other contributors, though everyone knows it to be difficult in practice. It requires a certain educational level, as well as a shared 'democratic spirit'. The Hebei county authorities in Shue's field research would likely assist in developing associations to represent emerging social groups with divergent interests. The users associations described by Manoharan are a possible vehicle. Another, functional, area which might see autonomous associations forming is cooperative insurance schemes. Perhaps it is really a good thing that the state is holding back in this sector, because it might permit the formation of genuinely cooperative associations. This would help to build the civil society which proved material in European democratization, helping incidentally to train peasants to express interests and formulate demands.

Impact of the countryside on post-Tiananmen politics

Where were the peasants in the events of May-June 1989? A quick answer would be: 'at the Spring harvest'. More accurately, they did not share the concerns of the demonstrators, except perhaps for the distaste for corruption. Furthermore, the impression made by the favourable policies between 1978 and 1985 still lingered. Income increases and freedom from supervision by cadres still gave the leadership of Deng Xiaoping a certain legitimacy. The short-term gains had had their effect, and no one in the top leadership attempted to mobilize the peasants. Since then the record 1989 grain harvest has filled the stores. 'Unrest in the countryside stems from problems in the countryside', as the saying goes. Those problems exist, but so far only in manageable blocks. There is anger at the one-child policy (though tempered by its modification), there is discontent over the uncertainty of policy which is never fixed in law, and there is the humiliation of political corruption around inputs and land contracts. In some places peasants have been forced to dismantle collective organisations which worked for *them*, in other places the lack of state investment is deeply resented or the lack of liquidity of state purchase organs and rural banks rankles. But nowhere does there seem to be organized discontent, or even information-networks , and sporadic rebellions can still be handled by show of force. The most volatile element is the 'floating population', which after a taste of towns, travelling and a fast life is now having to return to villages which hold nothing for them. Particularly not since the closing of millions of rural enterprises by decree or by credit strangulation. The floating population are not the only peasants to travel, and increasingly peasants are becoming aware, as never before, of the difference in their living conditions and those of the urban population.

Incredibly or inevitably, the post-Tiananmen regime in 1990 used the same medicine for the villages as for the rest of the country: a campaign to strengthen rural Party committees and branches, increased political controls on rural officials and people, and a building up of government and cooperative institutions at the village and township level. They had been crumbling, leaving Party members too close to peasants for comfort.

New agricultural policy?

Stagnation in grain and cotton output, and increased dependence on imports, led the central leadership to formulate a 'new' agricultural policy on the eve of the 1990s (Travers 1990). There would be no price rises on agricultural products, but the breakthrough was to come from increased yields on low- and medium yield fields. This was to come about mainly through increased investment, improved agricultural technology and better management.

The central government was not itself very eager to invest. In fact, an estimate of the 1989 investment showed 3.6 billion yuan from the central government and 11 billion yuan from the peasants. There was little cash to spare in 1990: local governments rely on village and township enterprises which had had declining growth rates in 1989. Peasants were scared off investing in land or irrigation in the reigning uncertain situation, and they did not feel at ease with the small voluntary cooperatives because they smacked of the 1950s start of collectivisation.

As to agricultural technological transfer, there were problems too, cf. Vermeer in this volume. Low yield regions also have less money for agricultural extension programmes. And government has not been keeping agricultural research abreast with sufficient funding. The risk-bearing capacity of the commune system was able to support agricultural technology-transfer in low-yield areas, but in its absence there were difficulties in implementing this part of the policy.

The third element, improving management needs, is conditioned on the possibility of improved education for children and grown-ups. Again, poorer low-yield areas relying on local funding could not easily achieve good, cheap schooling for everyone.

The premises of the entire policy seemed faulty: investment was not forthcoming, technologies were not there to be transferred and the extension services were lacking, in any case the end-users were among the less-educated farmers and nothing indicated that the available educational system would change that.

Agriculture, like the rest of China, seemed to be waiting for leaders with vision, imagination and political will.

References

William Parish (ed.), *China's Rural Development*, M.E. Sharpe 1985.

Lee Travers, "Reemphasizing Agriculture", *China Business Review*, July-August 1990.

AGRICULTURAL DEVELOPMENT: ISSUES AND PROJECTIONS

The Agricultural Crisis in China at the End of the 1980s

Claude Aubert

The bloody repression of the democratic movement on June 4th 1989 confirmed the Communist government's refusal to undertake any reform of the political system. This dramatic negation, which served to strengthen the dominant position of the gerontocrats espousing the most orthodox hard-line 'socialism', also jeopardizes the economic reforms and China's opening to the West, despite loud declarations to the contrary on the part of the present leadership, afraid of scaring off foreign investment. But were not economic reforms already stagnating well before June 4th, due to lack of political changes? These changes alone could have injected the reforms with new vigour and pull them out of the bureaucratic doldrums into which they had sunk. And this is precisely the case of agricultural reforms which, for the past four years, have been paralysed by a growing crisis.

An Agricultural Crisis or a Crisis of Crop Production?

The 1984 bumper harvests had magnified what was, rightly, considered to be the success of the agricultural reforms and particularly of decollectivisation which was carried out between 1979 and 1982 (Aubert 1984). At 407 million tons, grain production had advanced by nearly 100 million tons within a six year period, i.e., as much as in the 20 years that agriculture had been collectivised. Cotton and oilseeds had tripled their 1977 (pre-reform) levels at six and 12 million tons respectively. Meat production had also doubled following a period of stagnation which had lasted nearly 15 years (see table 1). Peasant rations had finally taken off and silos were literally overflowing (20 million tons of surplus grain production and over two million tons surplus cotton in 1984) (Aubert 1985). These successes ratified the policy of a return to household farming which had recently been rehabilitated, as well as the optimum use of the soil as a consequence of decreased centralised crop planning. These successes, which were founded on putting into effect the production potential which had previously been hampered by the collective structure of the Peoples' Communes, were to be of a short duration for the crisis set in as early as 1985.

In 1985, cereal production fell to 379 million tons (a decline of seven per cent) while cotton fell to four million tons (a decline of 34 per cent). Only oil seeds continued to advance with a record harvest of nearly 16 million tons, but the following year this fell to under 15 million tons. This was to be a long-lasting crisis for, up to 1988, none of these three Chinese main agricultural crops (which alone account for 87 per cent of the total cropped land surface) have recovered their record levels: in 1988, grains totalled only 394 million tons, cotton only four million and oil seeds, 13 million tons. In fact, all agricultural production was affected: jute, having peaked at four million tons in 1985, fell to one million tons, while sugar cane has been stagnating at around 50 million tons since 1985. Only beetroot, tea, tobacco and fruit production has risen in the last four years.

Table 1. Agricultural production and peasant incomes, 1977-1988

Year	1977	1978	1979	1980	1981	1982	1983	1984	1985	1986	1987	1988
Production (million tons):												
Grains	283	316	332	321	325	355	387	407	379	392	403	394
Cotton	2.05	2.17	2.21	2.71	2.97	3.6	4.64	6.26	4.15	3.54	4.25	4.15
Oilseeds	4.0	5.2	6.4	7.7	10.2	11.8	10.6	11.9	15.8	14.7	15.3	13.2
Sugarcane	17.8	21.1	21.5	22.8	29.7	36.9	31.1	39.5	51.5	50.2	47.4	49.1
Jute	0.86	1.09	1.09	1.1	1.26	1.06	1.02	1.49	4.12	1.42	1.14	1.08
Red Meat	7.8	8.6	10.6	12.1	12.6	13.5	14.0	15.4	17.6	19.2	19.9	21.9
Income/p	125	134	160	191	223	270	310	355	398	424	463	545
Index		100	117	132	150	179	202	225	232	233	237	235

Income/p = Income per capita, in current yuan prices
Index = Index of per capita income, in real terms

Sources: NYNJ 1980, p. 36; TJNJ 1989, p. 198-200, 213, 688, 743.

It is remarkable that the crisis appears not to have affected meat production, which increased from 15 to 22 million tons between 1984 and 1988. This agricultural crisis, therefore, is mainly a crisis of crops' production. Up until 1988 at least, the crisis did not concern either the entire rural economy since small-scale, non-agricultural enterprises in the countryside continued to grow and accounted for as much as 54 per cent of the total value of rural production, employing more than 90 million workers in 1988 (compared with 50 million in 1984) (RMRB 1 March 1989, TJNJ 1989, 246).

The crisis was none the less real for all that and has resulted in a stagnation of peasant revenues since 1984. True, because of the rise in agricultural prices, peasant nominal revenues have continued to increase sharply: from 355 yuan per person per year in 1984 (compared with 134 yuan in 1978), to 545 yuan in 1988. But in real terms this increase has been practically non-existent, for inflation has offset any increase whereas previously, between 1978 and 1984, peasant purchasing power had more than doubled (from an index of 100 in 1978 to 225 in 1984 and 235 in 1988; cf. table 1).

Natural Disasters

Was not this limited, but nevertheless real, crisis largely a result of climatic conditions? There is no doubt that the natural disasters which have befallen China since 1985 have been extremely serious. In 1988, an exceptionally severe drought affected the regions from the Hubei and Hunan basins up to Henan and Shandong in the northern plain, while Heilongjiang in the Northeast suffered from severe floods. A total of 51 million hectares were affected, of which 24 million severely damaged (five million deprived of any harvest whatsoever) (NMRB 27 February 1989). As a result of these calamities, five million tons of grain were lost out of a total harvest which fell by nearly ten million tons between 1987 and 1988. Similarly, in 1985, floods in Manchuria alone caused the loss of eight million tons of grain, out of a total which fell by 28 million tons in the same year. Since the damaged areas covered, on average, over 20 per cent of the total grain cropped area in the past four years, the impact of these natural disasters was, of course, far higher during this period than in the previous decade when the percentage of the damaged grain cropped area was only between 14 and 15 per cent (TJNJ 1989, 229).

It is hazardous to try and explain how natural disasters arise. Nevertheless, certain Chinese economists do consider that they may have been the consequence of poor upkeep of the irrigation network since the onset of the reforms, due to insufficient government funds and the lack of collective mobilisation on the part of the villagers (Zhou Zhiping 1989). Certainly government investments in 'agricultural basic construction' (land and water) fell sharply after 1980 from 6.24 billion yuan in 1979 to 2.42 billion in 1981, rising to only 4.72 billion in 1988. In terms of percentage of the state budget, these investments thus fell from 4.9 per cent in 1979 to 1.8 per cent in 1988 (the fall being of a comparable size when expressed in terms of percentage of national agricultural revenue: 5.1 per cent in 1979, 1.2 per cent in 1988) (TJNJ 1989, 29, 488, 657 and 669). The irrigation network certainly suffered as a result, reservoirs being poorly equipped to handle drought situations because they were silted up, wells being damaged, barrages weaker, etc. These factors all combined to intensify the damage when a natural catastrophe hit. Thus during the great drought of 1988, 70 per cent of the wells in Anhui province were not operational, just at the time they were most needed (Yang Zhenhuai 1988).

There was therefore, undoubtedly, a certain deterioration of the irrigation network. On the other hand, the stagnation of the surface of irrigated land since 1979 (45 million hectares, i.e., just under 50 per cent of the total cultivated area) is more a consequence of insurmountable geographic constraints than the result of this lack of investments. And, overall, the resilience of the Chinese agricultural apparatus has proved to be not so bad in the past few years if we consider that the figures concerning the natural disasters of 1985 and 1988 were the worst China has seen since the three black years of the Great Leap Forward. Under such unfavorable circumstances, production simply stagnated or fell by several percentage points while consumption remained at its high 1984 levels.

It would seem, therefore, that the above-mentioned hypothesis of the cause of the crisis (compounded by natural disasters), namely the government's disengagement from agriculture together with a decrease in investment following decollectivisation, should be viewed in context, even though, in the long term, there clearly is a problem with the level of investment in land and irrigation.

In fact, the fall in grain, cotton and oilseed production of the past few years was not solely due to climatic reasons, however serious these might have been, but was also due to variations in the cropped land area. And these variations were the direct result of decisions made by the peasants, which in turn were largely dependent on the price the state was offering for the various crops.

Grain Prices

According to the farmers themselves, grain prices have been the underlying reason for the growing disinterest in grain production and have resulted in the decrease in both the grain

Table 2. Grain procurements and prices, 1978-1988 (in million tons)

Year	1978	1979	1980	1981	1982	1983	1984	1985	1986	1987	1988
Output	316	332	321	325	355	387	407	379	392	405	394
index	100	105	102	103	112	122	129	120	124	128	125
Total gross proc. (1)	62	72	73	79	92	120	142	116	135	141	138
Idem, "maoy." (2)	51	60	61	68	78	102	117	108	115	121	120
per cent	100	100	100	100	100	100	100	100	100		
of which:											
quotas (3)	38	35	34	30	30	30	30	79	63	53	50
per cent	75	58	56	44	38	29	26	73	55	44	n.a.
above quotas (3)	13	21	23	33	42	67	77				
per cent	25	35	38	49	54	66	66				
above contract procurements (4)								12	32	42	n.a.
per cent								11	28	35	n.a.
free market	0	4	4	5	6	5	10	17	20	26	n.a.
per cent	0	7	7	7	8	5	9	16	17	21	n.a.
price yuan/ton (5)	263	331	361	382	392	393	395	416	466	509	564
index	100	126	137	145	149	149	150	158	177	193	214

1. Total gross procurements
2. Gross procurements in "maoyiliang" (commercial grains)
3. Quotas of procurements at list prices (volumes of contracts after 1984)
4. Above contract procurements paid at "negotiated prices"
5. Average price for all grain procured to the state (yuan/ton of "commercial grain")

Sources: TJNJ 1985, 547; TJNJ 1989, 198, 613, 615, 620, 714; SYNJ 1988, 55; WJNJ 1988, 121.

cropped area and the use of fertilizer for grain cultivation. Numerous Chinese economists, too, consider that the price problem is the source of the cereal crisis.

A comparison of the fluctuations in grain harvests with the average price paid by the state to the farmers (all types of procurement included) does not, at first glance, appear to corroborate this opinion. The massive price rise which accompanied decollectivisation did not immediately result in a sharp increase in production: there was a 45 per cent increase in cereal prices between 1978 and 1981, while the average level of the harvests did not progress really (an increase of three per cent only, with a peak year in 1979 and a fall in 1980). Conversely, the bumper harvests of 1983 and 1984 (up 30 per cent on 1978) coincided with a near stagnation of prices (the index, which had stood at 145 in 1981, only reached 150 in 1984). On the other hand, the stagnation or fall in grain production since 1985 occurred when the average price was soaring: from an index of 150 in 1985 to 214 in 1988 (table 2).[1]

In fact, both the farmers and the economists are right, and prices are the basic factor behind the current crisis: peasants respond well to cereal prices which serve as their point of reference and the basis for their activity. But the reference prices do not necessarily coincide with the average price they get from the state, as may be seen from examination of the grain marketing system and prices since the onset of reforms.[2]

The rise in the quota price for cereals (about 20 per cent) agreed to by the Chinese government in 1979, along with the first agricultural reforms, was amplified by the increase in the peasants' above-quota sales, which were paid 50 per cent more than the quota prices after 1979 and resulted in a sharp increase in the average price of cereals between 1978 and 1981. In 1978, the quotas represented as much as 75 per cent of peasants' sales, but in 1981 they only represented 44 per cent, while the above-quota sales rose from 25 per cent to 49 per cent (the remaining seven per cent being sold on the free markets; cf. table 2). The state, faced with growing decollectivisation, was unable to impose the mandatory quotas and was therefore obliged to supply the cities at a high cost by procuring an increasingly large proportion of above-quota grain.

This proportion was to continue to grow until 1984. It rose from 49 per cent of sales in 1981 to 66 per cent in 1984 and, in fact, doubled in volume because of the massive increase in procurement (above-quota purchases rose from 33 million tons in 1981 to 77 million tons in 1984, out of total state purchases which rose from 63 million tons to 107 million, while quota purchases stagnated at 30 million tons). Since only a limited amount of grain transited through the free market during that period, the reference price for the farmer was what he, individually, could obtain for his total sales to the state. This price was, in fact, indirectly (through the above-quota sales) indexed on the volume of sales to the state, so it is not surprising that, under the circumstances, these sales, and therefore above-quota sales, rose dramatically (although in reality, the average price for total sales only rose slightly).

If twisting the underlying logic of the quota system in this way benefited the Chinese peasants, and indeed, the harvests, the same could not be said for the state budget. For only a small portion if indeed, any, of the price rise was passed on to the selling price of the city dweller's rice and flour rations. The state was obliged to cover the surplus costs and consequently subsidies for cereals and oil rose considerably: from seven billion yuan in 1978 (six per cent of the budget) to 23 billion yuan in 1984 (15 per cent of the budget) (Wu Shou 1988) and was threatening to rise still further if a stop had not been put to the surplus procurements (over 20 million tons of surplus in 1984).

The 'Double Rail' System

In 1985, the state therefore decided to put an end to the system of mandatory quota deliveries which had become completely distorted, and restrict its agreements. It henceforth only bought fixed quantities from peasants, under contract, at an agreed price which was roughly the average price for the total sales of the previous year (in practice, 70 per cent of the price was determined on the basis of the previous above-quota price and 30 per cent on the quota price). Surplus would, eventually, be bought by the state at the free market price (an intervention price, the equivalent of the former quota price, could be applied in the event of a slump in prices).

This new system appeared to be fair and rational since surplus grain bought on the free market could have a regulating effect on prices since the free market price, in the event of shortages, would be higher than the contract price and could make up for any losses. Conversely, the contract price appeared to be a form of support price in case of surplus. Nevertheless, this system failed to work as early as 1985.

Fair though it might have been, the average contract price in 1985 was, in fact, down for producers or regions with large surpluses and selling a considerable proportion to the state at a price which was formerly close to the above-quota price (Hu Changnuan 1988). These producers therefore reduced their cropped land area in 1985. They were also encouraged in doing so by the sharp fall in the free market prices which occurred in 1984 as a consequence of the surpluses that year. Coupled with bad weather conditions, this reduction in cropped land provoked the dramatic fall in the harvest that we know.

In 1985, against a background of poor harvests and ensuing shortages followed by soaring free market prices, the recently-installed 'double rail' system (contracts plus free market) did not have the regulating effect intended and the crisis continued into the following years.

Certainly, under peasant pressure, poorly paid contracts (in relation to free market prices) continued to decrease, just as the proportion of quota procurements in total peasant sales had decreased previously. These contracts fell from 79 million tons in 1985 (73 per cent of sales) to 53 million tons in 1987 (44 per cent of sales). But the volume of sales truly paid for at free market prices had not increased proportionately as one might have supposed. For one part, private transactions on the peasant markets, which became far from negligible, did not succeed in supplanting sales to the state: 17 million tons in 1985, only 26 million two years later (21 per cent of sales). Thus it was the above-contract sales to the state which really grew both in volume and proportionately: 12 million tons (11 per cent of sales) in 1985, 42 million tons (35 per cent of sales) in 1987. But despite the measures taken in 1985 stipulating that above-contract sales should be done at free market prices, it appears that they were made at negotiated prices which were mid way between the contract and the market price. Quite often, these sales made at negotiated prices were even described as a 'second levy' imposed on the peasants after the 'first levy' i.e. the contract sales (which were a contract only in name) (Duan Yingbi 1988; example in Zhejiang, cf. NMRB 4 January 1989).

The fact is that the state grain marketing organisations, which have a virtual monopoly in the absence of any organised, large-scale private trading bodies, do not play the market game for above-contract purchases. Indeed, why should they? Faced with peasants who are unwilling to fulfill their contract obligations and hoping to sell a maximum amount on the free market, the state organisations have absolute powers to organise the marketing as they will. They therefore start off by closing down the peasants' free grain markets for as long as the contracts have not been delivered (the closing down of local markets generally lasts until the procurements have been completed at a higher level), and then try to purchase the remainder at the lowest possible price by imposing ceilings on the market price, or quite simply by obliging the peasants to sell a second quantity at a negotiated price. These measures are reinforced by 'customs barriers' erected to prevent peasants from selling in regions where they might obtain a better price (closure of markets in Hebei, cf. Ren

Xianliang 1989; customs barriers in Chuxian, Anhui, cf. Niu Xiaofeng and Zhao Yibo 1989).

Under such constraints, farmers are not interested in the average price at which the state will finally accept to pay them, but far more in the difference between the contract and negotiated prices which are imposed on them, and the market price. Needless to say, the difference is a dissuasive one for the cereal producers who see themselves being obliged to sell their harvests at prices between 25 and 50 per cent below those they could obtain on the free market.

Cost Inflation

But the state is far from being the winner at this game, for, despite a rise of about 43 per cent in cereal prices since 1984, neither harvests nor sales have recovered their record levels of that year. Certainly, the state has passed on a large portion of this price rise on to the selling price of rationed cereals, but subsidies for cereals (and oil) remain heavy: 21 billion yuan in 1987, 22 billion in 1988, representing more than eight per cent of the state budget (NMRB 22 February 1989; He Kang 1989).

The peasants have not benefited from this rise either. Indeed, most of the benefits have been offset by the increase in the price of inputs. These had remained stable until 1984, before taking off. The sharp rise was largely due to a transit through the black market. Thus urea, the fertilizer most in demand, was sold at the allocation price of 450 yuan per tonne up until 1984. In 1988, while this official price had already risen to nearly 700 yuan, most of the urea sold was at a black market price of between 1,000 and 1,100 yuan (Wu Si 1989a). The black market is supplied by the cadres in charge of allocating the inputs. They either distribute the quotas of urea among themselves or sell them off to friends, family or other government departments, which in turn, sell them back to the peasants at a higher price (Wu Si 1989b). Urea is far from being the only agricultural mean of production to be diverted in this way before being sold off, for all inputs are concerned and their prices consequently soared: bicarbonate of ammonia (poor quality fertilizer produced by small factories) sold at 190 yuan per tonne in 1986, in some places was sold for 360 yuan in 1988, while fuel oil sold at 0.08 yuan per litre in 1982, was being resold at 0.6 yuan in 1988 (report from Hebei, cf. Li Qiuyuan. 1988; report from Hubei, cf. Chen Jinqiao 1988; complaints of large-scale farmer Zhang Yucai of Shandong, cf. NMRB 5 January 1989).

As a result of price rise of inputs, the material costs of cereals doubled: thus reports from North China indicate that the costs for corn rose from approximately 450 yuan per hectare in 1984, to over 900 yuan in 1988, while wheat's ones rose from 650 yuan to nearly 1,200 yuan.[3] Because of the parallel increase of procurements' prices, average gross revenue rose from 1,500 yuan per hectare to about 2,000 for both corn and wheat. But this increase in agricultural prices was not sufficient and, as a result, net revenue stagnated or declined (the daily wage was sustained at the five yuan level only because of the decrease in the number of days devoted to these crops) (report from Shanxi, cf. Xinzhou 1988).

The stagnation or decline in net revenue from cereal cultivation lay, of course, behind the peasants' unwillingness to increase production. And the same phenomenon may be found in all other crops for which we have noted a decline in production. Cotton is an excellent example.

The Crisis in Cotton Production
As was the case with grain, cotton benefited from a substantial increase (approximately 20 per cent) in quota prices during 1979 together with the installation of an above-quota system in the same year (at a price 30 per cent above that of the quota sales) on top of bonuses for the production zones of Northern China. Consequently, in 1984, cotton was being paid 50 per cent more than in 1978. As with cereals, this rise gave way to an unprecedented increase in both production and sales. In 1984, state procurements were heavily in surplus (the state had always held on to the cotton marketing monopoly, which was not the case with cereals) and stocks reached four million tons, making a heavy dent in state finances. The cotton purchasing price was therefore downgraded (as was the case with cereals) and an end was put to the above-quota prices, to bonuses, preferential selling prices for cereals or fertilizer to producers, etc. In 1985, the average price went down then dramatically and the harvest fell back to four million tons, once again adjusting to demand (Mei Fangquan 1988).

Here, it seems, the price policy had the desired effect. The problem was that inertia on the part of the state decision-makers prevented this policy from being followed up and adjusted to changes in demand and increases in the cost price. Whereas domestic consumption has hardly risen since (about four kg of cotton per person per year), the sharp increase in cotton exports (fabrics, clothing, etc.) had instigated the rapid rise of small rural textile factories (28 million spindles in 1988) and inflated demand which reached 5.5 million tons of cotton in 1988 compared with a production figure of only 4.2 million tons. Stocks were depleted and the state was belatedly obliged to increase prices once again (Rosario 1989).

This increase was a slight one, in the region of 13 per cent in 1988 compared to the low 1985 level, and was not sufficient to offset the increase in the cost of inputs which had a greater impact on cotton, a crop with a more intensive need for fertilizer and pesticides than cereals. Thus in 1986, the cost of cultivating one hectare of cotton was 900 yuan, but in 1988 this material cost soared locally up to more than 1,500 yuan.[4] At the same time gross revenue per hectare only rose from 3,300 yuan to about 3,800 yuan, with net revenue declining.

It is hardly surprising under these conditions that, despite the pressure of demand, the cotton growing land area decreased again in 1989 by about six per cent (NMRB 27 January and 8 July 1989).

Monopolies and Corruption
The problem raised by the difficulties encountered in both cotton and cereal production is, of course, the state monopoly. It is only a partial monopoly for cereals, but no less of a burden for that, and a total monopoly in the case of cotton. Another state monopoly has been reinstated since the beginning of this year, supposedly in order to thwart speculators and the black market: the monopoly of selling the means of production for agriculture (NCNA 13 October 1988; NMRB 8 and 17 February 1989; for a critical commentary of the monopoly, cf. NMRB 13 February 1989). Although the state always ends up by having to raise its prices (and 1989 rises are considerable: over 30 per cent for rice, six per cent for wheat, six per cent for corn, seven per cent for rapeseed and groundnuts, 34 per cent for cotton) (NMRB 9 March and 9 August 1989), it always does so too late (this is the case with cotton, the announcement having been made in August 1989 after the crop had already been planted),

or the prices bear too little relation to free market prices (as is the case with cereals) for them to provide real motivation for the farmers and boost production out of its current stagnation.

Still more serious is the corruption of the state marketing cadres which render useless any policy to encourage a given crop. Thus the measures taken to sell fertilizer or fuel oil at list price to peasants growing grain for the state (three kg of fertilizer and 1,5 kg of fuel oil for 50 kg of cereals) as well as the advances which the peasants were entitled to (20 per cent of total contract sales) (JJNJ 1988 p.V-221) were never fully applied. Coupons for cheap fertilizers are the object of wheeling and dealing just like the rest of the fertilizer allocations and generally end up in the pocket of the village cadres (Qin Zunwen 1989). Government funds to pay for the advances on the harvests are generally used by the cereal marketing administration to offset amounts embezzled, and rarely reach the peasants (report from Hunan, cf. NMRB 12 July 1989). And even if these sums were to reach their destination, they would represent a very meagre compensation for losses resulting from the low price of cereals sold to the state, as against the free market. Thus it was estimated that, in an important region of Hubei, the sum total of all measures to encourage grain farmers represented less than 15 per cent of the losses they bore as a result of the low contract price (report from Jingmen, Hubei, cf. Qin Zunwen 1989; report from Hefeng, Hubei, cf. NMRB 5 August 1989). Under these circumstances, the announcement that cereal growers may receive double their ration of cheap fertilizer and fuel oil in 1989 (He Kang 1989) is unlikely to have any effect—no more than similar perks offered to cotton growers in 1988 (35 kg of fertilizer and 2.5 kg of fuel oil for 50 kg of cotton sold) (NCNA 22 March 1988), were able to prevent a decline in the harvest.

The Rise in Breeding

Conversely, the example of animal breeding shows that the farmers could benefit from a decrease in the state marketing monopoly. As we have seen, meat production, unlike crops production which entered a crisis, has continued to increase since 1984. This is true for all animal products: pork (92 per cent of meat production) rose from ten million tons in 1979 to 14.5 million tons in 1984 and reached 20 million tons in 1988. Corresponding figures for eggs are 1.8, 4.3 million and seven million tons respectively, while for milk they are 1.3, 2.6 and 4.2 million tons (NYNJ 1980, 118; NYNJ 1985, 172; TJNJ 1989, 217-218). Sustained growth after 1984 reflects the fact that since 1985 these products were allowed to be sold freely and prices were, therefore, aligned on those of the free market (before 1985 quotas for hog sales still existed and only surplus production was sold on the free markets, with specialised private middlemen appearing after 1983). Since 1985, the state has, in reality, lost its dominant position in this market: the proportion of state purchases out of total commercialised hog production fell from 88 per cent in 1983 to 52 per cent in 1986 (when the state retailed only 48 per cent of pork sold production). At the same time, the proportion for egg sales to the state fell from 65 per cent of sales to 30 per cent (Zhang Lechang 1989). This liberalisation resulted in a rise in the selling price which substantially increased the farmers' revenues. To take but one example, the purchasing price of live pigs, sharply stimulated by demand, more than doubled between 1978 and 1986, and the hog:feed price ratio rose from under four to one in 1978 to nearly five to one in 1986 (Yu Jiabao 1988; report from Sichuan, cf. Liu Jiang 1988).

Of course, pig rearing is not without problems. Firstly the state still tries to intervene in market prices (if only because it re-sells the city-dwellers' rationed pork at a loss in the state stores) and the local authorities sometimes reimpose hog quotas' procurements at low prices on the peasants (report from Fang Xian, Hubei, cf. NMRB 2 February 1989). Moreover, liberalisation of the market is not in itself enough to ensure the actual organisation of the marketing. The state, more adept at managing rationing or quota sales, than regulating markets, frequently triggered off the 'pork cycles' which began to occur after 1985 by its clumsy intervention (Zhang Lechang 1989; pork cycles in Shandong, cf. Chen Jiuqin 1989). These cycles affect the breeders on the fringes of the major cities who have to purchase their feed grains and who market almost all their production (unlike the peasants who kill a fat pig at the New Year for their own consumption and sell their second and last pig to make a bit of money). These cycles are accentuated by the state shortages of abattoir and storage facilities (total Chinese cold storage capacity for meat is only 1.15 million tons) (NMRB 17 February 1989). Pigs are quickly killed off in a period of heavy selling during a crisis and this contributes to the fall in prices. This is what happened in early 1989: the sharp rise in the cost of feed (up by more than 50 per cent over 1988 levels) led to bankruptcy for numerous pig farmers (survey by the Ministry of Agriculture in eight provinces, cf. NMRB 23 March 1989; other reports in Anhui, Jiangxi, Jiangsu, Guangdong, Shandong, etc. cf. NMRB 5, 24 and 30 January, 8 February, 12 April 1989).

The recent crisis in pig breeding highlights a major problem in this sector of agriculture, which is the contradiction between stagnation in grain production, paralysed by state monopolies, and the increase in meat production, stimulated by a demand which is itself inflated by the increase in revenues following the reforms. Consumption of grain fodder, which only reached 40 million tons in 1978 (13 per cent of production) exceeded 74 million tons in 1984 (18 per cent) and 100 million tons in 1988 (25 per cent) (provisional estimates; relevant comments on reserves of grain fodder, cf. Zhou Li 1989). Chinese grain reserves, which have decreased at a rate of nearly 20 million tons per year since 1985, will soon be exhausted (Ministry of Agriculture 1988). If the situation is not remedied quickly, the grain crisis will, ultimately, lead to shortages and jeopardise the social order of the whole nation.

Urban Privileges vs. Rural Interests

From what we have seen above, it is clear that any solution to this crisis in grain production (or any other crop for that matter), must necessarily include the removal of the state trading monopolies and the elimination of the double rail system (the co-existence of contract or negotiated prices with those of the free market). These prevent prices from reflecting supply and demand and, moreover, open the way to corruption and hence the manipulation and abuse of the peasants.

In the short-term, however, the removal of state monopolies is quite simply impossible, because of the negative impact this would have on the standard of living in the cities. This is something that the government could never allow, least of all after the events of last June. This contradiction lies at the core of the dilemma facing the Chinese government, which, until recently at least, was divided between the desire to pursue reforms (i.e. extend market mechanisms in the countryside as well as in the cities) and the need to pander to the urban bases.

Indeed, the free egg and meat prices cost the city-dweller a great deal of money. The retail price of these goods rose by 115 per cent between 1984 and 1988 (deduced from NCNA 28 February 1986, 22 February 1987, 23 February 1988, 1 March 1989). State retail stores, which had readjusted their prices considerably in the Spring of 1985, had lagged behind the free market prices again. A further readjustment was therefore necessary in the Spring of 1988, just after pork rationing had been reintroduced the previous winter (one kilo per person per month, representing about half of real urban consumption). Thus a kilo of fat pork which was sold in state stores for 2.8 yuan in 1984, cost nearly six yuan by the end of 1988 (and still more on the stalls of the peasant markets).[5]

It must be stressed, however, that when the state freed the retail prices of eggs and meat in 1985, it also granted direct subsidies to urban consumers to compensate their loss of purchasing power. In 1987, these subsidies reached five billion yuan, to which may be added the two billion yuan which the state was paying to cover the deficit of its meat retailing apparatus (Zhang Lechang 1989). After the price rise in the Spring of 1988, the state granted a further subsidy of ten yuan per worker per month (at least in the great cities), over and above the one granted in 1985 (NCNA 12 May 1988). Despite this direct aid, in Spring 1989 city-dwellers were still complaining bitterly of the high price of meat, vegetables and fruit (which, it is true, represented one third of household expenditure in 1988) (TJNJ 1989, 727), and this was, without any doubt, a contributing factor to the urban unrest which followed.

The cost of eliminating the double rail in grain prices and passing the price increases on-to the retail price (eliminating rationing and subsidies for grain and oil), is estimated at between 30 and 40 billion yuan (the alignment of contract and negociated prices on free market ones would represent alone an additional expenditure of approximately 15 billion yuan, cf. Duan Yingbi 1988). The upgrading of prices to producers and real pricing for the urban consumer would, in fact, mean that the latter would be paying 200 per cent more for flour, rice or oil than at present. In 1988, these goods represented only nine per cent of urban household expenditure,[6] and, in theory, an increase would be possible. Indeed, a reform of this nature began to be carried out in Guangdong and Fujian provinces (Yang Qirong 1988; Su Xiaohe 1988). But the ensuing two-fold increase in the price of white rice was offset by a direct monthly subsidy of seven yuan per urban worker. One may be justified in wondering whether what is feasible in these two rich Southern provinces, can really be applied to the rest of China? Nothing is less certain. The government, which is already spending nearly 25 billion yuan on subsidies for grain and oil alone, cannot pay an additional 15 billion yuan in direct consumer subsidies. Conversely, it is not politically realistic to pass on the full cost of free grain prices to the urban consumer, making an 18 per cent dent in the latter's budget.

The situation is thus at a deadlock, and the government, faced with a choice between the interests of the urban population and those of the peasants, has implicitly opted for the former (at least up to the events of June 1989). We have already seen that the increase in the price of meat and eggs was immediately compensated by direct subsidies to urban consumers. Total government subsidies to city-dwellers, both indirect (by covering the deficit of the state trading organisations) and direct in order to limit the rise in food prices, reached nearly 32 billion yuan in 1988, i.e. 12 per cent of the state budget (NCNA 4 July 1989). This figure should be compared with the four billion yuan in agricultural investment and the 16 billion yuan in aid to agriculture (Wang Binqian 1989) (and largely devoted to the expenditure of the local administrative bodies) which were allocated in the same 1988 budget.

The Effects of Inflation

This implicit choice on the part of the government was made even more clear during the recent spate of credit restrictions which the authorities have been using, since Autumn 1988, to eradicate the rampant inflation which is undermining the economy (21 per cent in urban retail prices in 1988 according to official data (RMRB 1 March 1989), 30 per cent according to our own estimates). These restrictions hit the rural economy particularly badly. Grain and cotton purchasing stations in particular, had already frittered away part of their funds (originally earmarked for purchasing harvested crops) in various costs and speculation. They found themselves unable to pay the farmers in full and gave them IOUs instead (NMRB 9 January 1989). In the spring of 1989, a number of these debts had still not been paid and, in desperation, the peasants sold off these IOUs to speculators at 60 per cent of their face value (NMRB 25 March 1989).

It is easy to imagine the anger of the peasants when they were paid for a portion of their harvest in 'white tickets' (*baitiao*) while having to pay cash for seeds and fertilizer for the October sowing (Zhan Zhongde 1989). Not surprisingly, the first signs of resistance to procurements were seen in the Autumn of 1988. In one village a gong was hung on a tree for the children to sound on the approach of the cadres coming to requisition grain, thereby enabling the villagers to hide in the fields. In another village, the same cadres were greeted with knives, whereas previously the ladder they had used to climb to the granary had been pushed down. (Liu Zifu and Wang Bin 1989).

Less directly, but with no less an impact for all that, the budgetary restrictions and ensuing industrial slowdown seriously affected turnover in the fertilizer plants supplying the farmers. Faced with electricity cuts and short of funds to cope with an unprecedented rise in the price of coal (from 80 to 150 yuan per tonne), the small factories producing bicarbonate of ammonia saw their operating costs exceed the mandatory out of mill price in some cases (270 yuan per tonne, with profits from black market sales going into the pockets of the intermediary organisations rather than those of the manufacturers). Numerous small factories were then forced to close during the spring of 1989 (reports from Shaanxi, cf. NMRB 1 and 23 February, 13 April 1989; report from Kaifeng, Henan, cf. NMRB 12 April 1989). Large plants, such as the one manufacturing urea in Cangzhou, Hebei province, were producing at low capacity. In the case of this plant, for example, the cost of the gas used as its principal raw material, rose from 0.135 yuan per cubic meter to 0.315 yuan, while the same gas is sold to urban consumers in the neighbouring city of Tianjin at 0.08 yuan (NMRB 3 March 1989). Once again, indirectly, the city-dwellers are privileged, while the peasants, faced with a serious shortage of fertilizer, have to pay even higher prices for their inputs in 1989 than they paid on the black market in 1988.

Generally speaking, the peasants are far from being the instigators of inflation, as certain city-dwellers, indignant at what they resent as exorbitant free market prices, would have it. On the contrary, they are its victims. The inflation is due to uncontrolled investment in public companies, with the resulting increase in wage costs and industrial 'overheating'. It in no way benefits the peasants who only obtain price rises when it is too late. The substantial increase in the price of grain and cotton granted in 1989, will hardly offset the soaring rise in the cost of inputs, whereas any measures to cool down the economy hit the peasants first and foremost. While peasants were being paid in IOUs, the (nominal) revenues of the city-dwellers rose again last year by about 22 per cent (RMRB 1 March 1989). The gap separating urban and rural revenues, which had begun to narrow since the onset of reforms, started to widen again after 1985. In 1988, the ratio between the annual expenditure of an urban household and that of a rural one (including self consumption), was 2.7:1 compared to only 2.3:1 in 1984 (2.9:1 in 1978, before the reforms) (TJNJ 1989, 720). Moreover, it should be emphasised that this ratio does not take into account the numerous indirect subsidies which benefit the city-dweller.

Favouring the Cities

The government's urban bias, its preference for the interests of the town dwellers over those of the peasants, is not a deliberate policy choice. Rather it is the result of the very inertia of the political and economic system still operating in China today. The entire political system is weighted in favour of the urban inhabitants, in the sense that any display of discontent on their part is far more dangerous to the regime than localised peasant uprisings, easily dispersed by the authorities. The events of May 1989 were a clear demonstration of this. This underlying principle may be found at the very core of the financial and commercial institutions which function to the detriment of the peasant. The apparition of IOUs, in a massive quantity in 1988, was not a new phenomenon: the first ones appeared as soon as 1985. The state commercial organizations have always given priority to the covering of their own internal costs, saddled with bureaucratic redundancies and wastes, at the expense of the payments to peasants (Zhao Zekun 1989). For their part, the Agricultural Bank and the Rural Credit Cooperatives grant most loans to highly profitable non-agricultural businesses which, in 1981, only represented 15 per cent of total loans, but rose to 24 per cent in 1988. Agricultural loans, proper, fell from 28 per cent to 22 per cent during the same period (Bank 1988). Peasants' savings with the Credit Cooperatives, which are intended to finance agricultural credit, are, for a non negligible part, recycled into the government's industrial investments. It has been estimated that by manipulating the reserves handed over to the central banking organisations and playing on interest rates, five billion yuan were syphoned off the Rural Credit Cooperatives in 1986 alone (Zhang Zhongfa 1989).

One should not be surprised by this urban and industrial preference or the transfer of peasants' savings, for they reflect the fact that agriculture is continuing to finance China's industrial development, as it has been doing for a very long time. It has been estimated that in the period 1952 - 1986, 687 billion yuan were transferred through the price scissors (582 billion) and taxes (105 billion) compared with total investment and state aid to agriculture of 233 billion yuan. If we are to believe these figures, 454 billion yuan were thus taken from agriculture, or the equivalent of 30 per cent of the 1,600 billion which the state invested in its own enterprises during the same period (Niu Ruofeng 1988). Still more worrying is the fact that the prices' scissors (under-estimating of the agricultural prices to the benefit of industrial ones), which tended to close between 1979 and 1984, are once again on the increase. Some economists have estimated that 85 billion yuan was thus surreptitiously tapped from agriculture in 1987, i.e., the equivalent of more than one quarter of the country's agricultural revenue (Xiong Jianyong 1989).

The Thwarted Development of Rural Industry

Although these figures may be contested, the dent made by the state on agriculture is none the less real, as are the constraints of the state monopolies. Constantly at a disadvantage, agriculture is hardly a lucrative activity for peasants who are tempted, when they have the opportunity, to take on other employment. A peasant earns at most five yuan for one day of actual agricultural labour, or, if we consider that labour in the fields only takes up half the year, an average daily wage of between two and 2.5 yuan. In comparison, a worker in a small rural factory earns between three and four yuan, a fish farmer or fruit grower between seven and eight yuan and an individual transporter (with his own hand-tractor), over ten yuan (Tian Zelin 1989).

The peasants' response to this crisis in agriculture was a mass exodus to the small rural industries or trades which had proliferated since 1984 in the expanding market towns (Aubert 1988). These enterprises, which only employed 25 million workers in 1980, counted 93 million of them in 1988, representing nearly one quarter of the total rural labour force. Half of these are family businesses, mostly in trade and services (12 million family employees out of 14 million jobs) or transport (six million out of seven million), while the remainder are employed in rural construction work (six million out of 15) and industry (22 million out of 57) (deduced from TJNJ 1989, 240 and 246). Added to this agricultural exodus was a rural one in which more than 20 million peasants obtained more or less permanent employment in the large cities of China (nearly two million of them in Shanghai and over one million in Beijing: one quarter of that city's population) (NCNA 22 January 1989). It goes without saying that instead of investing in agriculture (less than ten billion yuan in 1988) (Chong Anni 1989), the peasants preferred to invest in these non-agricultural industries. In 1988, fixed capital investment in this type of enterprise totalled 40 billion yuan, largely through private rural finance (tontines, etc.) (NCNA 7 May 1989). The other form of investment favoured by the peasants is housing (over 40 billion yuan was spent on the construction of new houses in 1988) (estimate from NCNA 12 April 1989; report from Jiangsu on the structure of peasants' investments, cf. Tu Yilin and Ju Weimin 1989).

Although agricultural potential has suffered from the lack of peasant investment (on average, a farmer only has 1,000 yuan in fixed capital assets, excluding land and irrigation equipment) (Chong Anni 1989), peasant revenues have been sustained by the growing proportion of non-agricultural revenue (nearly 37 per cent of households' total revenues in 1988) (TJNJ 1989, 743). Following decollectivisation, the peasants' newly found freedom of employment found an outlet in these non—agricultural rural activities. Unfortunately, it appears that, just as decollectivisation had exhausted its potential for developing agriculture as early as 1984, so the capacity of these rural businesses to expand in the long term has already diminished. Most Chinese economists already seem to have abandoned the hope of an 'urbanisation' of the countryside through the expansion of the larger market towns, with peasants 'leaving the land without leaving the countryside' *(litu, bu lixiang)* (the slogan is now that it is necessary to 'leave both the land and the countryside'; cf. Guo Shutian 1989; Gu Yikang 1989).

The service sector, largely filled by family businesses, has already made up for time lost during collectivisation and is in full employment. The small industries, which continued to flourish during the past two years, are now beginning to have difficulties. Collective workshops in the villages and market towns, drained by the cadres which manage them, are more and more frequently loss-making (cf. the crisis of the South Jiangsu model (*Sunan moshi*) in Shi Xunru 1989). The extremely dynamic private workshops are now being investigated for tax fraud (not without reason: a report states that tax fraud in Liaoning concerns 70 per cent of the earnings of private rural entreprises, cf. Cheng Xiangqing 1989) and a major operation is currently underway to check their accounts (NMRB 2 August 1989).

Still more serious, are the budget restrictions on rural enterprises, unjustly accused of weighing too heavily on the nation's finances and contributing to inflation. While in 1987 and 1988, public loans to them increased by 14 billion yuan each year, only seven billion in new loans were granted in 1989. Whereas rural workshops self-finance most of their development, they do resort to the official loan institutions for their day-to-day business. Many of them are now likely to get into difficulties and an estimated 20 per cent will probably have to close in 1989, making between 15-20 million people redundant and obliging them to return to the fields (Zhang Zhongfa 1989; Delfs 1989). The same restrictions will affect a number of urban work sites and send some four million workers back to their villages. It is easy to imagine the problems posed by growing under-employment in the countryside, with peasant non-agricultural revenue diminishing as well. Because of this, the agricultural crisis may well turn into a widespread rural crisis.

Peasant Autonomy vs. Bureaucratic Contracts

We have seen that the solution to the crisis would be the effective removal of state monopolies, but this is no longer on the cards. More fundamentally, a real stimulus to the rural economy should take the form of a genuine peasant autonomy with proper peasant organisations. But as we have seen too, the non-agricultural rural sector, the most autonomous and dynamic one in the whole rural economy, is in danger of suffocation, and China is undoubtedly going down the wrong path. Yet only a few months ago, numerous 'reformist' Chinese economists, the same ones who promoted the abolition of the double rail system and the extension of market mechanisms to the countryside, were stressing the need to form independent, professional agricultural organisations to defend the interests of the peasants and act as buffers between them and the government administration (Li Qinzheng 1988). It is true that only genuine purchasing and selling cooperatives (and not those which bear that name but are only appendages of the state trading organisations), organised by the peasants themselves, would be capable of doing battle against speculation and the black market sales of inputs, obtain the best agricultural prices for the peasants (assuming monopolies were removed) etc. And only independent farmers' unions could provide an efficient means of dealing with the arbitrary injustice of the local bureaucrats.

Yet even before the return to power of the conservative gerontocrats, all attempts at bringing democracy to the countryside tended in fact less to favour the growth of independent structures, than to create organisations which were mid way between local administrations and agricultural 'clubs'. A good example of this is the Association of Cereal Growers set up in Lingshi, Shanxi province, which the press had presented as 'the first autonomous professional association' of its kind. In fact, this association, despite its charter, management committee, departments and services with local branches, only consisted of a few major cereal producers (one thousand families only, but supplying 30 per cent of quota deliveries for the whole district) under contract to the local administration which, in turn, granted them supplies and loans on favourable terms (NMRB 10 February 1989). Generally speaking, official policy is to place the services of the township or district economic administration under contract to a limited number of 'advanced' farmers, entitling the latter to benefit from favourable prices and supplies (report on the application of this kind of technical contracts in Hebei, cf. NMRB 2 February 1989).

Whereas local experiments of this kind could meet with a certain success, it is hard to see how, given the current climate of corruption, putting services under contract could be applied throughout the country. Studies carried out on the enforcement of the contracts which bind the majority of peasants and oblige them to deliver their quotas, reveal that, as far as the local cadres are concerned, contracts are composed of hard and soft constraints (examples of 'double sided contracts' in Zhengzhou, Henan, cf. NMRB 12 January 1989, and their criticism in Wu Fangchun 1989). Hard constraints may be generally summed up as 'the three requirements, of the cadres in relation to the peasants: grain (which has to be delivered), money (which has to be paid in various taxes) and souls (i.e., new births, tightly controlled by the plan and penalised by fines if quotas are exceeded) (NMRB 27 March 1989). The soft constraints are the duties of the cadres in relation to the peasants, particularly where the supply of inexpensive fertilizer or inputs is concerned. Improving the administrative services in the villages or townships, by putting their services under contract, seems a fairly utopian vision in the present situation where village cadres reign supreme and the balance of power between the rulers and the ruled has not been altered greatly by decollectivisation. There is no shortage of examples of abuse of power on the part of village leaders or cadres of small market towns, even if the importance of these examples should be viewed proportionately. Arbitrary arrests and punishments are still common currency in the countryside (for a typical story of a commando raid to requisition grain and taxes with arbitrary fines and arrests, in Yingshan, Sichuan, cf. NMRB 9 July 1989). Even more flagrant is the practice of abusive taxation, either in collective levies (up to 200 yuan per family, example in Tanghe Xian, Henan, NMRB 3 April 1989), often embezzled by the village cadres for their personal use (example in Yichang, Hubei: 9,000 yuan for each cadre of village level and only 1,500 yuan per subordinate cadre, cf. NMRB 19 July 1989), or in other kinds of taxes for the township authorities. In one township in Jiangsu province, up to 39 separate taxes were counted (for birth control, the sterilisation of women, the families of the military, repairs of schools, culture, etc.), which were paid in the grain procurement stations when the peasants sold their grain, and totalled more than the peasants' earnings from their sales (report from Gaoyou, NMRB 3 August 1989).

How could cadres of this kind enforce a contract policy which would truly benefit the peasants? Even if many village heads are honest and not all rural administrators are corrupt, the enforcement of such a contract system must necessarily depend on all parties having equal status, and having this guaranteed by an efficient legal framework. Unfortunately, these conditions do not exist in China at present. Moreover, rational though it may appear at first glance, the government's current policy, which targets aid to agriculture by concentrating it on a handful of 'advanced' farmers (a core of ten million peasant households out of a total 200 millions, cf. NMRB 4 April 1989), bears the germs of a serious threat to the peasantry as a whole.

The Precarious Right to Land

The problem lies in the 'economies of scale' in agriculture which have become the pet topic of Chinese economists. The idea is, where possible, to favour large-scale farms which are easily mechanised and sell almost all their produce to the state in exchange for supplies and loans at favourable rates (Meng Fanqi 1988a; Wu Weidong 1988). In reality, such economies of scale are the exception rather than the rule in China. Indeed, how could it be otherwise in a country with an average of three labourers working one ha. of cultivated land? Generally speaking, these experiments have been limited to the suburbs of the larger cities where most of the rural population is already working in factories (example of a Beijing suburb, cf. Shunyi 1989), as well as the highly developed coastal areas in Eastern and Southern China (report from Jinhua, Zhejiang, cf. Zhang Baiqi 1988; report from Zhongshan, Guangdong, cf. Center 1988) or areas where it is still possible to clear virgin land for agriculture (report from Jingzhou, Hubei, cf. Peng Junxiang 1988). The size of these 'large-scale' farms is, in fact, fairly modest at between two and five ha. (compared with an average of less than two thirds of one ha. in China as a whole). Very few exceed 20 ha., like the one in Zhejiang province which employs eight permanent labourers and owns its own combine harvester (NMRB 3 January 1989). Experience has shown that these large farms do not produce more per ha. than small traditional ones (and operating costs are often far higher). But the large concentration of land does ensure a good man:land ratio and provides the farmer with a comfortable revenue while guaranteeing massive procurements to the state.

The development of these large-scale farms, which locally cover only between four and six per cent of the land in the few regions where such experiments have been carried out (but over 90 per cent of agricultural land in the outer suburbs of Beijing), is limited. Indeed, these would represent a marginal and inoffensive phenomenon were it not for the accompanying rhetoric used to justify the experiments and the practices they condone, which endanger a basic right won by the peasant during decollectivisation, i.e. the right to land, or failing that, at least the free use of it. Supporters of the economies of scale theory criticise the division of Chinese agricultural land into a multitude of small farms (over 200 million) which, moreover, tend to be neglected by the farmers who are frequently employed in rural industry and regard the land as a private allotment for the mere production of their own grain rations, at the expense of the state procurements (Meng Fanqi 1988b). This is a case of putting the chicken before the egg, since the low level of agricultural investment and application of inputs is the rational peasant response to low agricultural prices and expensive means of production. Nevertheless, the responsibility system is being reviewed more and more frequently, making land leases more precarious while inciting worker-peasants to relinquish their plots (which represented their sole security in the event of unemployment, Lu Nong 1988). Thus, in some villages, tiny parcels of land are distributed equally to all for private consumption, while the remaining land is auctioned off. This land is then subject to heavy contract quotas and collective levies. Formulas vary: in one place annual farm rental (the levy paid to the village) has to be paid in advance, the plot of land being attributed to the farmer offering the highest rent. In another, a deposit has to be paid by the applicant farmer (examples in Dingxiang, Shanxi, cf. Wu Yuming 1988; in Hebei, Henan, Hubei, Shanxi, cf. NMRB 1 November 1988, 13 February, 14 and 22 March 1989). In all cases, the duration of the leases (in theory 15 years according to a 1984 circular) is reduced to five years, three years or even one year. As often as not, this also gives rise to an increase in the individual peasant's total levies (up to 750 yuan per hectare, or nearly half the net total revenue of two annual harvests). On the positive side, of course, a few peasants in the village will find themselves operating a farm two to three times larger than those of their fellow-villagers, and double their own revenue as a result.

The fact that this distribution of land is enforced by village cadres who are obliged, on such a sensitive issue, to take local opinion into account, limits the spread of this practice, or at least makes excesses rarer (report on abusive concentration of land and subsequent peasants' anger in Jilin, cf. Song Xunfeng 1989). There is, however, a far more serious threat hanging over the right to land, in the form of land nationalisation which a number of economists are promoting. The reasons they give in support of this are (not entirely without foundation) the discrepancies in the collective ownership of the land which give the village cadres ample scope for the abuse of power, embezzlement etc. in the absence of any clearly defined regulations. These economists therefore suggest nationalising the right to ownership of agricultural land, individual farmers then renting the land they till directly from the state. Lease and rent management would be transferred to Land Offices. According to the supporters of this measure, the advantage lies in being able to implement regulations governing a rational utilisation of the land, while creating a quasi-property market with the possibility for individual farmers to sell their 'farming rights' (subject to certain conditions) if they decide to change occupations (Zheng Zhenyou 1988; An Xiji 1988; Wei Zhengguo 1989; Yang Xun 1989).

Attractive though it might appear on paper, this project could be extremely dangerous in practice since the allocation, renewal (or non-renewal) of leases would be in the hands of the local township bureaucracy which, as we know, is corrupt, and would, in the event, no longer be submitted to village pressure. The land administration offices would thereby have the perfect means for obliging the peasant-workers to give up the allotments which enable them to be self-sufficient. This is what happened in Shunyi where, in 1986, 180,000 part-time farmers cultivating cereals, in this district of outer Beijing, were obliged to give up their land to a mere 24,000 of their number. As a result, the worker-farmers now only have their factory wages to live on while the remainder have become full-time salaried farmers, (with an individual responsibility system for production contracts) on vast, heavily mechanised farms of nearly 200 ha., under unified management (Shunyi 1989).

Of course, this is an exceptionnal occurence and the supporters of the 'nationalisation' of farmland stress that the individual farmers' rights would be garanteed. And up to now, the household farming is still the basis of present agricultural policy (a few doubts remain, however, since a recent editorial thought it necessary to remind its readers of this continuing policy, cf. NMRB 18 August 1989). But it goes without saying that the creation of Land Offices would deal a fatal blow to the minimum peasant autonomy which, in the vast majority of Chinese villages, still guarantees the equal distribution of land.

Conclusion

Fortunately, this proposal to nationalise land is still at project stage. Current agricultural policy, deprived of the imaginative capacities and stimulii of the reformists which instigated it and who are now reduced to silence, is characterised more by total paralysis and an incapacity to find long-term solutions to the current crisis, than by a desire to reimpose strong controls on the countryside. This immobility can only serve to strengthen the grip of the rural administrative bureaucracy on village life and aggravate the situation, but without making way for a return in force of effective planification for all that.

In the Autumn of 1989, the situation in the Chinese countryside was less reminiscent of a 'great leap backwards' (after all, there has not been a return to collectivisation and production has not collapsed), than of a dramatic bogging down of the previous reforms. The present regime no longer has the political volition to pursue the liberalisation which it started ten years ago with decollectivisation, and which it was unable to guide towards a true market economy. But neither does it have the means to enforce the authoritarian mobilisation of yesterday. The government is thus reduced to short-term measures for dealing with emergencies as they arise in order to prevent the economic crisis from leading to another outburst of social unrest.

From this point of view, the rise in agricultural prices in 1989 reveals the extent of the government's weakness. The highest price increase (nearly 30 per cent) was for rice, which is the cereal producing the highest net revenue, whereas the lowest price increases were for wheat and rapeseed oil which are the least paid crops (Li Yingjie 1988). This discrepancy is not the result of a rational price adjustment, but may be explained by the simple need to retain peasants' sales in the major rice producing regions of the Yangzi river basin and prevent their peasants from selling their crops in the southern 'liberalised' provinces (despite all the existing 'customs barriers') where rice prices are twice as high (examples of sales by peasants from Hunan on the markets of Guangzhou, cf. NMRB 30 January 1989). Similarly, rampant inflation in the cities seems to have been stopped for the time being by the massive increase in subsidies for urban food products. In the short term, supplies to the cities are therefore assured at the cost of a later increase in the budget deficit, thus paving the way for still greater problems in the future.

But does the future really count for a government which is entirely occupied by the immediate problem of maintaining its own authority?

Notes

1. The official index of grain prices given in the Chinese Yearbooks (TJNJ 1989, 706, 710; WJNJ 1988, 91-93) includes probably free market prices without any indication about the method used for computation. Therefore we prefer to use the average price of all procured grains for the State (total sum paid by state commercial organs, divided by volume of procurements measured in 'commercial grains').

2. This analysis has already been presented in an unpublished study carried out by the author for the OECD in July 1989.

3. For 1986, the material costs indicated in the Agricultural Yearbook for wheat and corn, as well as for other crops (NYNJ 1987, 383 and 387), are not reliable, being far below the actual levels observed during our personal investigations as well as the indications of the surveys published in Handbook (1986, 38-40, 47-48, 58-60).

4. As indicated previously, for 1986, the material costs for crops indicated in the Agricultural Yearbook are quite under-estimated, and for this case of the cotton we are refering to our own observations and to the figures of Handbook (1986, 140).

5. Author's trips notes and interviews. During the fall of 1989, the free markets' prices for pork were down to the level of those of the state's retail stores, due to the crisis in breeding and massive subsequent slaughtering of hogs in the vicinity of the cities.

6. In 1988, rationed grain and oil expenses cost about 90 yuan per urban person per year (of which 75 yuan for grain alone), out of a total budget of about 1,015 yuan (estimates and TJNJ 1989, 727).

Bibliography

An Xiji (1988): An Xiji, 'Lun tudi guoyou yongdianzhi'. *Zhongguo Nongcun Jingji*, No. 11, 22-25

Aubert (1984): Claude Aubert, 'La Nouvelle Politique Economique dans les Campagnes Chinoises'. *Le Courrier des Pays de l'Est*, juillet-août 1984, 3-32.

Aubert (1985): Claude Aubert, 'Chine: le décollage alimentaire?'. *Etudes Rurales*, vol. 99-100, 25-71.

Aubert (1988): Claude Aubert, 'Villes et Campagnes en Chine'. *Cahiers d'Economie et Sociologie Rurales INRA*, vol. 6, 75-113.

Bank (1988): 'Heli kongzhi xindai guimo, tiaozheng jiegou, zujin nongcun jingji wending fazhan'. *Zhongguo Nungcun Jingji*, No. 7, 15-19

Center (1988): 'Zhongshan Shi nongcun tudi guimo jingying yanjin ji mianling de jige wenti'. *Zhongguo Nongcun Jingji*, No. 12, 16-22.

Chen Jinqiao (1988): Chen Jinqiao et al., 'Yizhi he xiaohua nongye shengchan ziliao zhangjia de duice yu jianyi'. *Zhongguo Nongcun Jingji*, No. 12, 47-48.

Chen Jiuqin (1989): Chen Jiuqin, in: *Nongmin Ribao*, 31 july 1989.

Cheng Xiangqing (1989): Cheng Xiangqing et al., 'Siying qiye fazhan mianling de zhuyao wenti'. *Nongye Jingji Wenti*, No. 2, 24-26.

Cong Anni (1989): Cong Anni, 'Woguo nongye zijin yunxing de tezheng he chouzi duice'. *Zhongguo Nongcun Jingji*, No. 5, 11-14.

Delfs (1989): Robert Delfs, in: *Far Eastern Economic Review*, 2 march 1989, 43ff.

Duan Yingbi (1988): Duan Yingbi, 'Dui liangshi jiage gaige de yixie kanfa'. *Nongye Jingji Wenti*, No. 10, 19-23.

Gu Yikang (1989): Gu Yikang et al., 'Dui xiangzhen qiye—xiao chengzhen daolu de lishi pingpan'. *Nongye Jingji Wenti*, No. 3, 11-14.

Guo Shutian (1989): Guo Shutian, 'Dui nongcun gongyehua, chengshihua yu nongye xiandaihua de jidian sikao'. *Zhongguo Nongcun Jingji*, No. 2, 20-23.

Handbook (1986): *Quanguo nongchanpin chengben shouyi shouce, 1986*. Beijing: Wenhua Jishu Chubanshe, 1988.

He Kang (1989): Interview with the Minister of Agriculture, He Kang, in: *Nongmin Ribao*, 22 March 1989.

Hu Changnuan (1988): Hu Changnuan, 'Ping jiu nian lai nongchanpin jiage juece de chenggong yu shiwu'. *Nongye Jingji Wenti*, No.6, 7-11.

Li Qinzheng (1988): Li Qinzheng, 'Rang nongmin xuanze'. *Zhongguo Nongcun Jingji*, No. 9, 25-32.

Li Qiuyuan (1988): Li Qiuyuan, 'Gu jian shang nong'. *Zhongguo Nongcun Jingji*, No. 11, 56-58.

Li Yingjie (1988): Li Yingjie, 'Zhiding nongchanpin jiage ying yi pingjun lirun wei biaozhun'. *Nongye Jingji Wenti*, No. 6, 12,53.

Liu Jiang (1988): Liu Jiang, 'Sichuan yang zhu shengchan ji qi ke gong jiejian de jingyan'. *Nongye Jingji Wenti*, No. 8, 9-13.

Liu Zifu and Wang Bin (1989): Liu Zifu and Wang Bin, in: *Nongmin Ribao*, 31 March 1989.

Lu Nong (1988): Lu Nong, 'Tudi shidu guimo jingying shi ge jianjin guocheng'. *Nongye Jingji Wenti*, No. 5, 42.

Mei Fangquan (1988): Mei Fangquan et al., 'Woguo liangshi he mianhua wenbu xietiao fazhan wenti de yanjiu'. *Nongye Jingji Wenti*, No. 6, 20-24.

Meng Fanqi (1988a): Meng Fanqi, 'Lun fazhan nongye guimo jingying'. *Zhongguo Nongcun Jingji*, No. 6, 33-36.

Meng Fanqi (1988b): Meng Fanqi, 'Woguo nongye guimo jingji de qianjing yu tudi zhidu de xuanze'. *Zhongguo Nongcun Jingji*, No. 12, 11-15.

Ministry of Agriculture (1988): 'Liangshi duanque ji jingji zhengce de tiaozheng'. *Nongye Jingji Wenti*, No. 5, 3-9.

NCNA: *New China News Agency.*

Niu Ruofeng (1988): Niu Ruofeng, 'Woguo nongye jieduanxing bodong yu jingji fazhan zhanlüe de guanxi'. *Nongye Jingji Wenti*, No. 10, 9-13.

Niu Xiaofeng and Zhao Yipo (1989): Niu Xiaofeng and Zhao Yipo, in: *Nongmin Ribao*, 17 january 1989.

NMRB: *Nongmin Ribao* (Peasants' Daily).

NYJJWT: *Nongye Jingji Wenti* (Problems of Agricultural Economy; monthly).

NYNJ: *Zhongguo Nongye Nianjian* (Chinese Agricultural Yearbook).

Peng Junxiang (1988): Peng Junxiang et al., 'Tudi shidu guimo jingying xianzhuang yu duice tanxi'. *Zhongguo Nongcun Jingji*, No. 11, 16-21.

Qin Zunwen (1989): Qin Zunwen, 'Liangshi dinggou "sanguagou" toushi'. *Zhongguo Nongcun Jingji*, No. 3, 7-9.

Ren Xianliang (1989): Ren Xianliang, in: *Nongmin Ribao*, 9 February 1989.

RMRB: *Renmin Ribao* (People's Daily).

Rosario (1989): Louise de Rosario, in: *Far Eastern Economic Review*, 26 January 1989, 55-56.

Shi Xunru (1989): Shi Xunru et al., 'Weiji, zhengjie, chulu'. *Zhongguo Nongcun Jingji*, No. 6, 5-11.

Shunyi (1989): 'Shunyi Xian nongye shidu guimo jingying de diaocha'. *Zhongguo Nongcun Jingji*, No. 6, 34-40.

Song Xunfeng (1989): Song Xunfeng, in: *Nongmin Ribao*, 30 January 1989.

Su Xiaohe (1988): Su Xiaohe, 'Guangdong liangjia gaige mubiao moshi ji qi yingxiang yu duice'. *Nongye Jingji Wenti*, No. 10, 28-30.

SYNJ: *Zhongguo Shangye Nianjian* (China's Commerce Yearbook).

Tian Zelin (1989): Tian Zelin and Yang Shiyou, 'Zhili jingji huanjing, jianli nongcun shangpin jingji xin tiexu'. *Nongye Jingji Wenti*, No. 1, 29-34.

TJNJ: *Zhongguo Tongji Nianjian* (Chinese Statistical Yearbook).

Tu Yilin and Ju Weimin (1989): Tu Yilin and Ju Weimin, 'Butong shouru shuiping nonghu zijin jilei he touxiang de tedian ji qi guilüxing', *Zhongguo Nongcun Jingji*, No. 1, 44-49.

Wang Bingqian (1989): Report by the Minister of Finance, Wang Bingqian, in: *Renmin Ribao*, 7 April 1989.

Wei Zhengguo (1989): Wei Zhengguo, 'Woguo nongye tudi guoying siyong lun'. *Zhongguo Nongcun Jingji*, No. 5, 15-22.

WJNJ: *Zhongguo Wujia Tongji Nianjian* (China's Prices Statistical Yearbook)

Wu Fangchun (1989): Wu Fangchun, in: *Nongmin Ribao*, 10 february 1989.

Wu Shou (1988): Wu Shou, 'Zhongduanqi liangshi wenti de peixi he duice'. *Nongye Jingji Wenti*, No. 11, 14-18.

Wu Si (1989a): Wu Si, in: *Nongmin Ribao*, 23 March 1989.

Wu Si (1989b): Wu Si, in: *Nongmin Ribao*, 24 March 1989.

Wu Weidong (1988): Wu Weidong, 'Nongye guimo jingying de chencixing ji woguo nongye guimo jingying de fazhan daolu'. *Zhongguo Nongcun Jingji*, No. 6, 37-40.

Wu Yuming (1988): Wu Yuming et al., 'Shixing tudi jingzheng chengbao de diaocha'. *Nongye Jingji Wenti*, No. 5, 36-39.

Xinzhou (1988): 'Xianxing liangshi jiage dui fazhan liangshi shengchan de yingxiang ji qi gaige shexiang'. *Nongye Jingji Wenti*, No. 10, 31-33.

Xiong Jianyong (1989): Xiong Jianyong et al., 'Jianxi tonghuo pengzhang dui woguo nongye fazhan de weihai'. *Nongye Jingji Wenti*, No. 2, 44-47.

Yang Qirong (1988): Yang Qirong et al., 'Liangjia gaige: tupo yu fansi'. *Nongye Jingji Wenti*, No. 10, 24-28.

Yang Xun (1989): Yang Xun, 'Guoyou siying: Zhongguo nongcun tudi zhidu gaige de xianshi xuanze'. *Zhongguo Nongcun Jingji*, No. 5, 23-29.

Yang Zhenhuai (1988): Interview with the Minister of Irrigation, Yang Zhenhuai, in: *Nongmin Ribao*, 1st November 1988.

Yu Jiabao (1988): Yu Jiabao et al., 'Quanguo dongwuxing shipin jiage biandong qushi he duice'. *Nongye Jingji Wenti*, No. 5, 15-18.

ZGNCJJ: *Zhongguo Nongcun Jingji* (Chinese Rural Economy; monthly).

Zhan Zhongde (1989): Zhan Zhongde et al., in: *Nongmin Ribao*, 16 January 1989.

Zhang Baiqi (1988): Zhang Baiqi, 'Nongcun tudi guimo jingying zhong de nixiang xianxiang'. *Nongye Jingji Wenti*, No.5, 40-41.

Zhang Lechang (1989): Zhang Lechang, 'Woguo chengshi fushipin (rou, dan, nai) liutong tizhi gaige de jinzhan he mubiao moshi xuanze'. *Zhongguo Nongcun Jingji*, No. 5, 35-40.

Zhang Zhongfa (1989): Zhang Zhongfa, 'Woguo nongcun jingji zai zhili zhengdun zhong de duice yanjiu'. *Zhongguo Nongcun Jingji*, No. 5, 3-10.

Zhao Zekun (1989): Zhao Zekun, in: *Nongmin Ribao*, 17 July 1989.

Zheng Zhenyuan (1988): Zheng Zhenyuan, 'Tudi shangpinhua he shehuizhuyi tudi shichang'. *Zhongguo Nongcun Jingji*, No. 11, 13-15.

Zhou Li (1989): Zhou Li, 'Xushouye mianling de nanti he chulu'. *Nongye Jingji Wenti*, No. 6, 35-39.

Zhou Zhiping (1989): Zhou Zhiping, 'Nongcun gaige shinian zhong de shuili wenti'. *Zhongguo Nongcun Jingji*, No. 5, 30-34.

China's Agriculture Towards 2000: Projecting the Unprojectionable

Jørgen Delman

"It is difficult to make predictions, especially about the future" (Robert Storm-Petersen)

Introduction

In recent years, much effort has gone into projecting agricultural development, globally by FAO (Alexandratos 1988) and at national level by institutions and experts all over the world. Basically, such projections have all been rooted in a wish to see if we will still have bread on the table in the years to come.

In view of the importance of China's agriculture in the country's overall development, not to mention the impact of China's food production on the world food security and trade situation, foreign and Chinese experts and institutions have carried out extensive studies aimed at predicting the future of China's agriculture.

Of the few foreign projections of China's agricultural development, a World Bank study published in 1985 is the best known and most comprehensive, and it is recognized as a standard work on China's contemporary agriculture (World Bank 1985). The OECD has also published a study, which looks at the prospects for food consumption and production in relation to future agricultural trade (OECD 1988).

The FAO study includes a number of data sets on China in its analysis of the global situation in agriculture. But the author argues that 'the unavailability as yet of detailed data on land use limits the depth of production analysis for this country' (Alexandratos 1988, 1). Because of this constraint and in view of its general approach, the FAO study offers more insight into the impact of China's agriculture on global agricultural development than it does into the prospects for China's own agriculture.

Being a socialist country with a planned economy, China has always used projections as an integral part of the physical and economic planning process, but during the first three decades of the PRC, they were never made public. Only during the last decade have details of the national and specific sectoral plans, including the agricultural section of the seventh five-year plan (Seventh FYP 1986), become known to a wider audience, as have numerous statistics which enable us to assess past developments and current performance.

Furthermore, China's academic circles have shown a growing interest during recent years in projecting long-term agricultural development until the year 2000 to identify the future path for agricultural growth, primarily within a reformist policy framework. This article reviews some of the projections focusing wholly or partially on agricultural development. They are mostly representative of reformist thinking in the 1980s, but also, to some extent, of critical reassessments of trends and options towards the end of the decade, but before the political upheavals of 1989.

The most comprehensive and sophisticated of the Chinese projections to be reviewed is a study by the Chinese Academy of Agricultural Sciences. It is confined to grains and economic crops (CAAS 1985). The data are analysed within different scenarios for the year 2000, and various analytical models are used: extrapolation of historical and current trends, simulation, and expert judgement. The study is strong on quantitative analysis, but, unfortunately, the scenarios do not always correlate, which limits their predictive capacity.

A later study by the Academy of Social Sciences emphasizes qualitative aspects, strategic analysis, and assessment of options (CASS 1986). The base-line data are few, but the study offers a comprehensive analysis of institutional and economic factors and constraints in the development process, and lists a number of proposals for institutional change which may promote agricultural development towards the year 2000.

Another comprehensive study focuses on structural development in rural areas. It is the result of a joint effort by two major reformist 'think tanks': The Rural Policy Research Office (RPRO) under the Secretariat of the CCP Central Committee and the Rural Development Research Centre (RDRC) under the State Council. This study integrates extrapolation of long-term development trends, analysis of growth patterns of sectoral interrelationships, and simulation excercises based on these analyses. The aim is to create a basis for defining policies which may contribute to configuring a rational sectoral composition in rural areas in the year 2000 (RPRO 1987).[1]

Finally, some minor studies, mostly based on a limited number of parameters, are primarily concerned with projecting quantitative growth within a qualitative framework and with identifying constraints on future development as well as policy options to alleviate these constraints (Guo Shiping 1985; Xiaokang 1988; Cong Anni 1989; Lin Longji 1989).

Most projections are made to serve as tools for policy-makers. China's recent political history has shown that clearly formulated development objectives focusing on qualitative aspects are often crucial to attract political interest, and that such objectives determine the framework for subsequent identification of quantitative targets. For example: The need to ensure self-sufficiency in grain, which is a commonly accepted development objective, has wide-ranging implications for the setting of targets for both grain and non-grain crops. Some articles, which primarily identify such objectives or policy options for future development, have also been included here to add to the qualitative dimension of the review (Gu Jingde 1985; Li Chuanzhang 1986; Liu Guanghui 1986; Fu Zhengde 1988; Li Yuanzhu 1988; Zhang Xuequan 1989). These studies offer little or no detail regarding their theoretical foundation or the underlying methodologies, and they only carry few source references, which is still quite common in Chinese social science literature. It is surprising, though, that there is little, if any, trace in the texts of the rich international literature on agricultural development in the Third World. In this respect, China's professionals appear still to live in splendid isolation.

Most of the projections under review are sympathetic to goals defined by China's reformist leadership in the 1980s. They are far from being impartial, and most appear to be excessively optimistic about future potentials. However, a number of the authors have attempted to strike a balance between political dictums on the one hand, and the need to pursue objectivity, accuracy, and scientific reliability on the other, and, all in all, the studies offer: (1) valuable data and information on the contemporary agricultural situation; (2) knowledge of the estimated resources available for future agricultural development; and (3) insight into the knowledge base for short-term and long-term agricultural and rural policies. However, sluggish growth in grain production and in some branches of cash crop production since the mid 1980s, as well as an excessive natural population growth rate, loss of agricultural land, and environmental degradation make some of the studies little more than testimonials of how difficult it is to project what often seems unprojectionable. This review explores how qualitative objectives and quantitative targets are linked in the projections, and appraises them on the basis of current performance in agriculture. The projections are also assessed in the light of findings and conclusions of the World Bank study and the recent global study by FAO. Since the issues involved are complex and the available data quite comprehensive, the focus is on basic objectives, options, and parameters, as well as on a few major crops, particularly grains, in order to confine the review within manageable limits.[2]

The Hierarchy of Development Objectives

Objectives and targets pertaining to agricultural development are linked together vertically and horizontally, like in a web, which may be called the 'hierarchy of development objectives'. No matter which objective or target is changed or redefined, corresponding objectives and targets at the same or other levels of the hierarchy may also have to be redefined or changed.

Here the 'hierarchy' image is used to link the arguments of the different studies in a coherent manner and to add contextual perspective to the individual arguments and propositions. The 'hierarchy' is shown in Figure 1. In the subsequent sections, the objectives for the future development of China's agriculture are presented in the order of the hierarchy. The focus is primarily on objectives that pertain to agricultural development, and, more specifically, on those that have a bearing on crop production.

Global Development Objectives

Population control is one of the basic global development objectives. The official 1.2 billion population target for the year 2000 was first announced at the Fifth National People's Congress in 1978 (Yan 1988, 165). Soon after it became evident, however, that the target was unrealistic, based as it was on the assumption that the natural rate of population growth could be confined to one per cent annually. Between 1978 (962 million) and April, 1989 (1,100 million), the rate of growth was 1.23 per cent. At the end of 1989, official sources estimated that the total population had reached 1,112 million and that the natural annual rate of growth was 1.43 per cent.[3] Some of the studies take the uncertainty about the natural rate of increase into account, as does the seventh five-year plan, which assumes an average growth rate of 1.16 per cent.[4] The lowest alternative projection for the year 2000 is 1,250 million at an annual rate of growth of 1.2 per cent (Xiaokang 1988), and the highest is 1,305 at a rate of growth of 1.4 per cent (Lin Longji 1989). Yan Hao offers an educated guess of 1,250 - 1,270 million, whereas the United Nations has projected a population level of up to 1,300 million on the basis of the 1982 population census data (Yan 1988, 182). The FAO study estimates the figure to be 1,256 million in the year 2000 at the fairly conservative annual growth rate of 1.1 per cent between 1985 and 2000 (Alexandratos 1988, Table A.1). However, if the rate of increase continues to remain at the 1989 level of 1.43 per cent, which

Figure 1. The hierarchy of development objectives

A. Global Development Objectives

B. Rural Development Objectives

B.1 Societal	B.2 Economic	B.3 Inter-	B.4 Environmental
Political		sectoral	
Institutional			

C. Sectoral Objectives

C.1 Agriculture (primary)   C.3 Service Sector (tertiary)
C.2 Industry (secondary)

D. Objectives Relating to Inputs/Factors of Production

D.1 Land	D.2 Labour/	D.3 Capital	D.4 Technology/material
	human resources		technical inputs

E. Objectives Relating to Individual Branches of Agricultural Production

E.1 Crop	E.2 Animal	E.3 Aquatic	E.4 Forestry
Production	Husbandry	Production	
1. Wheat	1. Cattle		
2. Rice	2. Pigs		
3. Coarse grains	3. Poultry		
4. Oilseeds	4. Milk		
5. Cotton	5. Eggs		

is not implausible, the figure will reach 1,300 million at the end of 2000, i.e. close to the UN estimate and the highest Chinese estimate—1,305 million (Lin Longji 1989).

All scenarios in the CAAS study presume that the total population will be confined to 1,200 million in 2000. Although it is acknowledged that demand for food will increase if the 1,200 million target is surpassed, the implications are not analysed (CAAS 1985, 389), thereby severely limiting the reliability of the detailed scenarios in the study.

The significant differences in food requirements in terms of grain at different population levels is demonstrated in Lin's projection, in which the need for grain at a total population of 1,305 million in 2000 is calculated to be 30-33 million tons higher than the approximate state target scenario using a 0.91 per cent population growth rate (Lin Longji 1989). Similar consequences can be observed from the World Bank projection which calculates the total grain requirement in 2000 to be 459 million tons at a one per cent population growth rate and a 3.5 per cent GNP growth rate, and 498 million tons if the GNP growth rate increases to

5.5 per cent. The requirement will rise significantly—to 536 million tons—if the population growth rate increases to 1.4 per cent in conjunction with a 5.5 per cent GNP growth rate (World Bank 1985, 25).

The FAO study estimates the annual 1985-2000 population growth rate of all developing countries (including China) to be 1.9 per cent. The rate for Asia (including China) will be 1.8 per cent, and that for low-income developing countries (including China) 1.7 per cent. If China was excluded from the latter two categories, the corresponding rates would be 1.8 per cent and 2.1 per cent respectively (Alexandratos 1988, 61). Hence, China's one per cent target growth rate is extremely low by comparable international standards. As a higher growth rate in China will not only have implications for China's food demand, but also for world food demand, it is surprising that the FAO study used a conservative estimate, especially considering that a higher actual growth rate was already evident.

Most of the studies refer to a number of qualitative global development objectives, which are politically and ideologically significant. Among these, the most important seem to be: the need for continued and accelerated growth—reflected in such objectives as 'agricultural modernization' and 'quadrupling of gross industrial and agricultural output value (GIAOV)' by 2000, both of which were announced at the Fifth National People's Congress in 1978. In a poor country like China, it is natural that development policies focus on growth, but in contrast to most other countries, where the indicator for growth is gross national product, the Chinese leadership understands economic performance in terms of GIAOV growth. If China is to attain the much-celebrated 'quadrupling' target, the growth rate should be in the range of 6.5 to 7 per cent for the rest of the century,[5] a rate which is significantly higher than the average gross domestic product growth rate of 4.4 per cent projected in the FAO study for 93 developing countries excluding China (Alexandratos 1988, 61).

Some of the studies describe the level of development to be attained by 2000 in terms of: 'Xiaokang', which means—literally translated—'small wealth' or 'small well-being'. The 'xiaokang' objective was propagated officially for the first time by the now demoted General Secretary of the Communist Party, Zhao Ziyang, in his report to the Thirteenth Party Congress in 1987.[6] The concept implies that China should move from 'wenbao' (litterally, 'having warm clothes and eating one's fill'), i.e. the basic needs strategy pursued during the Cultural Revolution, to that of 'xiaokang' in the year 2000, and from there to the stage of a medium-level developed country at the middle of the 21st century (Gu Jingde 1985).

'Xiaokang' comprises some loosely defined objectives for improvement of life quality, such as an improved diet, better and more varied clothing, higher levels of education, and a richer cultural life (Gu Jingde 1985). Furthermore a number of quantitative targets have been set for the year 2000, mostly on a per capita basis: The average annual income shall be in the range of 800—1000 yuan; expenditures on food shall decrease from 60 per cent to 40 per cent of per capita income, whereas that of non-food items shall increase from 40 to 60 per cent, or the ratio shall be at least 50:50 (Gu Jingde 1985; Xiaokang 1988); average food consumption per person shall reach over 400 kg of grain (including indirect consumption through animal products and liquor) and 45 kg of animal products (Xiaokang 1988), which is double the level of consumption in the early 1980s, but only about half of the demand projected by the World Bank on the basis of consumption patterns of analogous Chinese populations (World Bank 1985, 20).

The studies vary with regard to their quantitative definitions of 'xiaokang', but all relevant computations (Guo Shiping 1985; Xiaokang 1988; Huang Peimin 1985; CAAS 1985, 384) show that the expected changes in future dietary composition following increased personal incomes and, hence, an increased demand (CAAS 1985, 380; Gu Jingde 1985; RPRO 1987, 35; Xiaokang 1988; Lin Longji 1989)[7] will lead to higher demands for grain because of the conversion ratios of feed grain (World Bank 1985, 23). To this comes the extra demand for grain for direct human consumption (*kouliang*) which may arise when population growth exceeds the official one per cent target.

Although the official 400 kg per capita target is part of the 'xiaokang' scenario, one study argues, in an attempt to temper excessive optimism, that at a grain consumption level of 400 kg per capita, each Chinese will only be able to eat half a kg of grain and 100 g of meat per day in 2000, which may still be considered rather basic, i.e. 'wenbao' (Cong Anni 1989).

Such a reminder may help keep a proper perspective, but nevertheless, the importance of the 'xiaokang' objective cannot be underestimated. It is a meaningful conceptualization of the future growth path. By focusing on human needs as the basis for projections, it qualifies the somewhat fancy 'quadrupling' objective which makes little sense as a development objective beyond its catchy character.

Rural Development Objectives

Institutional arrangements in relation to farm management are discussed extensively in some of the studies. It is generally agreed that conditions shall be created for gradually expanding the scale of management, so that the typical farm will change from being 'small and complete' (*xiao er quan*), which has been the standard since decollectivization in the early 1980s, to become larger and engaged in specialized and socialized production. The need to promote and facilitate voluntary cooperativization is also underlined. The problem is, however, to define the ideal farm size in each of China's major regions. Not surprisingly, the best answer seems to be rather vague: somewhere between too big and centralized, like under the collective system, and too small and scattered, like the small-scale family farms prevalent now (Li Chuanzhang 1986).

The study by the Academy of Social Sciences (CASS 1986, 26-30) argues that private land ownership is unsuitable for overcoming the current small-scale management constraint (see also Delman 1989, 55-56), since it impedes the rational transfer of land, reduces investments in land, and begets land speculation. Instead, the CASS study contends, the scale of management can only be increased by vesting the state ownership in independent, regionalized land companies which can rent out their land to farmers in accordance with specific land use plans and through public bidding. The land companies would be share-holding enterprises with the original collective land-owners as share-holders. Such an arrangement would have several benefits, it is argued: the affiliation between land companies and farmers would become a simple, commercialized relationship between landowners and tenants; land companies would be in a position to control land use; and the rent collected could be used for land maintenance and improvement (CASS 1986, 26-30).

However, the CASS study also argues, somewhat self-contradictorily, that farmers should be allowed to keep their land as a personal insurance even if they leave agriculture to work in other sectors. Although this would appear to be a serious obstacle to enlarging the scale of management in view of the increasing population and the large number of redundant agricultural labourers who have retained their land, the study maintains that it would be detrimental to rural and personal security if non-active farmers were not allowed to retain their land. The risks involved in leaving agriculture are still considered to be too high (CASS 1987, 22-23).

No matter how crucial an expanded scale of management may be for future agricultural development, the ultimate feasibility of the proposition rests with the issues of population, which seems insolvable within the short-term perspective, the land constraint (see page 48), and the current fifteen year land contract period, which renders changes in the structure of land use almost impossible (Kojima 1988, 707).

A few authors see the safeguarding of peasants' democratic rights—e.g. electoral rights, property rights, and the freedom to speak—to be an important prerequisite for future agricultural development (e.g. Li Chuanzhang 1986). Currently, farmers are in a subordinate position, one study calls it a 'colonial relationship' (Liu Guanghui 1986), vis-à-vis the various government agencies they deal with. However, both farmers and cadres in local government agencies must learn to take personal political and economic risks, if they want to enjoy democratic rights and if China's rural areas are to break the present constraint of small-scale, risk averting farming. But the fostering of such a mentality may be impaired by the lack of willingness among large sections of China's rural bureaucracies to relinquish their control over farmers and to open markets, as well as by the absence of clear price signals at the macro-economic level (Delman 1989; Aubert in this volume).

Since political and socio-cultural developments are difficult to forecast and often too sensitive to be discussed within the framework of the kind of studies reviewed here, they have been largely neglected. The belief is that, given correct and stable policies, peasants will act as willed by the policy-makers (see e.g. CAAS 1985, 421-422). However, the rural situation is often quite different. The current, rather flexible, policies of decentralization have indirectly allowed peasants to pursue traditional organizational and institutional counter-strategies opposed to the policies propagated by the state (CASS 1986, 37). For example, over recent years, China's rural areas have seen the reemergence of 'secret societies' (*huidaomen*) on a scale never experienced before under the PRC (Munro 1989), and members of such secret societies and other similar organizations may not necessarily be interested in so-called 'democratic rights' and 'voluntary cooperativization', since they may enjoy entirely different social, political, and economic rights within the secret society they belong to. Whether such organizations will engage in direct political action, remains to be seen, however.

At the macro-economic level, the majority of the studies argue for the need to further strengthen the transition from direct administrative control to indirect regulation through economic levers and the market, a process which is already underway—at least it was until early 1989. A basic tenet in the market-oriented model is that society should strive for economic efficiency and profitability rather than pursue the equitable goals of the past (Fu Zhengde 1988). In the transition from a centralized to a market economy, the status of farmers as legal persons is a major issue to be dealt with. In principle, farmers are responsible for their own profits and losses, but should the government allow farmers to go bank-rupt if they prove to be poor and inefficient farm managers? And if so, how would traditional peasant society respond? The question is crucial, when discussing the viability of the market economy. Whereas the advantages and disadvantages of using the 'bankruptcy mechanism' in industry have been discussed for years, the same has not been the case for agriculture. Only the CASS study addresses this issue, and argues that the state should fix minimum prices on agricultural products covering the basic production cost (*chengben*), thereby preventing farmers from going bankrupt (CASS 1986, 39). In doing so, the study is in line with current practice, but if the market does not offer a mechanism for sifting out inefficient farmers, it will be difficult to expand the scale of management. In addition, it may well be the most educated and best farmers who will feel tempted to leave agriculture for more profitable occupations (Delman 1989, 57-58).

Sectoral Objectives

In line with other studies, the RPRO study argues that China should strive for coordinated development of the primary, secondary, and tertiary sectors and gradually move towards an industry-based sectoral structure. In two growth scenarios, a high and a low, the share of the primary sector in rural gross national product will fall dramatically: from 62 per cent in 1985 to between 42 and 38 per cent in 2000, whereas the share of the secondary and tertiary sectors will grow correspondingly, from 24 and 14 per cent in 1985 to between 37 and 39 per cent in the low scenario, and between 21 and 23 per cent in the high in 2000.[8]

Thus both the tertiary and particularly the secondary sector will play increasingly important roles in rural economic development. The same trend is evident in the CAAS study, which projects that the share of crop production in GIAOV will drop from 63.7 per cent in 1980 to between 24.9 and 28.3 per cent in two different scenarios in 2000 (CAAS 1985, 412). The tendency is already evident in real life: in 1987, the share of crop produc-tion in rural gross industrial and agricultural output value had already dropped to 35 per cent.[9]

The structural composition of crop production, i.e. the ratio between grain, economic crops, and other crops, will remain fairly stable, however, according to the CAAS project-ion. The share of grains in the total value of crop production will only drop from 72 per cent in 1980 to 69 per cent in 2000 (CAAS 1985, 412). Grains will continue to be the major crop group due to dietary preferences, the increasing demand mentioned previously, and the professed self-sufficiency policy. Furthermore, the CAAS study only projects fairly moderate annual growth rates of gross output value for crop production (2.92 per cent) between 1980 and 2000 as compared to those of GIAOV (between 6.5 and 7 per cent, see page 42), as well as compared to those for the primary sector in the RPRO study mentioned above.

The Environment

Severe environmental degradation is one of the factors constraining China's crop production most (Smil 1984; Delman 1989, 58-60), and a number of studies argue that environmental considerations are essential for guiding future agricultural development. Attention shall be shifted towards the development of eco-farming through a combination of traditional farming practices with modern technology. Another priority task is environmental protection, and one author argues that China should turn a new leaf and strive to create a new man-made eco-system capable of regenerating itself (Liu Guanghui 1986).

Although the awareness of the impact of environmental degradation on future agricultural development is growing, the resource base for implementing protection measures is extremely weak. Furthermore, farmers are hardly aware of the issues at stake. On the other hand, the science and human resource bases for developing eco-farming technologies may prove much better, and farmers are already familiar with the basic farming techniques involved.

Despite the various propositions, none of the projections analyse the viability of eco-farming given the land and population constraints. At least two issues are at stake: (1) Can high growth rates be sustained if agriculture intensifies the use of eco-farming technologies? Although highly productive eco-farming systems are in existence (see e.g. Chan 1988), there is little evidence that they can compete with farming systems based on modern inputs; (2) Does China's agriculture, particularly crop production, have the capacity to sustain high growth rates given the current rate of environmental deterioration, particularly through erosion and soil and water pollution?

Such analysis would be crucial since China will still have to pursue a strategy of inten-sified utilization of available resources for years to come in order to feed the growing population. As environmental degradation will continue in the foreseeable future, the regenerative capacity of the environment will be increasingly threatened. Therefore, relevant technologies will have to be developed to check deterioration. The focus of research may have to shift from growth capacity to regenerative capacity, and short-term gains may have to be sacrificed for long-term sustainability. However, such issues are hardly touched upon in the studies.

Agricultural Development

The 'two transformations' (*liange zhuanhua*) is a concept customarily used to designate two basic objectives of agricultural development: the transformation of (1) traditional into modern farming, and of (2) self-serving into commercial agriculture. The CASS study argues that commercialization of agriculture is a prerequisite for attaining agricultural modernization. A main criteria for assessing the degree of commercialization is the degree of commercial-ization of grain production, as it is the most important single branch of crop production. Only when more than 50 per cent of total grain production is marketed through commercial channels can China be said to have commercialized grain production, it is argued. 75 per cent would be the benchmark for so-called 'expanded reproduction' of grain production on market conditions. Currently, the figure is around 30 per cent including quota deliveries. Under the assumption that the composition of the rural population as well as the structure of grain production management remain the same and that total grain output grows at an annual rate of 2.9 per cent and population at a rate of one per cent, the 50 per cent target can be reached by 2000, it is argued. However, if the average size of grain producing farms is increased from the current 6.1 mu to 12.2 mu, and if 50 million households would concurrently dis-engage themselves from grain production, the 50 per cent target could be achieved in ten years (CASS 1986, 2 and 6-8). Since the population growth rate already exceeds one per cent and since grain production is stagnating (see page 53), such rapid commercialization seems to be little more than wishful thinking, however.

Another important objective is to ensure self-sufficiency in food, while improving the quality of products at the same time. The need for remaining self-sufficient is an objective shared by most of the studies. Pursuance of self-sufficiency is an international trend: A high level of self-sufficiency in basic foods is widely held to be an objective transcending purely economic considerations and most countries pursue it, despite the fact that food imports might be economically more viable given the depressed prices in the world food markets (Alexandratos 1988, 84-85).

China has strived for food self-sufficiency for decades, particularly during the Cultural Revolution when the 'grain first' strategy overruled most other considerations. Still it has proven difficult to satisfy the demand for grain. The years 1980-1981 and 1985-1986 showed a negative result on the national grain balance sheet, i.e. demand exceeded production, thus necessitating grain import (Cong Anni 1989). The trend persisted in the late 1980s, and grain imports continued. Undoubtedly, the problem has been aggravated by the decentralization of production management and the double pricing system, which has made procurement more cumbersome and costly for the state, and by the government's wish to stimulate other branches of agricultural production, e.g. economic crops and animal production. Infrastructural problems inhibiting the transport of grain from the countryside to the cities have also influenced the food supply situation negatively (Delman 1989, 48).

On a speculative note, it may be argued that, given the current declining returns on grain production (Aubert in this volume; Delman 1989, 49-51), farmers may choose to follow a different strategy. Not only do they attempt to avert risks by running their farms as 'small and complete', i.e. non-specialized, entities, they may also pursue their own self-sufficiency goals on a family, kinship and community basis as has always been the case in rural China (Thaxton 1987, 197-199). Such behaviour may not necessarily converge with the state self-sufficiency policy, since farmers will only grow what is needed for their own consumption and be uninterested in supplying what is needed by the state. Therefore, it may prove difficult to reverse the current trend of stagnation in grain production. At the same time, pursuance of the self-sufficiency objective will confine the major part of China's sown area, approximately 75 per cent of the total (CAAS 1985, 409), to grain production for decades to come, which will have a negative impact on the potential for diversification.

All the studies imply that increasing intensification of agricultural production is necessary to sustain anticipated growth. There is little willingness, however, to thoroughly examine the crucial issues embodied in this intensification: Can China's agricultural sector sustain such a development? Can the environment? Can the socio-economic infrastructure? And under which conditions?

One way of promoting agricultural development, a number of studies argue, is to develop an efficient tertiary sector capable of supporting pre-production, production and post-production operations. Traditionally, there has been too much emphasis on production, whereas linkages with marketing, circulation, and consumption have been neglected. Furthermore, the agricultural sector often lacks inputs. The marketing infrastructure, including storage, processing, and transport facilities, also lags behind, and farmers experience difficulties in buying inputs and in selling produce, called 'nanmai nanmai' in Chinese (Delman 1989, 51-53). Following the growth in production during recent years an increasing amount of agricultural produce deteriorates before reaching the customer. It is estimated that ten million tons of vegetables, fruit and aquatic products are spoilt annually due to lack of handling facilities (Liu Guanghui 1986). CAAS projects that 12.5 to 14 million tons of grain will be lost annually in the coming years (CAAS 1985, 387). Although it is difficult to quantify the different types of losses, there is no doubt that a large portion will be lost due to lack of proper handling facilities.

To meet the demand for more and better products, there is a strong need to make research and extension systems more efficient in order to generate and supply sufficient quantities of new technology in a timely manner. Urgent interventions in this respect are supported by all the studies, but they lack detailed analysis of resource requirements (see also Delman 1989 and 1990). The establishment of an infrastructural capacity within the tertiary sector is necessary to escape the 'small and complete' syndrome of self-serving agriculture and to speed up commercialization. Since relevant technologies are available, the future development of the service sector will depend on the availability of investment for expansion and upgrading. Since competition for capital is fierce, allocation of sufficient amounts of capital to this important sector will not only depend on establishment of an efficient capital market, but also on politcal good-will.

Factors of Production/Inputs

It is generally agreed in the studies that agricultural productive forces should be developed both qualitatively and quantitatively. In this respect, the CAAS study argues the need to increase the multiple cropping index to alleviate the serious land constraint. The multiple cropping index fell from 151 in 1978 to 148 in 1985 (Crook 1988, 15), possibly because marginal returns in sophisticated multiple cropping systems were too low to be sustained in a decontrolled economy. The CAAS study estimates that two thirds of the total grain output and one half of the total output of economic crops can be ascribed to multiple cropping practices. It is further argued that the multiple cropping index should not be pushed beyond limits of viability (CAAS 1985, 451). Given the man/land constraint and the potential decrease in arable land, the multiple cropping index will, however, still have to be increased to the level of about 155 in 2000 (CAAS 1985, 396), i.e. to the 1977 level.[10] Currently, the multiple cropping index shows an upwards tendency, and in 1987 it was 151.[11] Nevertheless, it must be considered an extremely arduous task to achieve a significant multiple cropping index increase given the declining total arable land (see also Walker 1988, 619-620; CAAS 1985, 395), as well as to retain the area sown to grain.

There is, however, considerable uncertainty about the actual size of China's arable land. Based on data from satelite photographs and qualified guesses made in China, the World Bank Study claimed that the total arable area might be anywhere from one fourth to one third larger than the current official estimate (World Bank 1985, 28). In August 1989, the State Land Administration Bureau brought out data which seemed to confirm this estimate. The Bureau explained that significant underreporting had occurred because local authorities feared that they would have to pay more agricultural tax and provide more quota grain if figures on arable land were revised upwards.[12] Therefore, the multiple cropping index may prove to be much lower than calculated in the preceding paragraph. More significantly, the uncertainty concerning the size of the total arable land as well as with respect to the actual size and rate of increase of the population may further rock the basis of the projections under review—in this case in a positive direction. However, it would be pertinent to ask why both the CAAS and the World Bank did not create scenarios taking these uncertainties into consideration?

Apart from increasing the multiple cropping index, land productivity can also be optimized by adjusting the land use structure as already discussed, and by improving soil quality. The current ratio between good, i.e. high-yielding, medium, and poor soils is 2:5:3 (Liang Mouqian 1988). High-yielding soils produce more than 2.2 tons of grain per crop per ha., medium-yielding lands produce grain in the range of 1.2 to 2.2. per crop per ha., and poor soils yield less than 1.2 tons per crop per ha. and are subject to frequent droughts, water-logging, or flooding (World Bank 1985, 28). The CAAS study argues that investment should be put into improving the quality of medium-yielding soils, whereas comparatively less attention should be paid to improving poor soils, since the investments needed are significantly higher and benefits proportionately lower (CAAS 1985, 419-421).

Irrigation can also be expanded and improved. In 1987, 44.4 mill ha. were effectively irrigated (Rural Statistical Yearbook 1988, 242), i.e. 46.2 per cent of the total arable land. Out of the total irrigated area, approximately 58 per cent of the high-yielding lands, 45.5 per cent of the medium-yielding and, 22.8 per cent of the low-yielding were irrigated in 1985. In order to sustain the projected growth in crop production, CAAS estimates that 13 million ha. will have to be added to the currently irrigated area (CAAS 1985, 417-418). Since water management facilities have deteriorated significantly over recent years, and since investment in maintenance and new facilities has also been cut (Delman 1989, 54-55), it may prove an impossible task to expand the irrigated area on such a scale. Finally, to qualify the projection, it should be noted that the seventh five-year plan only foresees an aggregate increase of 1.3 mill ha. of irrigated area during the five-year plan period from 1986 to 1990 (Seventh FYP 1986, 179). All the same, expansion of irrigated area is not necessarily a more important or a more viable option than improving management of current facilities to increase the efficiency of water distribution to the users (World Bank 1985, 33).

It is difficult to calculate gains to be obtained from each of the land augmenting measures, since the final outcome depends on an appropriate relationship among individual interventions. Outcome is also linked to the application of other inputs, such as seeds, fertilizers (see below), machinery etc. It is argued by CAAS, however, that all of these measures are essential to attain projected output targets (see page 52). Furthermore, the viability of the various land improvement measures proposed should be assessed in the light of the serious depletion of China's soils over recent decades. At present, good soils are being depleted, whereas poor soils are not being improved sufficiently (Delman 1989, 58-60).

The CAAS study estimates that it is necessary to open up 13 million ha of new land before 2000 to make up for projected land losses, but concedes that the target will be difficult to achieve (CAAS 1985, 394-395). The World Bank study estimates that only 3-5 million ha. of wasteland are suitable for sustained cultivation of annual crops (World Bank 1985, 29). In fact, it will be difficult to achieve any net gains from land reclamation measures given the current annual losses of arable land, which amounted to an annual average of 0.4 per cent, i.e. 341,000 ha. from 1986 to 1987 (Rural Statistical Yearbook 1988, 218).

As for the second important factor of production: labour, the RPRO study estimates that the total rural labour force will increase from 398 million in 1985 to 450 million in 2000, i.e. by 0.82 per cent annually, whereas the agricultural labour force in rural areas will decrease from 307 million to 230 million during the same period (RPRO 1987, 33), i.e. by 1.9 per cent annually. In 1987 the agricultural labour force was 308.7 million, i.e. slightly above the 1985 figure (Statistical Yearbook 1988, 220).

According to the RPRO study, 220 million rural labourers will have to be employed outside of agriculture in 2000 as compared to 91 million in 1985 (RPRO 1987, 33). Although assumptions with respect to changes in the structural composition of the rural labour force in the RPRO study are unknown, it appears that calculations are based on projected needs in the secondary and tertiary sectors, and not on needs in the agricultural sector. If this is true, a large part of the projected agricultural labour force may still be redundant in agricultural production in 2000.

Whichever the assumption, it is evident that lack of labour is not a constraint for the development of any of the sectors. With the falling agricultural labour force, however, there will be some room for improvement of labour productivity should either of the CAAS projections on sown area—143.3, 151.3, or 153.6 million ha. in 2000 (CAAS 1985, 409)—materialize. In that case, the average amount of sown area per agricultural worker would increase from 0.469 mu per capita in 1987 to 0.623-0.667 mu in 2000 for these three CAAS scenarios. Projected productivity gains in agriculture may be attained through a combination of increasing levels of labour saving technology in conjunction with the land augmenting measures mentioned previously. But better training of farmers is also an important factor influencing productivity. The educational level of the rural population is to be heightened through universalization of primary education before 1990, and of lower middle school education before 1995 (Li Chuanzhang 1986). To this should be added the need for technical education at all levels of the agricultural system.

The availability of capital for agriculture is crucial to allow the other factors of production to be developed and deployed in sufficient quality and quantity, and to facilitate human resource development, infrastructural development etc. This issue has attracted considerable attention over the last few years, both in China and abroad, since capital input, particularly the state budgetary allocation for investment in absolute terms and in terms of its share of the total state budget has decreased since the late 1970s (Watson 1989, 95-98; Delman 1989, 53-55), as has collective investment (Watson 1989, 99-100).

CAAS estimates that capital requirements for irrigation, production of farm chemicals, and new agricultural machinery during the period 1980 to 2000 will amount to 1,010 billion yuan., and it will be acquired through four channels: (1) rural industries (12 per cent); (2) eight per cent of the total government budgetary allocation for capital construction (6 per cent); (3) production funds raised through agricultural credits (15 per cent); and (4) funds provided by farmers at an annual rate of eight per cent of total GAOV (67 per cent). Altogether these four sources will possibly contribute 1,470 billion yuan during the period, which would amply cover the estimated needs (CAAS 1985, 424). The figures offered in the CAAS study are of limited value, however, since they only cover part of the needs and since no comparisons are made with the current level of investment.

Furthermore, farmers have been extremely cautious about capital investment since the reforms started in the early 1980s, and most of their investments in fixed assets have gone into non-productive housing. One source estimates that in 1983 the total rural investment in fixed assets was 40 billion yuan of which 26 billion yuan (60 per cent) went into housing and only 14 billion yuan (40 per cent) into productive investment (Yan Duanzhen 1987).

On the basis of the 1983 figure of 14 billion yuan in productive investment, Nicholas Lardy has calculated the rate of gross investment in agriculture in 1983 to be a modest seven per cent as compared to the global investment rate of the economy, which was 30 per cent. Out of the 14 billion yuan worth of productive investment, 47 per cent came from private households, 29 per cent from rural collectives, and 24 per cent from the state (Lardy 1986, 451-457).

Despite considerable uncertainty about these figures, it is worth speculating whether farmers will be able to sustain or even increase their proportion of gross agricultural investment given the prevailing depressed market conditions and the various constraining institutional arrangements. Since the current level of private investment is well below the projections in the CAAS study, despite the boom in agriculture in the early 1980s, it may prove difficult for farmers to do so. Furthermore, experience has shown that farmers may prefer to invest in non-agricultural assets and activities. The question is, then, which incentives will the government devise to motivate farmers to increase their productive investments? Unfortunately, none of the studies give the subject more than superficial consideration.[13]

A variety of technology objectives are identified in the studies which mostly reflect well-established policies as outlined in the seventh five-year plan (Seventh FYP 1986, 231-241) and in science and technology plans (e.g. Zhongguo Kexue 1986, 44-48). With respect to the most crucial technologies, one author argues that in 2000 China should attain the level of the advanced countries in the late 1980s, and that the mechanization level should reach that of medium-level developed countries in the 1980s (Li Yuanzhu 1988).

There is surprisingly little substantial analysis or discussion of options and strategies for developing new or existing technologies in the studies. What are, for example, the long-term socio-economic and ecological implications of an 'oil-based' as compared to an 'eco-farming' strategy and of choosing between modern bio-technologies and traditional or proven 'intermediate' technologies? Even more importantly: What are the energy requirements for sustaining continued growth propelled by modern technology and will energy supplies be able to meet the increasing demands?

Given the potential benefits of increasing technology inputs, such analysis is essential. For example, one Chinese analyst tentatively estimates the contributions of various factors of production to productivity growth during the period 1952-1985 to be as follows—Technology: 29.32 per cent; increased investment in land improvement: 0.21 per cent; investment in human resource development: 11.39 per cent; and capital investment: 59.08 per cent. The importance of technology in productivity growth reflected in this analysis is significant, but the author argues that the percentage is still far below that of the developed countries (Feng Haifa 1989). Although difficult to compare, evidence suggests that the rates of return on technological development are indeed substantially higher in developed economies (Ruttan 1982, 241-249).

The ever-increasing use of technology inputs is particcularly manifest in the case of chemical fertilizers, one of the 'pillars' of the success of Green Revolution technologies in

China over the last three decades. Application rates for chemical fertilizer doubled between 1977 and 1981. By 1983, 115 kg of nutrients were being applied per ha., which equalled the level of USA. India only used a third of this amount per ha., whereas application levels in South Korea and Japan were three times as high. Thus China's application level is already high by world standards, but still behind comparable farming systems in East Asia. Chemical fertilizer is supplemented by organic fertilizer in amounts corresponding to 40 per cent of the total amount of applied chemical fertilizer (nutrients). In 1983, 70 per cent of fertilizers were used on grain crops. In 1981, the N:P:K ratio was 100:31:4 as compared to a world average of 100:52:10. In Japan the ratio was 100:112:83. The composition of fertilizers in China is disproportionate and impedes efficient utilization of the large nitrogen component (World Bank 1985, 34-35).

The CAAS study estimates that fertilizer application will increase to about 300 kg per ha. in 2000,[14] and argues that the N:P:K ratio will have to be more balanced. The target for 2000 is 100:60:20, and it is estimated that the fertilizer industry will have the capacity to supply the required quantities (CAAS 1985, 417). However, the energy requirement to meet the increased demand is not established.

Given environmental constraints and the amounts of unutilized nutrients already being washed out of China's soils (Delman 1989, 58), the strategy of steadily increasing fertilizer application may prove detrimental to the environment and result in quickly diminishing economic returns, reducing the proportionate contribution of technology to total agricultural growth. Furthermore, there appears to be a contradiction in the CAAS scenario between the fertilizer strategy (reality) and the eco-farming strategy (the ideal), which will have to be reconciled in the long-term perspective.

Output Targets and Current Performance

All scenarios in the CAAS projections envision growth for the major crops included (rice, wheat, cotton and oilbearing crops)—in terms of both per-unit yields and total output—but the average annual growth rate for grain yields per hectare are expected to decelerate in the 1990s, from about two per cent during the period 1983—1990 to 1.43 per cent between 1983 and 2000 in the lowest CAAS scenario and to about 1.8 in the two highest scenarios.[15] The study does not explain whether this trend reflects anticipated declining returns on inputs, lack of resources for sustained growth (e.g. technological or land resources), or saturation of demand. The Chinese case is not unique, however. A similar declining trend in per hectare growth rates may be observed at the global level (Alexandratos 1988, 120-123).

The annual increase of per hectare yields for grain from 1966 to 1984 was 3.6 per cent, well above the annual averages projected by the CAAS study for the remaining years of this century. During those years, China benefited from the availability of emerging Green Revolution technologies combined with steadily increasing supplies of inputs. A 0.2 per cent annual decline during the subsequent three years (1984—1987) held less promise for the future, however. Growth rates for rice and wheat were sluggish, whereas those for cotton and oil bearing crops were negative.[16]

A variety of computations in the studies of the total grain requirement for 2000 shows a lowest requirement of 480 million tons (Guo Shiping 1985) and a highest of 593 million tons (Gu Jingde 1985). CAAS projects the total requirement to be between 498 and 526 million tons (CAAS 1985, 383-389), whereas the World Bank's estimates are between 459 and 536 million tons using a low and a high growth scenario respectively (World Bank 1985, 25). As the projections base themselves on incongruous sets of assumptions weighing individual parameters differently (such as population, availability of resources, gross national product growth rate, demand elasticity etc.), they escape direct comparison, and it would be pointless to judge which is most likely to materialize, if any.

However, if the government target for consumption of grain in 2000 is taken as the basis, i.e. 400 kg per capita (or approximately 35 kg more than the current level of consumption), the total requirement would amount to 520 million tons for a population of 1.3 billion, which seems to be a likely figure. Using 1989 as the base year (407 million tons),[17] the total annual output will then have to grow at a rate of 2.25 per cent to meet the government target scenario. If we ignore the uncertainties presented previously with respect to various parameters, the two high CAAS scenarios on projected production performance for grain—507 and 527 million respectively (CAAS 1985, 397)—are closest to the estimated requirement. They both presuppose an annual per ha. yield increase of about 1.8 per cent from 1983 to 2000. The low figure is based on a grain area of 109 million ha. and the high on a grain area of 114 million ha. In comparsion, the OECD calculates the total grain requirement in 2000 to be much higher—570 million tons—on the basis of a 1.3 billion population figure (OECD 1988, 11).

Given the land constraint, increased total outputs will have to come from increased per-unit yields in the future, as is the case in other parts of the world (Alexandratos 1988, 120-121). As we have seen, most of the studies argue that these should come from intensification of land use and cultivation methods, as well as from higher levels of technology application—including consumable inputs. All the Chinese studies contend, directly or indirectly, that the capacity and potential to follow such a growth path exists. The World Bank study is basically in agreement with this assessment provided that technological development and application can follow suit, particularly the expansion of the area sown with hybrids, and that distribution of available technologies becomes more efficient (World Bank 1985, 57-64). In this respect, the World Bank appears to have been smitten by the optimism characteristic of China's agricultural circles in the mid-1980s.

Given current performance on total output and per-unit yields, there is reason to be pessimistic, though, about China's capacity to attain the more optimistic of these estimates. Grain production has continuously fluctuated below the 407 million tons record in 1984 and only hit 407 million tons again in 1989. It is now certain that the lowest target for 1990—425 million (Seventh FYP 1986, 94)—cannot be attained. Furthermore, the population growth rate has already exceeded one per cent, and there is no solid evidence available to testify that the rate of specialization in grain production is increasing. Therefore, current performance is a warning sign that the future may not be as bright as expected, and it may be surmised that China will just be able to sustain the current level of per capita availability of grain, i.e. 366 kg in 1989. This would result in a total harvest of about 476 million tons in 2000 with an average annual increase of 1.43 per cent, which corresponds to the lowest CAAS scenario for the period 1983 to 2000 (CAAS 1985, 397). In that case, the Chinese diet would remain more or less the same as today—with the already existing regional variations (CAAS 1985, 427).

Summary and Conclusion

This review of projections of agricultural development in China has primarily focused on objectives and targets pertaining to crop production, particularly grains. By pooling studies only published over a five year period (1985-1989), the advantages of historical perspective are of course lost. But this is of minor importance considering the purpose, which was to look at the state-of-affairs in this particular field and to assess the viability of objectives and targets identified by the various studies.

There is evidence of some conceptual development during the period: Chinese planners have moved from the quantitative concept of the 1970s: 'quadrupling of GIAOV', to the more qualitative concept of the 1980s: 'xiaokang'. Otherwise, however, the basic conceptual configuration was already there in the mid 1980s. The objectives identified are quite comprehensive and relate to all levels of the 'hierarchy of development objectives'. Although the selected source materials were far from exhaustive, they fully reflect reformist thinking in China in the 1980s.

Most of the projections reviewed lack methodological clarity, particularly in explaining the underlying assumptions. There are only few source references, and the general approach makes it difficult to identify different schools of thought, emerging traditions, and theoretical breakthroughs, which have advanced the knowledge base of China's policy-making community. Data are often handled indiscriminately to underpin and not to validate or test ideas, concepts, and objectives, and to support current policies, rather than to prove or disprove their viability. To a certain extent, the same is the case for the CAAS study. It does stand out against the other studies, however, in being by far the most comprehensive study and in offering well documented scenarios for future development, which are quantitatively substantiated.

Although projections often sacrifice objectivity and scientific reliability to allow for quantification and qualification of policy objectives, they may, nevertheless, be usefully regarded as catalogues of policy options which represent the anticipated convergence of reformist developmental goals and policies with growth potentials and potential structural adjustments to future needs.

If the current stagnation in crop production persists and if projected increases in sown area for all crops in most scenarios fail to materialize, grain production will barely be able to follow suit with the increasing population. In that case, other branches of production, such as coarse and minor grains, other economic crops, and animal products will be negatively affected. Since grain will have to be grown at almost any cost to feed the increasing population, the diet may eventually remain more or less as it is, instead of swinging towards higher consumption of animal products as forecasted, thereby making it impossible to attain the 'xiaokang' objective with its associated benefits.

It may be asked whether the implications of the excessive population growth, the decrease in arable land, and the current stagnation in grain production could not have been designated more clearly as risks by the 'projectors', if they had not been so preoccupied with validating development objectives and policies? If they claim that these risks could not have been identified, then they have indeed been true performers of the art of projecting the unprojectionable.

Notes

The author is indebted to Ole Odgaard, Dirk Betke, Clemens Stubbe Østergaard, and Flemming Christiansen for their useful comments and suggestions on the draft of this article. Special thanks to Claude Aubert for drawing the author's attention to the OECD (1988) report.

1. I am aware of two other comprehensive projections dealing with aspects of rural development, but not directly with agriculture (Deng Yingtao 1988; Li Bingkui 1988).
2. The original conference paper carried numerous tables from the various sources used for this review. They have been taken out by the editors to economize on space. The tables are available upon request from: The Secretary, Institute of East Asian Studies, University of Aarhus, 8000 Aarhus C., Denmark.
3. SWB (*Summary of World Broadcast*) FE/0681, B2/5, 6 February 1990.
4. Computed on the basis of an estimated population of 1,113 million in 1990 (Seventh FYP 1986, 92).
5. Computed on the basis of data in Statistical Yearbook 1988, 25.
6. The China Quarterly, no. 113, 1988, 144.
7. See also Kueh (1988) for a discussion of changes in pesants' food consumption patterns and dietary consumption as well as of the adequacy of current nutritional levels.
8. A number of different scenarios are analysed on the basis of international comparisons of the structural composition of the three sectors at various levels of national incomes. The lowest of these projections has a gross output value of 753 billion yuan in 2000 (RPRO 1987, 28-31)
9. Calculation based on data in Statistical Yearbook 1988, 214 and 216. Computations on the same set of data show that crop production accounted for 56 pct. of GVIAO in 1980.
10. Walker (1988) has calculated four scenarios elaborating on the same set of data as in the CAAS study: 154.5, 158, 164.4, and 170.1 (CAAS 1985, 619). The latter two assume that the arable area will decrease while using the same projections for sown area. Therefore, they are particularly high. See also Walker's discussion on the potential decline in arable area (Walker 1988, 593-599).
11. Calculation based on an arable area of 95.88 million ha. and a sown area of 144,95 million ha. (Agricultural Statistics 1987, 17 and 34).
12. SWB/FE/W0090, 16 August 1989, A/3.
13. For a discussion of the issues involved, see Watson (1989).
14. Calculation based on data in CAAS (1985, 417), and Rural Statistical Yearbook (1988, 238).
15. Computed on the basis of data in CAAS (1985, 397).
16. Computations are based on the following sources: *1966-1984:* Rural Economic Handbook (1989, 146-147, 150-151, 152-153, 189-190, 191-192, 240-241 and 256-259); *1987:* Rural Statistical Yearbook (1988, 81-82, 83, 85 and 68); Agricultural Yearbook (1988, pp. 277 and 295); *1990:* Seventh FYP (1986, 94, 129 and 141).
17. SWB/FE/W0110, 10 January 1990, A/3.

References

Agricultural Economics: *Nongye Jingji*. Beijing: Zhongguo Renmin Daxue.

Agricultural Statistics (1987): *Zhongguo Nongye Tongji Ziliao 1987*. Beijing: Nongye Chubanshe, 1988.

Agricultural Yearbook (1988): *Zhongguo Nongye Nianjian 1988*. Beijing: Nongye Chubanshe.

Alexandratos (1988): Nikos Alexandratos (ed.), *World Agriculture: Toward 2000. An FAO Study*. London: Belhaven Press.

CAAS (1985): 'Wo guo liangshi he jingji zuowu fazhande yanjiu'. In: *Zhongguo nongcun fazhan zhanlüe wenti*. Beijing: Zhongguo Nongye Keji Chubanshe, 377-456;

CASS (1986): *Zhongguo nongye fazhan zhanlüe wenti*, Beijing: Zhongguo Shehui Kexueyuan.

Chan (1988): George Lai Chan, 'Energy Aspects of the Integrated Farming System in China'. Paper presented to the International Conference On Renewable Energy and Local Production, Ydby, Denmark, 18-24 September 1988.

Cong Anni (1989): Cong Anni et al., 'Lengjing yuce nongye xingshi—shenzhong jueze zhanlüe juece'. *Caizheng yanjiu*, No. 2, 34-39. Reprinted in *Agricultural Economics*, 1989:8, 11-16.

Crook (1988): Frederick W. Crook, *Agricultural Statistics of the PRC 1949-1986*, Washington D.C.: United States Department of Agriculture.

Delman (1988): Jørgen Delman, *The Agricultural Extension System in China*. London: Overseas Development Institute. (*Agricultural Administration (Research and Extension) Network paper*, No. 3).

Delman (1989): Jørgen Delman, 'Current Peasant Discontent in China: Background and Political Implications'. *China Information*, IV:2, 42-64.

Delman (1990): Jørgen Delman, 'Agricultural Extension in China—A Perspective From Renshou County'. *Copenhagen Papers in East and Southeast Asian Studies*. (Forthcoming).

Deng Yingtao (1988): Deng Yingtao, *Xin fazhan fangshi yu Zhongguode weilai*. Beijing: Guowuyuan Nongjiu Zhongxin Fazhan Yanjiusuo. (*Fazhan Yanjiu Baogao*, No. 4).

Feng Haifa (1989): Feng Haifa, 'Lun jishu jinbu yu nongye fazhan'. *Nongye Jishu Jingji*, No. 2, 1-5.

Fu Zhengde (1988): Fu Zhengde, 'Ershiyi shiji fazhanzhong guojiade nongcun qushi'. *Weilai yu Fazhan*, No. 6, 1-5.

Gu Jingde (1985): Gu Jingde, '2000 nian wo guo nongcun fazhande qige da qushi'. *Ganjiang Jingji*, No. 2, 28-30. Reprinted in *Agricultural Economics*, 1985:5, 20-23.

Guo Shiping (1985): Guo Shiping, '2000 nian wo guo heli shiwu jiegou liangde queding ji shengchan nenglide gujia'. *Nongye Xiandaihua Yanjiu*, No. 3, 23-26. Reprinted in *Agricultural Economics*, 1985:13, 122-125.

Huang Peimin (1985): Huang Peimin et al., 'Shiwu goucheng yu nongye shengchan'. *Nongye Jishu Jingji*, No. 6, 24-27. Reprinted in: *Agricultural Economics*, 1985:13, 118-121.

Kojima (1988): Reeitsu Kojima, 'Agricultural Organization: New Forms, New Contradictions'. *The China Quarterly*, No. 116, 707-735.

Kueh (1988): Y.Y. Kueh, 'Food Consumption and Peasant Incomes in the Post-Mao Era'. *The China Quarterly*, No. 116, 635-670.

Lardy (1986): Nicholas Lardy, 'Prospects and Some Policy Problems of Agricultural Development in China'. *American Journal of Agricultural Economics*, 68:2, 451-457.

Li Bingkui (1988): Li Bingkui, 'Xiangzhen qiye: Zou xiang 2000 niande zhengce sikao'. *Jingji Yanjiu Cankao Ziliao*, No. 1834 (March 1988), 1-21.

Li Chuanzhang (1987): Li Chuanzhang, 'Wo guo nongcun shehui fazhande mubiao tixi'. *Fujian Luntan: Jingji-Shehui Ban*, No. 12, 49-51. Reprinted in *Agricultural Economics*, 1987:1, 7-9.

Li Yuanzhu (1988): Li Yuanzhu, '2000 nian wo guo nongye fazhan mubiao'. *Jingji Yuce yu Xinxi*, No. 3, 10-11. Reprinted in: *Agricultural Economics*, 1988:4, 111-112.

Liang Mouqian (1988): Liang Mouqian, 'Wo guo nongcun huanjing ji ziyuan chuxian quanmian weiji'. *Jingji Yanjiu Cankao Ziliao*, No. 34, 32-39.

Lin Longji (1989): Lin Longji, 'Zhongguo chengxiang jumin liangshi xuqiu qushi yuce'. *Shanghai Jingji*, No. 1, 60-64. Reprinted in: *Agricultural Economics*, 1989:3, 176-179.

Liu Guanghui (1986): Liu Guanghui, 'Shilun nongye xiandaihuade duo mubiao tixi—jian tan wo guo nongye xiandaihuade mubiao xuance'. *Nongye Jingji Xiaoguo*, No. 6, 17-23. Reprinted in: *Agricultural Economics*, 1987:2, 153-160.

Munro (1989): Robin Munro (ed.), 'Syncretic Sects and Secret Societies'. *Chinese Sociology and Anthropology*, 21:4 (Summer 1989).

OECD (1988): *Food Consumption and Agricultural Output Targets in China for 1990 and 2000, and Their Impact On China's Agricultural Trade*, Paris: OECD.

RPRO (1987): *1986-2000 nian Zhongguo nongcun chanye jiegou yanjiu*. Beijing.

Rural Economic Handbook (1989): *Zhongguo Nongcun Jingji Daquan 1949-1986*, Beijing: Nongye Chubanshe.

Rural Statistical Yearbook (1988): *Zhongguo nongcun tongji nianjian 1988*. Beijing: Zhongguo Tongji Chubanshe.

Ruttan (1982): Vernon W. Rutttan, *Agricultural Research Policy*, Minneapolis: University of Minnesota.

Seventh FYP (1986): *Di qige wunian nongcun jingji fazhan zhuanti jihua*. Beijing: Nongye Chubanshe.

Smil (1984): Vaclav Smil, *The Bad Earth—Environmental Degradation in China*, London: Zed Press.

Statistical Yearbook (1988): *Zhongguo Tongji Nianjian 1988*, Beijing: Zhongguo Tongji Chubanshe.

Thaxton (1977): Ralph Thaxton, 'The World Turned Downside Up—Three Orders of Meaning in the Peasants' Traditional Political World'. *Modern China*, 3:2, 185-228.

Walker (1988): Kenneth R. Walker, 'Trends in Crop Production: 1978-86'. *The China Quarterly*, No. 116, 592-633.

Watson (1989): Andrew Wason, 'Investment Issues in the Chinese Countryside'. *The Australian Journal of Chinese Affairs*, No. 22, 85-126.

World Bank (1985): *China—Agriculture to the Year 2000*. Annex 2 in: *China: Long-term Development Issues and Options*. Washington D.C.: The World Bank, 1985.

Xiangzhen fazhan (1987): *Dutede lishi nanti yu yansude xianshi juece—2000 Zhongguo nongcun xiangzhen fazhan yanjiu yu baogao*. Beijing: Guowuyuan Nongcun Fazhan Yanjiu Zhongxin.

Xiaokang (1988): 'Xiaokang shenghuo zhanlüe mubiao yu nongcun jingji fazhan'. *Xiaofei Jingji*, No. 2-9. Reprinted in *Agricultural Economics*, 1988:8, 163-170.

Yan (1988): Yan Hao, 'China's 1.2 Billion Target For the Year 2000: "Within" or "Beyond"?'. *Australian Journal of Chinese Affairs*, No. 19/20, 165-183.

Yan Duanzhen (1987): Yan Duanzhen, 'Nongye fazhan sudu yu nongye touzi biandongde guilü'. *Zhongguo Renmin Daxue Xuebao*, No. 4, 30-37. Reprinted in: *Agricultural Economics*, 1987:10, 97-105.

Zhang Xuequan (1989): Zhang Xuequan, '2000 nian nongcun shehui jingji fazhande mubiao moshi'. *Weilai yu Fazhan*, No. 3, 14-19.

Zhongguo Kexue (1986): *Zhongguo kexue jishu zhengce zhinan (Kexue jishu baipishu di yi hao)*. Beijing: Kexue Jishu Wenxian Chubanshe.

THE STATE
AND RURAL CHINA

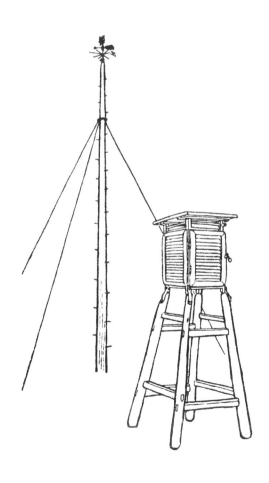

Emerging State-Society Relations in Rural China

Vivienne Shue

Premises

Even very strong states can exhibit some profound weaknesses. And even weak (or weakened) societies may adapt old structures and devise new strategies of resistance, evasion, and cooptation that serve to constrain, or to confound, a dictatorial state's freedoms and forms of action. More attention to the frailties of even such a universally acknowledged 'strong' state as that which has now managed to govern the Chinese mainland for more than forty years, may help give rise to interesting comparative insights. Several able students of other third world systems, both socialist and non-socialist, have already noted that new states may be both strong and weak at the same time—along different dimensions.[1] A reappraisal, then, of the Chinese state's particular mixture of demonstrated power and simultaneous impotence, could bring it more fruitfully into the field of comparative political study and analysis. Such hopes and assumptions as these are among the underlying premises of this essay. Another theme, however, is that the very process of consolidating even a broadly welcomed and popularly based regime in a post-colonial or post-revolutionary setting can (and almost certainly will) trigger social responses and adaptations to the new state's power that ultimately work to set important limits on state capacities. Control provokes resistance; even in cases where the last known political alternatives were widely held to be unrepresentative, unjust, inchoate, or anarchic.

This essay sketches some of the main lines in that process of state consolidation and social response as it has unfolded in the Chinese case. The intent is to suggest that it is not merely to 'state-society relations' at a given time (or at several points in time) that we will have to look in order to see how and why a state is strong or not-so-strong. But rather, that it is to the entire unfolding of the reflexive interactions between state and society over time:actions --> adaptations --> reactions --> readaptations, that we must give our attention. And further to suggest—although this is a point which will have to be given less attention here—that an adequate approach to the interactive processes involving state and society must include consideration of both the relevant structural and the phenomenological dimensions of the political experience.

A difficult conceptual and analytical task such as this may, perhaps, be most concretely and most confidently grasped by looking toward the lower levels of a polity, where state and society can be said to connect with the minimum of attenuation and abstraction. This essay focuses, therefore, on the interplay between local state and rural society in Mao's China, and after.

The 'Thin' State of the Mao Era

Structurally and procedurally speaking, the state that Mao built was long but not very wide. The Mao era saw the extension of effective state organization further down into rural society than ever before in China. But that organization achieved little structural differentiation at the bottom and actually routinely interacted with only a very limited range of social groups and associations.

The hierarchy of command relations itself was, of course, impressive. Looked at from the bottom up—from the individual household to the supreme State Council, as it were—all of China was apparently organized into a single command hierarchy of nested territorial units that almost fully blended party/state and society into one. Every peasant household belonged to a production team, which collectively owned and farmed its assigned land, and which was headed by a team leader selected by the party and agreed to by the households; several such teams constituted a brigade, which was still a collective but almost invariably was headed by a party secretary; a number of brigades made up a commune, where party and state agencies (as well as collective and state ownership systems) generally converged, to create at least a small semblance of local government presence at commune headquarters, including perhaps a police station, a tax and commerce control office, and an elementary school; thirty or more communes made up a county, where the local-state apparatus was much more fully elaborated; a number of counties comprised a prefecture; several prefectures made up a province; and every province reported finally to what was referred to as 'the center' in Beijing.

This basic vertical command hierarchy of geographically or horizontally demarcated units was then supplemented by a second set of vertically articulated governmental systems—the score or so ministries (such as Education, Public Health, Agriculture, Second Light Industry, etc.) with headquarters in Beijing and direct command relations extending to branch offices at least as far down as the county level. These two systems of vertically- organized ministries and horizontally-demarcated jurisdictions meshed at levels such as the county, where a ministerial branch office functioned simultaneously as a bureau of the county government. Together these two hierarchies formed the basic gridwork of state power in the rural periphery.[2]

At first this may seem like a more than sufficiently elaborated structure to enable a wide range of state interactions with social units and groups as well as a 'thick' integration of state activities with those of non-state actors. And all the more self-evident might it seem that Chinese state and society were indeed intimately integrated when we recall just how ambitious the Maoist state's economic planning and social change agenda was, and how often the party/state made use of giant mobilization drives and of mass political campaigns. Yet several specific trends and factors seem to have contrived over time to make such a thick integration of state and society rather more apparent than real.

First, state organs in the countryside almost always remained skeletally staffed.[3] Rural cadres were invariably burdened with multiple administrative roles and responsibilities. An austerely streamlined local government was the goal; generalist omni-competence was glorified; functional specialization was decried as a vice; and positive disincentives were offered to state functionaries for the acquisition of administrative expertise. The state may, in some sense, have been 'everywhere' in the Chinese countryside; but wherever it was, as a rule, it was spread pretty thin.

Second, the very spareness and formalism characteristic of the Maoist state structure in the countryside was matched by a certain structural simplification and artificial sameness that came gradually to be imposed on rural society itself. The redistributions of wealth and opportunity entailed in the early land reform movement and then in collectivization did not yield a *perfect* social leveling, of course, but the homogenizing and equalizing effects on the rural population were nonetheless very striking. And new regulations and policies, intended precisely to prevent any 'repolarization,' or reemergence of richer and poorer strata in rural society, were continually implemented over the ensuing years.

The early classification of every rural dweller into one or another of the party's official class categories also had its simplifying and homogenizing effects. A small percentage of village people were given 'bad' class labels as exploiters or counter-revolutionaries; and they and their families were made into pariahs for more than a generation. The vast majority, however, were given 'good' class labels as 'poor' peasants or 'lower-middle' peasants; and thus, conferred upon them with a stroke, were not only an automatic presumption of political rectitude and reliability, but also a certain degree of social status in the 'New China'. (Lost, of course, in this mass classification process, were most of the ornate subtleties of the prior systems of social stratification by which a peasant patriarch might consider it a good match to marry his daughter into a farm family owning two oxen but not into one with a sideline in tanning ox hides; into a carpenter's household, but not a shepherd's, and so on). The collectivization of agricultural production not only sealed the fate of the old landed elite, it gave to almost all rural dwellers the *same* occupation and thus, at least overtly, it enormously simplified the categories of social stratification and the entire structure of social life in the countryside.

Since it tied the fate of each individual household to the fate of the entire collective unit, collectivization also greatly enhanced the salience of the small community and its welfare for rural people. Since the harvest was pooled and then shared, the real income of each family depended not only on its own efforts and its own good or bad luck, but also on the quality and quantity of the labor of all the other members of the collective community. The 'household registration system,' the means for enforcing the late-fifties' interdiction on peasants' cityward migration, even further magnified the little community's importance. Peasants were in effect tied for life to the land and to the local collective into which they were born. No longer available were the old society's meagre (but frequently lifesaving) options for temporary family migration to safer havens in hard times, or for sending a son to the nearest coastal town after a disastrous harvest, to put in some months of coolie labor on the docks. Chinese peasants, in the two decades of the sixties and seventies, had little choice but to identify their own welfare and that of their families entirely with the fortunes of their village units.[4]

Additional Mao-era proscriptions against private productive activity and non-state regulated trade also cut down on the normal means of the rural dweller's connection to the outside, through market exchanges, peddling, or short-term hiring. The ties binding each peasant household to its own collective production unit became increasingly strong and compelling while the ties linking them to outside units and communities grew more attenuated or dissolved. From the early fifties through the late seventies, rural communities clearly became more and more inward-looking and isolated from one another. This peculiar parcelization of rural social life into innumerable small, similar, but discrete units was well noted by Western observers who characterized the Chinese socio-economy of that period as 'cellular' in structure, or as 'fragmented,' or as resembling a 'honeycomb'.[5]

The vigorous and sustained party/state pursuit of nationwide economic development through 'local self-reliance' imparted a similar cellularity to the organization and activities of higher-level units too—communes, counties, and even whole provinces.[6] Local governments in these units ceaselessly exhorted their people to strive for grain self-suffic-iency, in accord with national policy. County officials promoted the building of small low-tech workshops to produce tools, motors, ploughs etc., so as to avoid having to rely on procuring them through the unreliable state supply system. Small localities established their own little fertilizer factories, cement pipe works, breweries, chemical plants, and coal mines—using machinery and materials produced locally whenever possible—to satisfy local needs without recourse to imports from other localities.

Alongside this strangely parcelized socio-economic structure, not surprisingly, there developed a highly cellularized pattern of political authority too. Without significant lateral ties of mutual dependence with surrounding units, the influence and authority of local cadres, however great at home, generally stopped at the county line. The pattern of political power, like the pattern of rural local factory development sloganized at the time, tended to be 'small but complete'. Cadre abuses and petty tyrannies might readily flourish in such a cellularized polity. Inability to wipe out this malady of the system was one of the ways in which the strong state showed its weakness. And the system's toleration for local tyrannies was to be one of the key elements in its ultimate delegitimization.

Of course, most local cadres did not become local tyrants. Many became local advocates instead—lobbyists, apologists and mini-system-builders aiming to serve the interests of their local constituents within the larger bureaucratic system. This local protectionist tendency, in its own way however, could be every bit as undermining of central state policy, and as corrosive of central state capacity to realize its goals at the periphery, as the tendency to petty tyranny and abuse.

Numerous rural social adaptations emerged in response to these twin patterns of economic cellularization and power parcelization. Two may be noted here in particular. First, the cultivation of 'connections' or *guanxi*—networks of personal relationships based on the exchange of information, gifts and favors—helped to pierce the barriers that had been erected dividing society from itself. The use of *guanxi* ties had always been a characteristic of Chinese society; but the practice became much elaborated and intensified as a social (and political) coping mechanism during the Mao era.[7] Second, localistic protectionism and little-empire building were raised to a new level of social and political importance. Local people in and out of government routinely hoarded resources, misreported local conditions, evaded higher-level exactions, and deflected or distorted commands and policies from above—the better to serve local ends and needs.

Both localism and *guanxi* networking greatly undermined the central state's capacity to gather information and to implement its policies in the countryside. And the very fact that such questionable or quasi-illegitimate methods were finally so widely resorted to by bureaucrats and people alike—in pursuit of noble ends as well as selfish ones—served only further to delegitimize the entire regime.

To improve its governing effectiveness, then, as Mao's own inevitable departure from the scene menacingly approached, the leftist-dominated state center heightened its demands on the population for public-spiritedness and altruistic service, to combat personalistic networking and localistic protectionism. At the same time, however, it introduced new decentralizing reforms into the organization and routines of state administration that allowed an even greater accumulation of funds and other resources in the hands of low-level, localist or clientelist officials.[8] The scope of the problem only widened as so many (administrative and ideological) partial fixes, working at cross purposes with one another, were introduced during those turbulent years.

The radicalization of the official public ethos did not salvage the system's social losses. On the contrary, it only worsened the popular sense of personal alienation and regime illegitimacy as more and more people found themselves, in both the public and the personal aspects of their lives, having to engage in intricate forms of special protectionism and networking simply to get by, or to get around, the exaggerated expectations of the official ideology and the exasperating formalities of the official bureaucracy. Both programatically and in terms of reinvigorating the party/state's valuable personnel, the mobilizational excesses, the exclusionary rhetoric and the discriminatory politics of the Cultural Revolution era actually intensified the state's earlier frustrations and its weaknesses. Despite the left's claims to the contrary, it was beginning to seem to many people that the revolutionary state's most important founding promises to society—to develop the economy and improve the people's livelihood—had gone largely unmet for two long decades following its undeniably brilliant victories in land reform and collectivization. Meanwhile, the state's own skeletal administrative organization and its cellular restructuration of rural society had been leaving more and more urgent and latent social demands with only indirect (and often illicit) means of expression.

In very abstract summary then, the Mao era saw the evolution of a 'thin' state command structure, with an internally parcelized pattern of authority, increasingly struggling to govern a rural society first artificially homogenized and then cellularized by state policy and action. Social groups, demands, or problems that could not legitimately or effectively be articulated or presented through such formally universal yet actually highly segmented structures and channels, came instead increasingly to be expresssed through informal and quasi-illicit means and behaviors which, once generalized, in turn, furthered the popular delegitimization of the system as a whole.

The State Thickens

The post-Mao economic and political reforms have shaken both state structure and social structure in the countryside. The old familiar patterns of governmental command hierarchy and of socio-economic cellularization are now under vigorous assault by the forces of horizontal (economic, social, and administrative) integration. The decollectivization of agricultural production, the quickening release of surplus labor from the land, and the deliberate diversification and commercialization of the rural economy are producing marked tendencies toward privatization in property-ownership and enterprise management, enhanced divisions of labor, and consequent occupational differentiation and specialization. The new official importance accorded to market-based relations and interactions, as opposed to territorially—or communally—defined socio-economic development, has given much greater respectability and attraction to participation in the service and trade sectors of the rural economy. Profit, not physical production, is now much more often taken as the appropriate measure of growth; and this changed perception has put a premium on learning to work the webs of commercial interdependence where before the emphasis had been so decidedly on fostering relative local autonomy and self-reliance.

New socio-economic groupings are in the process of rapid formation all across rural China now. The old division of rural production and ownership relations into 'state' and 'collective' no longer even begins to capture the complexity of the emerging situation. Individual farming households now sign their own contracts for production and delivery to collective and state units. Their individual rights to make unilateral decisions about their land and other means of production are becoming ever more firmly respected also.[9] Individual farmers, even whole peasant households, have left the land entirely to go into private enterprise. Most are peddlers, street-stall vendors, or other petty traders; but many are more than making a go of their ventures, reinvesting, diversifying, and turning their operations into quite ambitious enterprises that employ dozens of non-family members as workers. Other enterprises have taken form as cooperatives in which workers and managers own shares (of varying proportions) in the company, paying dividends out of net profits.[10] Other companies and corporations are really para-statal contrivances. Originally established by a particular local government or ministry bureau, they now nonetheless operate for profit as discrete enterprises with a certain independence from their parent bureaus or state offices. Still other enterprises continue to remain entirely within the socialist state sector. Wholly-owned subsidiaries of the state unit that established them, they still receive most of their production inputs from state supply sources and still turn over all or most of their profits directly to the state organs to which they belong. But even they are now having to face the tough realities involved in paying more attention to the bottom line and in learning to compete with other hybrid business formations and non-state owned companies.

The release of surplus labor from the land is rapidly producing a major realignment in the rural-urban distribution of China's massive population. There is an enormous floating population now.[11] Millions of people hold papers permitting them to travel from place to place on business. And ever-growing numbers of former peasants who are now involved in private or semi-private business ventures have moved into towns and cities and taken up steady (if not, technically, 'permanent') residence there. 'Urban' populations are literally shooting up all over China.[12] Many rural counties that in 1979 would have counted town-dwellers as a mere eight to ten per cent of their total population now face proportions of 35-50 per cent and higher!

All this physical mobility and multi-form restructuring of economic relations is confronting local government officials with a host of literally unprecedented administrative challenges. As society becomes more differentiated and more complex, local state organizations are challenged to do the same. Many have begun to introduce greater differentiation into their own procedures and services. The structural sameness and the near uniformity of interests, of responsibilities, and of wealth that were characteristic of the old commune-brigade-team organization are now past. No longer can a few universalistic policies, slogans, and regulations be expected to apply effectively to all relevant rural units. No longer can local government administrations expect to maintain such a thin profile. Increased specialization of function and application of technical expertise, a greater division of labor, and more organizational complexity are sanctioned and emerging within China's local-state structure itself, in response to the rapid socio-economic changes unleashed a few years ago by the reforms.

The old unitary hierarchy of command relations is giving way to greater variety in the modes of the local state's interaction with productive units, enterprises, and groups in society. In place of commands now, local-state offices employ an array of indirect levers of social manipulation—everything from contracts and bonuses to tax concessions and preferential credit arrangements. In place of commands now, local-state offices may go into a variety of kinds of partnership with more or less independent actors in the new rural socio-economy—everything from setting up joint stock companies to negotiating the cost-sharing formula for local road construction. And in place of commands now, local-state offices maintain a demeanor of disinterest in many areas of social policy and practice where political imperatives formerly intruded. The post-Mao deradicalization of Chinese political ideology has led to a marked depoliticization of Chinese social life and to the expansion of what Tsou has called the zone of the state's 'indifference' as to how citizens choose to behave in their public and private lives.[13] More local-state activity is, thus, neutral and regulatory now, rather than hortatory and condemnatory.

But depoliticization has most certainly not been tantamount to debureaucratization in rural administration. 'Streamlining the bloated bureaucracy' has been a professed policy goal and a popular slogan under the reformists, as under Mao. But as White points out, there is an inescapably direct tension between streamlining on the one hand, and raising levels of functional specialization and technical expertise among local cadres, on the other.[14] Many recent studies and reports in the Chinese press confirm that bureaucratic streamlining has been approached half-heartedly and has made little progress in the reform years.[15] In fact, the apparent trend is quite contrary. Far from becoming smaller, local-state bureaucracies are steadily growing. The funds and other resources at their disposal are mushrooming. And the projects they are undertaking are *much* more ambitious than before.

As local-state organizations more thickly knit and interweave their own activities with those of a widening variety of non-official actors, then, a new fabric of state-society relations can be seen taking shape before our eyes. This thickening and interweaving should mean that at least some of the localistic and particularistic vices of the artificially simplified and parcelized state-society relationships of the past may well be overcome, with important consequences for rebuilding state capacity and legitimacy in the countryside. But while it seems clear enough that a tighter, more flexible and more durable knitting of state and rural society will be the result if present trends continue, it remains very unclear which patterns this knitting is most likely to follow.

Perhaps this thickening in rural state-society relations will lead to the creation of local bureaucracies that are more responsive to social pressures emanating from all sources and which can serve local needs and interests more sensitively and effectively than in the past. Or perhaps local-state structures will be captured by successfully rising social groups and forces—the town-dwelling entrepreneurs, the bigger villages, the richer lineages—to consolidate their interests as against those less favored in the first phases of the market reforms.

Perhaps, again, state organs themselves will continue stressing their own roles in production and trade, becoming more effective competitors in the market, and engaging the newly-rising social forces in various head-to-head struggles for economic and organizational dominance. The situation in the Chinese countryside is in such flux at present that any one, or any combination, of these outcomes seems not only possible but quite plausible.[16] Since no clear nationwide patterns have yet emerged to view, we must have recourse to local cases to help in piecing together a picture of the range of possibilities.

Shulu and Guanghan:
Two Emerging Patterns of Thickening State-Society Relations in Rural China

Here, then, let us turn briefly to a comparison of recent trends in local political economy and in state-society relations in two different Chinese counties, using material gathered through fieldwork interviews in both localities in the summer of 1979 and the winters of 1982 and 1986.[17] Since a comprehensive study of just one, not to mention a fruitful comparison of these two diverse localities, would constitute a major analytical and narrative undertaking,[18] what follows here should be regarded as merely a review of a few of the highlights of their recent development.

The two counties do make a good comparison because they are very close to each other in size and other basic indicators and characteristics. Both traditionally farming counties located in good agricultural areas, they are each also well situated for the development of trade and commerce. Shulu County[19] lies on the North China Plain and is linked to its provincial capital city (some 65 kilometers away) by a good network of paved roads and railroads. Guanghan County[20] is located in the very fertile and well-watered Sichuan Basin, and is easily reached by road or train from its busy provincial capital just 30 kilometers distant. In 1985 each county reported its total population at just over half a million, although the population density in Shulu County in the north—537 persons per square kilometer—was much lower than Guanghan County's crowded 925. Yet, before the reforms Shulu County was a distinctly poorer place than Guanghan County, and despite its recent impressive gains, in terms of general standard of living it remains so. In 1978 the average per capita income for Shulu County people was just 88 yuan; by 1985 it had risen to 522 yuan. But in Guanghan County, the growth registered over the same period was from 164 to 602 yuan.[21]

The major indicators of both state and economic development for the two counties have been very similar over recent years. In 1978 the gross value of industrial and agricultural output (GVIAO) in each county was right around 250 million yuan. By 1985, Shulu was reporting its GVIAO at 692 million, and Guanghan, at 669 million yuan. Between 1978 and 1985, a period of rapid commercialization of the economy in both counties, the total value of local retail sales rose from 95 million to 210 million yuan in Shulu; and from 86 million to 219.5 million yuan in Guanghan. Although the commercial sector is the one growing fastest in both places, agriculture remains an important, if no longer dominant, component of each local economy. With more land available, but a colder, dryer climate, and a multi-cropping index of just 1.5, Shulu County's 1985 sown area was 250,000 acres, and its total value of agricultural output, 306 million yuan. In Guanghan County, where food grows all year round, the multi-cropping index was 2.0, the sown area just 175,000 acres, and the 1985 agricultural output stood at 221 million yuan.

Shulu and Guanghan can be usefully compared in terms of county level finance and organization, as well. From 1979 to 1985, total Shulu County financial revenues rose from 28 million to 38.5 million yuan; and Guanghan County's, from 15.9 million to 33.8 million yuan. Total county government expenditures, which in 1979 had been 9.6 million yuan in Shulu County and seven million yuan in Guanghan County went up steeply in both localities, to 19.5 million yuan in Shulu and 19.4 million yuan in Guanghan.[22] And finally, as the total number of personnel working in state organs within the county rose between 1978 and 1985 from about 1,000 to 2,219 in Shulu County, it climbed in parallel in Guanghan County from 1,155 to 2,421.[23]

There are, however, also some intriguing differences in the recent patterns of local state and economic development in these two apparently comparable districts.

Shulu: The Coordinative Local State

In Shulu County the clear emphasis has been on the local state's role as coordinator and facilitator of county commercial and economic development. Not themselves usually very directly involved in profit-making, local-state agencies have devoted their efforts to improving the environment in which individuals, enterprises, or other social forces could interact and compete, and in which the public at large could enjoy the benefits of eco- nomic development.

The most impressive example of the local government's success in this realm was in the building and operation of Shulu County's famous 'Hebei Supreme' Market constructed in 1985 in the heart of Xinji town, the county seat. This marketplace—which is dominated by inexpensive ready-to-wear clothing vendors, but where everything from candied apples on a stick to fine carved seals and scroll paintings is on sale—is a giant complex by local standards, covering some 36,000 square meters of prime real estate at the town's central intersection. The idea to build such a shopping center originated in the Shulu County Commerce Bureau. It was provoked by the fact that commercialization of the local economy and the rise in local consumer buying power and demand had attracted hundreds and hundreds of peddlers and hawkers to the county seat where business was conducted haphazardly on the town's narrow and muddy streets. The congestion was becoming an unpleasant obstacle to necessary traffic, and the garbage and dirt left behind by itinerants was causing the Bureau to receive more and more complaints from local townspeople. The problem was attacked in two phases.

First the county government negotiated and coordinated a plan to widen several of the main streets downtown by 'persuading' all units owning buildings fronting on those streets to sacrifice their brick and adobe walled courtyards. (These windowless but spacious front courtyards are an architectural convention throughout the towns and cities of Northeast China. They afford residents some privacy and seclusion, even as they confront urban commuters and passers-by with an apparently endless expanse of forbidding gray and ochre walls.) The space gained was very substantial and the effect was quite dramatic. Sidewalks and some street lights were put in. Wheeled and four-footed traffic were confined to the newly-paved roadbeds. Townspeople and business people passing through both benefited from improved speed and convenience.

But the crowds of peddlers and hawkers were still a problem. The Bureau suggested setting up a unified marketplace in a central location. Engineers and architects were consulted. A price tag of seven million yuan was put on the plan, which included construction of a six-storey building nearly a city-block long and built (in this earthquake-prone region) to withstand a shock of 8.0 on the Richter scale. In architectural design the building would eclectically combine ancient Chinese and Western features. The color-scheme was to be the traditional lucky red and yellow, with several great arched entryways reminiscent of old China's massive city walls, and with a series of towers topped by upturned tiled roofs decorated with dragons and phoenixes. Yet in the middle was to rise—that very symbol of commercial revolution in the West—a clock tower of splendid proportions, whose round white face, black hands, and Arabic numerals were to look out in four directions over the town. At the front of this great building there would be a broad, landscaped boulevard, and behind it (perpendicular to it) were to be built some twenty two-storey blocks with small shops on the ground floor and apartments above—351 units in all. The idea was to sell these units like condominiums to families who would undertake both to run small businesses in them and to live on the premises. In the rows between these two-storey blocks were to be added a complex of covered but open-air stalls some 10,000 meters in length where space would be rented out to small retailers and service people.

The county committee liked the plan, but could not possibly finance any major portion of it out of existing or anticipated county budgeted funds. And in accord with the national tight-credit policy at the time, local-state offices could not even contemplate applying for bank loans to cover such a large outlay. The local state, thus, was not in a position to serve as a major investor; but it *could* help find investors, big and small, to put up the necessary capital jointly and it *could* help to procure the necessary construction services at a discount.

The Bureau of Commerce received permission to advertise the scheme at home and all across the country, and within a month peasant households wanting to buy in responded in the hundreds. Collective and even state-run factories and enterprises were invited—urged, perhaps—to purchase space also to set up retail outlet stores featuring their products. And several local government organs bought space too so that a police station, a tax collection office, a post office and a bank branch could be included among the service conveniences available at the shopping center. The initial investment coordinated by the Shulu County Commerce Bureau consisted of some 3.3 million yuan from private householders; 800,000 yuan from state and cooperative enterprises and units; 540,000 yuan from collective enterprises and units; and 280,000 yuan from state agencies. In addition, the county committee prevailed upon the county government's own construction company to do the work on a *non-profit* basis. Investors must have benefited substantially from this deep discount on the cost of materials and labor.

The 'Hebei Supreme' Market was a great success. Business was booming in 1986, and was attracting even more commerce to the county, while the downtown streets remained unusually clean and orderly. Government officials claimed also that licensing and regulation of petty traders, the prevention of theft, tax evasion, and black market activity, were all greatly enhanced by the physical concentration of market activity. Legitimately licensed private traders working out of 'Hebei Supreme' formed a Trade Association both to regulate themselves and to try to articulate their needs and interests in interactions with various bureaus and offices of the local government.

One point to note here is that while the county government orchestrated the entire project, it did not directly invest in it with a view to making a profit. It literally planned and created the space in which market competition could take place, but it did not enter the competition itself, nor did it apparently attempt to pitch the competition in favor of state-owned and managed businesses, nor would it be collecting any dividends on the investment.

This is not to say that the local-state apparatus took only a coordinative role and made *no substantial* financial contribution to the undertaking. On the contrary, in association with the downtown redevelopment scheme and the construction of the 'Hebei Supreme' Market, the Shulu County government had contributed a great deal of its own (extrabudgetary) funds to new buildings and public installations. Right across the boulevard from 'Hebei Supreme'—on what presumably would otherwise have become some of the most valuable real estate in town—the government constructed quite a pleasant public park, with children's amusement rides, a goldfish pond, and a small zoo including a modern-style monkey island. Right around the corner was a brand new, very spacious, and literally sparkling-white cultural center featuring art and technology exhibitions and a library. Its large open courtyard, graced somewhat incongruously in this drought-prone region with a sculptured fountain, was lined with bicycle racks to accommodate the public. Up the street a little further was a big new movie theater built also with county government (extrabudgetary) funding, where touring rock bands from Canton performed, and other live entertainment could be staged. People coming to shop at 'Hebei Supreme' would be able to find more to do in town than just to spend their money. The county government had also recently financed construction of a new youth center, a (second) public hospital in the county seat, an elementary school and kindergarten, a TV relay station, and two underpasses under the railroad line at the south end of town.

All this building created a change in the appearance of the town center since 1979 that was quite dramatic. The alleys just off the main boulevards, of course, remained narrow, winding, and dusty with many adobe houses in need of repair. But there was nothing Potemkin-like about the downtown scene. The Shulu County City Construction and Environmental Protection Office cadres reported, in careful detail, on their development plans for 1990 and for the year 2000, when the urbanized areas are expected to contain 33 per cent and 46 per cent respectively of the total county population. They had the harassed air of people who know they are working against the clock, but they certainly were not without clear direction. The town plan they said they intended to phase in featured residential and shopping expansion to the north (so that the railroad would run around the town, not through it); relocation of a few large industrial plants to join a planned factory and warehouse section of town downwind of the residential and commercial neighborhoods; the planting of parks and other green spaces; construction of a sports stadium, an athletic field, a public swimming pool, and an ice rink (behind the cultural center); the paving of new roads and parking lots; and the strict enforcement of national and local environmental protection regulations.[24]

The government's attention to roadbuilding, vital to further commercial development in the area, was not confined to the county town. Between 1980 and 1986, some 73 kilometers *outside* the county seat had been paved at government expense. A paved road by then extended to every township in the county, and a cost-sharing plan had been launched to help townships in paving the smaller roads that link them to their constituent villages.

The county government had a hand in promoting commercial development in other ways as well. A number of local-state investments had been made and other measures adopted, for example, to induce Shulu County farmers, who have long made a specialty of growing cotton, to plant a new variety that yields longer, stronger fibers. Orchard expansion and irrigation were high on the list of government-backed development efforts also. The nationally prized Tianjin pear grows well in Shulu County, at least when water is abundant, and the county's agriculture officials were looking forward to rapid development in local pear production. Irrigation there, as elsewhere on the North China Plain, is a pressing problem however. The underground water table in Shulu County has been dropping at the alarming rate of one meter a year since 1975. Surface irrigation is wasteful, so a plan was developed to subsidize and coordinate installation of an underground drip irrigation system (based on technology perfected in Israel) on some 10,000 acres of fruit orchards. This first experimental phase, of what could become an even more widely adopted answer to the Shulu County water shortage, should be completed by 1990 at a cost of about nine million yuan. The county government, through its Water Conservation Bureau, planned to subsidize 90 per cent of the interest on the loans farmers took to get this underground pipe system installed on their contracted land. No government agency or bureau, however, would ever net any direct profit from the research, development, planning, training, coordination, and investment it had put into this project, which could, if it succeeds, give Shulu County farmers a big competitive boost in the regional and national wholesale fruit market.

The Shulu County local-state apparatus has by no means been bowing out of local economic development planning and coordination during the recent years of reform. On the contrary, it is involving itself in projects now that are far more ambitious than ever before. (The largest known previous irrigation project coordinated by the county, for example, cost only about half as much as the estimate for the first phase of the underground drip system.) But in Shulu County, government agencies themselves had kept a discrete distance from market competition and profit-making.

Shulu County officials encouraged competition, but they did not generally join in it. They encouraged investment, but they did not seek to monopolize it. They promoted local products, but they did not insist on brokering sales. They channeled and coordinated local capital investment, but they had no contact with external capital markets and they raked off little if any commission for their services. And all this showed—or rather, it didn't show—in the Shulu County government's trappings of office. The official government guest house in 1986 was the same spartanly furnished dormitory that had served the purpose in 1979. Frequent power outages made light, heat, and running water only intermittently available to cadres holding meetings there. And the county government's motor pool consisted of just two old Shanghai sedans. The dramatic rise in the standard of living of Shulu County's farmers had not yet been reflected in the life-style of their local officials. Things, however, were rather different in Sichuan Province's model of reform, Guanghan County.

Guanghan: The Competitive Local State

The official Guanghan County guest house is entered through sliding glass doors that open automatically onto a carpeted lobby of gilt and mirrors and a wood-paneled desk staffed by young female attendants. Every room comes with a modern private bath, comfortable sofas and chairs arranged into a lounge area for entertaining guests, a TV, and a small refrigerator. The county government headquarters are recently refurbished, and as for the motor pool, it consists of a small fleet of shiny Japanese cars and vans. All these perks are perhaps to be expected in a locality selected early to be a model of the post-Mao reforms. Then Sichuan Provincial Secretary (later Party General Secretary) Zhao Ziyang first tapped Guanghan County as a keypoint for experimentation in institutional restructuring in the late seventies. As his career has prospered since, so have the Guanghan County cadres back in Sichuan.[25]

It is more than a little ironic that Guanghan County was selected to be a model of how to get government *out* of the economy at the end of the Mao era, however, because by 1986 it certainly appeared that the local-state apparatus was more intimately and more directly involved in economic life than ever. One accent in Guanghan County was on the competition—and how to beat it. The other was on venture capital—and where to get it. And county-level cadres were right in the thick of the fray on both fronts.

Guanghan County officials were on the lookout for outside investors of all sorts. Little direct foreign investment appeared to have found its way into the county so far, but visitors might be shown a sentimental video, aimed particularly at overseas-Chinese businessmen, which suggested pointedly that Guanghan County afforded a host of excellent investment opportunities. Perhaps it is not surprising, then, that one of the most interesting business ventures underway in the county in 1986 involved the construction of a ten-storey hotel and convention center in the county seat.

This project was being directly underwritten and orchestrated by the county-level office of the Federation of Rural Supply and Marketing Co-ops—a para-statal unit that in earlier years had been merged with the Ministry of Commerce. On the rather dubious premise that the convention center was to include a local products exhibition hall, the county office of the Federation maintained that the venture would promote sales of Guanghan County goods around the region and the nation. The real purpose of the project, however, appeared to be simply that of making money on the high-class hotel trade, and the shops, bars, and restaurants in the complex.

The project was to cost about three million yuan. Some 800,000 yuan had been raised through syndicated loans (paying 12 per cent interest) from peasant investors who were told that they stood a chance, if the project succeeded, of realizing as much as 15.7 per cent on their investment. Another 1.2 million yuan was borrowed from the bank, which must have involved the establishment of a dummy corporation since, according to national policy at the time, bank loans were not to be extended to state 'administrative' agencies such as the county office of the Federation. The remaining million yuan was put up by the county office itself, though some of it came from additional loans from rural investors who were to be paid 17.9 per cent interest! To minimize borrowing at this exorbitant rate, and because capital for construction outside the state plan was otherwise so difficult to secure, additional sums were raised through loans from banks located in poor minority areas of northern and western Sichuan—Aba and Ganzi Autonomous Regions, Tibetan nationality homelands. The interest rates charged on such inter-bank loans was 'negotiable', which is to say variable, but for this venture in 1985 it was set at 11.35 per cent, making it a very good deal for the Guanghan Federation which was having to pay its own local peasant investors even more.

According to the Director of the Agriculture Bank in Guanghan County, there was excess liquidity in banks located in remote areas like Aba and Ganzi because good investment opportunities were lacking there. Bank branches in such peripheral and backward regions therefore had difficulty meeting their assigned profit targets. So, starting in 1984 official policy permitted them to loan funds to other banks in more prosperous core areas where the demand for credit was high. Guanghan County had to compete as a potential borrower on this inter-bank financial market. Credit worthiness was not easy to establish. But one or two Guanghan County bank officials had once worked in Aba, and their personal connections and *bona fides* helped seal the deal. (By contrast it is worth noting that in 1986 such inter-bank credit transfers were as yet unheard-of in Shulu County, not of course a reform experimental keypoint. Branch banks in Shulu County had not yet even begun receiving targets for profits.)

It was not entirely clear how the profits earned on the convention center project would be split. But the county office made no secret of being in it for the earnings. The same office, after all, was taking a 30 per cent commission on the wholesale business it did in local products purchased by its own co-op 'partner' branch offices in the villages. And, according to the county Director, it had also established several food processing plants 'to make money'. Their object, they said, was to concentrate resources at the county level so as to gain visibility and a better market share for Guanghan County's special products in the intensifying regional and national competition with other counties. But the Federation was by no means the only Guanghan County office that appeared to put profit first. As one other official said, 'whatever brings money into the county's finance office is all to the good.'

The breathless pursuit of venture capital, however, and the determination to make a profit and beat the competition sometimes seemed in danger of pitting the county government against its constituent communities, and even against itself. The government office in charge of assisting and monitoring the development of little factories and enterprises located in the smaller towns and villages of the county (*xiang zhen qiye*) was justifiably proud of its accomplishments through 1986 and was continuing then to encourage peasant investment in home village ventures. But the Federation office at the county worked in direct competition with such village-based development efforts. They, as described above, were actively attempting to lure peasant private investment away from the smaller towns and into more ambitious schemes (like the convention center) by offering higher interest rates than the fledgling village enterprises could afford. Many people, Federation officials claimed, actually preferred to invest outside their home villages—presumably so that their family's total worth would not be so transparent to their neighbors and village leaders. (In Shulu County, by contrast, Federation officials admitted that they would have liked to attract more peasant investment than they had so far, but their own regulations obliged them to offer no more than ten per cent interest, and so peasants were often choosing to put their money into village ventures where they hoped to earn more. The county officials accepted this trend and expressed no intention of competing with it since, as they saw it, village-based enterprise development was necessary and good for the county economy too.)

Another interesting undertaking in Guanghan County was the establishment of a new nylon conveyor belt factory by the county's Second Light Industry Bureau. Since funds for fixed capital investments outside the state plan such as this were tightly restricted, Guanghan County's Second Light Bureau came up with the idea of forming a 'joint venture' with its counterpart Second Light bureau in another county located to the northwest-Wenchuan County of the Aba Tibetan Autonomous Region. This was also just another way of getting 'excess liquidity' from Aba channeled into Guanghan County's fast-moving and credit hungry economy. Each of the two county Second Light bureaus borrowed the necessary funds from its own local banks, in apparent contravention once again of the proscription on loans to state agencies for projects outside the state plan. The Wenchuan bureau contributed nothing more than this necessary supplemental financing; the technical expertise and the workers were available in Guanghan County where the factory was built. The Wenchuan bureau therefore remained the junior partner in the arrangement, even though its contribution to the initial investment was 550,000 yuan, to the Guanghan County bureau's 450,000 yuan. In this case also, Guanghan County government entrepreneurs appear to have been successful in attracting funds for development from a relatively poor area into their own relatively rich and buoyant local economy.

There was a great deal of construction going on within the county town and all over Guanghan County in 1986. But it was not proceeding according to any clearly discernible plan, and county officials reported no recent public works undertakings to compare with Shulu County government efforts. Of course, Guanghan County was much more urbanized and prosperous to start with, and was situated much closer to its provincial capital city, so it is fair to assume perhaps that such basic amenities as hospitals, parks and cultural centers may have existed in adequate supply or may not have been high priorities for the local population. In the area of roadbuilding, however—a Shulu County government pre-occupation—Guanghan County officials seemed soon to face a genuine crisis. In 1979 it took about forty minutes to travel by car between Guanghan County and downtown Chengdu; in 1986 it took more than twice as long to do the journey. Local economic devel- opment had brought with it a spectacular increase in road traffic of all sorts. Trucks, bicycles, carts, oxen, motorcycles, and pedestrians carrying shoulder poles engulfed the main highway creating serious (if entertaining) traffic jams, especially where the road passes through Xindu Town, Xindu being another populous county on the outskirts of Chengdu undergoing its own commercial revolution. Guanghan County officials bewailed the traffic situation in 1986, but were making no apparent moves to remedy it. They may well have been calculating that if they waited long enough a major part of the necessary investment in roads for the whole region would finally be picked up by provincial officials in Chengdu, rather than by the surrounding counties.

Guanghan County's annual reports do include references to improvements not only in the standard of living but also in the general welfare and quality of life of its people—more schools and kindergartens, more doctors and nurses, more homes for the elderly, movie houses, magazine subscriptions, etc. But most such improvements were privately financed or carried through by town and village governments. County government officials claimed little credit or involvement and instead were more likely to emphasize the *relative* financial and decision-making autonomy of the county's constituent towns and villages under the reforms. The main concerns of Guanghan County officials in various bureaus and offices were, rather, to find ways of concentrating financial and other resources in their own hands, to find the cheapest possible credit sources to leverage their competitive advantage, and then to invest and reinvest for quick profit. And it was Guanghan County's local-state banking officials who were at the very center of play.

Two Potential Patterns of Local-State Power and Social Resistance

In neither of these two counties have the depoliticizing and commercializing reforms of the last decade produced a diminished role for the local state in the development of the local economy. On the contrary, in both cases the local-state apparatus has been getting bigger and doing more. Enhanced *local-state capacity* has clearly come along with greater *state legitimacy* in the post-Mao countryside. But these two local-state apparatuses appear to be following some very different-colored threads in contemporary China's tapestry of economic reform. This difference in emphasis, in turn, seems likely to leave its mark on the future fabric of their relations with local society.

In Guanghan County the thread of reform most highlighted is that which calls for the pursuit of profit in accord with comparative advantage, enhanced market-like competition, and commercially-based outreach and integration across the old cellular boundaries of the early socialist state's administrative structure. Guanghan County casts the local state as competitor, investor, and entrepreneurial agent. In Shulu County, by contrast, the thread of reform most highlighted is that which calls for the state to assume an indirect, guidance role in the economy while remaining the guardian of the general public welfare. Shulu County casts the local state as coordinator, facilitator, and regulator.

Because in Guanghan County the very bureaus and offices of local government themselves are avidly involved in the creation of venture capital and the pursuit of investment profits, the situation seems set up for the gradual emergence of a little local power elite, with the county government apparatus itself as the focus of influence, reward and opportunity—the place where the real action is. Able village entrepreneurs and others who are financially successful are very likely to be drawn into partnerships and cooperative ventures with local government agencies, as if to a magnet. As individuals, they may even seek official status since being on the state payroll no longer necessarily rules out maintaining private interests and investments. And in any case, the various cadre 'responsibility systems' (or bonus schemes) now ensure that the profits pulled in by the bureau or state agency in which one works will make a positive impact on personal income. But it may be more the privileges and perks of county official status that actually decide the matter. Access to a car, to a more spacious apartment in town, and to social contact with powerful people in Chengdu—these are the sorts of incentives likely to attract members of the upwardly mobile local economic elite into the county-level state apparatus. A partial merger, or at least a heavy overlap, between the rising local socio-economic elite and the official administrative elite would seem to be in the cards for state-society relations in Guanghan County. And, of course, a state-corporate synthesis could well be a formula for making the most out of the opportunities now being presented to communities like Guanghan County, located on the edge of one of China's great metropolises.

In Shulu County the local-state apparatus had remained more aloof from economic competition. State offices and agencies were not becoming so heavily involved in commerce or other direct profit-making activities. Even as new groups and interests were emerging out of the changing local socio-economy, local officials appeared to have held onto something of the old ethos of government work as a form of service. Where the local state casts itself in the role of city planner and chamber of commerce combined, citizens may find it expedient to organize so as to influence state decisions. And already new social entities, such as an association of private retailers, had begun to take shape and to articulate and represent new interests in the Shulu County community. There the state apparatus in no way resembled a power elite; instead it held the ring for the action of other socio-economic forces. It promoted trade *in general* and lived on the general revenues, earning its keep by arbitrating disputes and preserving a modicum of social harmony. Emerging social groups with potentially divergent interests can be expected, however, increasingly to organize or otherwise express their demands for state backing and support in the county.

These two different patterns of the local state's relations with local society are likely also to give rise to different patterns of conflict between state and society, and eventually to different forms of social resistance to state authority. Individual and group anti-state resistance in Guanghan County seems quite likely to take the form of private corrupt practices and other evasions of the remaining socialist state restrictions on individual social and economic behavior. Socially legitimizing rationales for such behavior might well feature appeals to a purer form of *laissez-faire* and freedom of competition. In Shulu County, by contrast, social conflict and resistance seem likely to take more organized forms of public demonstration and dissent. Socially legitimizing rationales for such behavior could well feature appeals to a more comprehensive form of democratic representation and even concern for human rights.

But all this, of course, is speculation; and the situation in China is changing so fast as to make speculation even more than usually foolhardy. Guanghan County is an experimental keypoint—a vanguard unit trying out policies and procedures that may well be officially permitted elsewhere before long. Even if this should occur, however—we may continue our speculations—Shulu County's recent interlude of coordinative rather than competitive state action can be expected to leave its mark on both the structure of local society and the style of local administration.

Conclusion: Rethinking State-Strengthening

One of the general assertions this essay has sought to illustrate is that 'state-strengthening' can occur in state socialist systems *even* during periods of massive decentralizing and depoliticizing reform such as that occurring in China now. On the one hand, centralization of authority into a recognizable hierarchy of public decision-making and administration is an essential prerequisite for the creation of any modern state. And the tendency toward state power centralization—one might say over-centralization—has certainly been one of the hallmarks of the development of modern socialist states. But on the other hand, it clearly is not the case that the more centralized the exercise of state authority becomes the 'stronger' or more capable that state can be said to be. And in fact the *very most* centralized states of the twentieth century have plainly shown themselves to be prone to a variety of now quite familiar inadequacies, incapacities, and fallibilities. By devolving certain central powers to lower levels of the system then, it is very possible, indeed probable, that such states may be able to make important gains in their actual ruling capacities: capacities to acquire accurate information and evaluate it in a timely fashion; capacities to make sensitive policy recommendations and intelligent policy adaptations; and capacities to pursue state goals and administer state policies with enhanced efficiency, fairness, and thus legitimacy.

To Western social scientists, such a mildly paradoxical observation about the state-strengthening potential entailed in the administrative decentralization of state socialist systems may by now seem highly unsurprising. Some may even be inclined to say they always guessed as much. But for a host of party/state cadres in China as little as a decade ago, and for many others today in Gorbachev's USSR, there has been nothing so self-evident about it.

An even more general suggestion here—one for social scientists only, not for party bureaucrats - has been that the very concept of state-strengthening can bear some rethinking. In particular, we should approach the development of modern state capacities not as a once-and-for-all process, but as a process that can (and very likely will) proceed in waves.

The particular patterns of regime consolidation pursued beget their own forms of social adaptation and resistance. As they, in turn, become refined, those mechanisms of social resistance may more and more effectively dull or deflect the consolidated state's real power. If the system in question can be flexible and responsive enough, then social resistance may be made manageable through incremental state and social reforms. But if incremental reform is successfully fought by entrenched elites, it may be postponed too long. Then a reform of the magnitude now being witnessed in China and the Soviet Union may be undertaken—one in which the old regime in its fundamental structure and ethos may appear to be undergoing qualitative change.

Even if, as this essay has attempted to show, such great and qualitative changes do contribute to making the still statist regime in place stronger and more resilient than before, we should not expect the final outcome to be simply a more perfect (and certainly not a more permanent) consolidation of control. As observed earlier, control provokes resistance. State control provokes social resistance. Social adaptations to the reformed regime, with the potential to carry protest and resistance, will be shaped anew. In China now, we can already (almost) glimpse them in formation.

Notes

1. See e.g. Rudolph and Rudolph (1987), Migdal (1989), and Nee and Stark (1989).
2. Many of the main points and arguments made in this section concerning state and society in the Mao era are much more fully elaborated in Shue (1988). For more on the gridwork of vertical and horizontal units, see especially Chapter 2.
3. And in the final years of the Mao era, during the Cultural Revolution, this phenomenon could often reach exaggerated proportions in the countryside. In Shulu County, discussed below for example, with a population at the time of just under a half million people, the entire county party/state staff was reduced and held for an extended period to just 86 cadres.
4. See Shue (1988), especially Chapter 4.
5. 'Cellular' was the adjective used by Donnithorne (1972). The term 'fragmented'is employed to describe some similar and related characteristics by Lyons (1987). 'Honeycomb' is adopted in Shue (1988).
6. See especially Lyons (1987, chapters 1 and 2).
7. The *guanxi* phenomenon has also been widely discussed and analyzed in contemporary Chinese studies.

For a helpful recent treatment see Gold (1985). See also Oi (1985), and for an especially sensitive treatment of the morality of *guanxi* and its distortions in the countryside, Madsen (1984). Also, Chan, Madsen and Unger (1984). For more on the dimensions of *guanxi* in an urban setting, see Walder (1986).

8. See e.g., Shue (1984a), Wong (1982), and the descriptions of Longyong's behavior in the seventies given in Chan, Madsen, and Unger (1984).

9. Some of the many available sources on the Chinese reforms in agricultural production include, Hartford (1985), Shue (1984c), Nee (1986), Burns and Rosen (1986, 251ff), Zweig (1986), Gray and Gray (1983), and Selden and Lu (1987).

10. For some discussions of these cooperatives see Johnson (1986) and Howard (1988).

11. Moran (1988). Compare Banister (1987), where the 'permanence' of migration is emphasized.

12. See Banister and Woodard (1987).

13. Tsou (1986).

14. White (1988).

15. On problems associated with bureaucratic streamlining, see Lee (1983), Manion (1985), Burns (1983), Manion (1988), Manion (1984), Harding (1987, chapter 8), and White (1988). A brief discussion with documents can be found in Burns and Rosen (1986).

16. For an excellent discussion of some of the possibilities and combinations, see White (1987).

17. The 1986 work was only accomplished thanks to the invaluable assistance of my two co-researchers, Marc Blecher and Wang Shaoguang.

18. A comprehensive study of Shulu County is now in an advanced stage of preparation under the general editorship of Marc Blecher and with the working title, *The Tethered Deer: The Political Economy of a North China County*. Some partial studies of this county have been published. See Shue (1984a) and Blecher (1984). A partial study of Guanghan County is available in Shue (1984b). And for a preliminary comparison of the two localities along the lines of that offered here, see also Blecher (1988).

19. Shulu County was recently designated a Municipality and renamed Xinji.

20. Guanghan County is in Deyang Municipality of Sichuan Province.

21. Inflation over the same period in Guanghan County, however, was roughly estimated by local officials at 20 per cent. Shulu County officials also complained of higher prices, but inflation did not seem so severe a problem there. Without considerably more background information, therefore, these formerly very useful and reliable *shenghuo shuiping* (standard of living) figures routinely reported by Chinese localities, are actually becoming less helpful for direct comparisons.

22. The Shulu County figure reported here is for 1986. The figure for Guanghan County, where 1986 statistics were not yet available, is for 1985. This way of presenting the comparison actually exaggerates the similarity in their growth trajectories. In Guanghan County, expenditures appeared to have moved up sharply and steadily throughout the period. In Shulu County, big increases in outlays began only in 1985, and that after a period of some decline. In the absence of complete data, the 1984 figures, then, provide something of a corrective; they were 10.8 million yuan in Shulu County and 16.8 yuan in Guanghan County.

23. While figures could not be secured for Guanghan County, Shulu County admitted that expenditures on county administration had precisely doubled between 1979 and 1986, rising from 1.4 million to 2.8 yuan. And some of the other Shulu County budget data reviewed suggests that these are conservative figures that by no means overstate the case.

24. Arsenic in the effluent from Shulu County's many leather tanning shops and factories had been a problem in the past. And disposal of solid waste from the town's large chemical plants remained a challenge without a clear solution.

25. Details on Zhao's time in Sichuan can be found in Shambaugh (1984, chapter 6).

References

Banister (1987): Judith Banister, *China's Changing Population*. Stanford, CA: Stanford University Press.

Banister and Woodard (1987): Judith Banister and Kim Woodard, 'A Tale of New Cities: Rapid Urbanization Is Changing the Contours of the China Market'. *China Business Review*, March-April 1987, 12-21.

Blecher (1984): Marc Blecher, 'Peasant Labour for Urban Industry: Temporary Contract Labour, Urban-Rural Balance and Class Rela- tions in a Chinese County'. In N. Maxwell and B. MacFarlane (eds.), *China's Changed Road to Development*. Oxford: Pergamon Press.

Blecher (1988): Marc Blecher, 'Developmental State, Entrepreneurial State: The Political Economy of Socialist Reform in Xinji Municipality and Guanghan County'. Unpublished paper.

Burns (1983): John P. Burns, 'Reforming China's Bureaucracy, 1979-82'. *Asian Survey*, vol. 23, 1983, 692-722. Burns and Rosen (1986): John P. Burns and Stanley Rosen (eds.), *Policy Conflicts in Post-Mao China*. Armonk, NY: M.E. Sharpe.

Chan, Madsen and Unger (1984): Anita Chan, Richard Madsen and Jonathan Unger, *Chen Village: The Recent History of a Peasant Community in Mao's China*. Berkeley, CA: University of California Press.

Donnithorne (1972): Audrey Donnithorne, 'China's Cellular Economy: Some Trends Since the Cultural Revolution'. *China Quarterly* No. 52, 1972, 605-619.

Gold (1985): Thomas B. Gold, 'After Comradeship: Personal Relations in China since the Cultural Revolution'. *China Quarterly*, No. 104 (December 1985), 657-675.

Gray and Gray (1983): Jack Gray and Maisie Gray, 'China's New Agricultural Revolution'. In Stephan Feuchtwang and Athar Hussain (eds.), *The Chinese Economic Reforms*. London: Croom Helm.

Harding (1987): Harry Harding, *China's Second Revolution: Reform after Mao*. Washington, D.C.: Brookings.

Hartford (1985): Kathleen Hartford, 'Socialist Agriculture Is Dead; Long Live Socialist Agriculture!'. In Elizabeth Perry and Christine Wong (eds.), *The Political Economy of Reform in Post-Mao China*, Cambridge, MA: Harvard University Press.

Howard (1988): Pat Howard, *Breaking the Iron Rice Bowl*. Armonk, NY: M.E. Sharpe.

Johnson (1986): Graham Johnson, 'The Fate of the Communal Economy: Some Contrary Evidence from the Pearl River Delta'; paper presented at the Annual Meeting of the Association for Asian Studies, Chicago, Mar. 1986.

Lee (1983): Hong Yung Lee, 'Deng Xiaoping's Reform of the Chinese Bureaucracy'. In R. A. Morse (ed.), *The Limits of Reform in China*. Boulder, CO: Westview Press.

Lyons (1987): Thomas P. Lyons, *Economic Integration and Planning in Maoist China*. New York: Columbia University Press.

Madsen (1984): Richard Madsen, *Morality and Power in a Chinese Village*. Berkeley, CA: University of California Press.

Manion (1984): Melanie Manion, (ed.), 'Cadre Recruitment and Management in the People's Republic of China'. *Chinese Law and Government*, vol. 17:3, 1984, 1-128.

Manion (1985): Melanie Manion, 'The Cadre Management System, Post-Mao: The Appointment, Promotion, Transfer and Removal of Party and State Leaders'. *China Quarterly*, No. 102, 1985, 203-233.

Manion (1988): Melanie Manion, 'Retirement of Party and State Officials'; paper presented at the Annual Meeting of the Association for Asian Studies, San Francisco, Mar. 1988.

Migdal (1989): Joel S. Migdal, *Strong Societies and Weak State*. Princeton, N.J.: Princeton University Press.

Moran (1988): Thomas Moran, 'Urbanization in China in the 1980s: Beijing's Floating Population'. Unpublished paper.

Nee (1986): Victor Nee, 'Peasant Household Economy and Decollectivization in China'. *Journal of Asian and African Studies*, vol.21, 1986, 185-203.

Nee and Stark (1989): Victor Nee and David Stark (eds.), *Remaking the Economic Institutions of Socialism*. Stanford, Cal.: Stanford University Press.

Oi (1985): Jean C. Oi, 'Communism and Clientelism: Rural Politics in China,' *World Politics*, vol. 37:2, 1985, 238-266.

Rudolph and Rudolph (1987): Lloyd I. Rudolph and Susanne Hoeber Rudolph, *In Pursuit of Lakshmi: The Political Economy of the Indian State*. Chicago: University of Chicago Press.

Selden and Lu (1987): Mark Selden and Aiguo Lu, 'The Reform of Land Ownership and the Political Economy of Contemporary China'. *Peasant Studies* vol. 14:4, 1987, 229-249.

Shambaugh (1984): David L. Shambaugh, *The Making of a Premier: Zhao Ziyang's Provincial Career*. Boulder, CO: Westview Press.

Shue (1984a): Vivienne Shue, 'Beyond the Budget: Finance Organization and Reform in a Chinese County,' *Modern China*, vol. 10:2, 1984, 147-186.

Shue (1984b): Vivienne Shue, 'The Fate of the Commune'. *Modern China*, vol. 10:3, 1984, 259-283.

Shue (1984c): Vivienne Shue, 'The New Course in Chinese Agriculture'. *The Annals*, No. 476, 1984, 74-88.

Shue (1988): Vivienne Shue, *The Reach of the State: Sketches of the Chinese Body Politic*. Stanford, CA: Stanford University Press.

Tsou (1986): Tang Tsou, *The Cultural Revolution and Post-Mao Reforms: A Historical Perspective*. Chicago: University of Chicago Press.

Walder (1986): Andrew G. Walder, *Communist Neo-Traditionalism: Work and Authority in Chinese Industry*. Berkeley, CA: University of California Press.

White (1987): Gordon White, 'The Impact of Economic Reforms in the Chinese Countryside: Towards the Politics of Social Capitalism?'. *Modern China*, vol. 13:4, 1987, 411-440.

White (1988): Tyrene White, 'Political Reform and Rural Government: The New Matrix of Power'. Unpublished paper.

Wong (1982): Christine P. Wong, 'Rural Industrialization in the People's Republic of China: Lessons from the Cultural Revolution Decade'. In Joint Economic Committee Selected Papers, *China under the Four Modernizations*. Part I, 394-418, Washington, D.C.: Government Printing Office.

Zweig (1986): David Zweig, 'Prosperity and Conflict in Post-Mao Rural China'. *China Quarterly*, No. 105, 1986, 1-18.

'Never mind if it's a girl, you can have another try'

The Modification of the One-Child Family Policy
and its Implications for Gender Relations in Rural Areas

Delia Davin

Introduction

It is now ten years since Chinese couples were first called on to limit their families to a single child in response to what was perceived as a grim threat of demographic explosion. Demographers warned that as the bulge generations of the 1960s matured, over 10 million women annually would marry and would become potential childbearers. They projected that China's population of close on a billion would double within less than a half a century if each woman had just three children (Chen and Tyler 1982, 67). Since 1979, although the strictness with which the policy has been applied has varied both over time and from place to place, the one-child family has been maintained as an ideal. Parents have come under enormous moral and social pressure to comply with it and have also been offered considerable economic incentives to do so. Those who defy the regulations can be heavily penalised (see Croll 1985).

Population policy has a quite special significance for women. They are the child-bearers. Their lives are profoundly influenced by the number, sex and health of the children they produce. This is especially the case in the countryside where women's lives are more restricted to the family, and where the family is an economic unit relying mainly on reproduction to maintain or to increase its labour force. In the past, husbands and parents-in-law insisted on an influence over women's fertility, now the state does too. The family, especially the rural family, frequently desires more children than the state will allow and females are very much the victims of this conflict of interest. Women bear the main psychological and physical burdens involved in the use of contraception, abortion and sterilisation. The contempt which mothers of girls may experience within their families and communities is well expressed in the story of a Sichuan woman who underwent nine pregnancies, defied birth control regulations and paid a heavy fine in her determination to produce a son (Zhang and Sang 1989, 130-134). Some women who give birth to girls may even suffer serious mental or physical abuse at the hands of disappointed husbands or in-laws. The policy also adversely affected girl children in a variety of ways. Because under the one-child limit the birth of a daugther precluded her parents trying for a boy, her presence could be very much resented. In some much-publicised cases parents desperate for a boy even got rid of their infant daughters. Changes in the size and sex composition of sibling sets brought about by state policy have, as I will show, specific implications for girls.

My intention in this paper is to review the past ten years of the one-child family policy's development, with a particular focus on the way it affected females. I will show that recent modifications of the law were made at least in part out of a concern of these effects, but I argue that the major modification is in effect a concession to son preference, and itself has problematic implications for gender roles in rural China.

Developments in Chinese Population Policy: 1979-1989

'To keep the country's population at about 1.2 billion by the end of the century, China must strictly carry out the policies of promoting later marriages and restricting each couple to only one child'. (Li Peng, Report to the National People's Congress, March 1988; cf. Hardee-Cleaveland and Banister 1988, 251).

'I would like to emphasise that ... it was never a requirement that all couples should have only one child. So it is a misunderstanding that our policy is a one child policy'. (Peng Peiyun, the Minister in charge of the State Family Planning Commision, in an interview she gave in October 1988; cf. People 1989, 11).

Together these two statements illustrate the difficulties encountered in research on China's population policy. Official comments on the policy and its success tend to differ according to the context in which they are made. Birth control workers may be congratulated on their achievements and regaled with optimistic statistics and projections, or, more commonly, rebuked with pessimistic ones and urged on to greater efforts. Statements targeting foreign audiences veer between attempts to reassure and to play down severity of the policy, and attempts to awaken foreign sympathy by emphasising the magnitude of the problem. China is sensitive to international reactions in part because she has been criticised for violations of human rights and because her funding from the United Nations Population Fund could be at stake (see Crane and Finkle 1989). Difficulties arise also because not only has policy undergone considerable fluctuations over the last ten years, it has always been dependent on local regulations which differ from province to province, and quite commonly from one area to another within a single province. It is however possible to discern certain broad trends in policy development. Despite Peng Peiyun's disclaimer, I will use the term 'one-child policy' to denote the population policy of the last ten years. The term cannot reflect the full complexity of the requirements, but does not seem an unfair shorthand for a policy which has consistently advocated the one-child family as at very least an ideal to which all should aspire.

The single child family policy attempted to impose on Chinese peasants a family size considerably at variance with their own wishes, and in a country where son preference is strong, required that almost half the population be denied a son, leaving parents without support in their old age and breaking the male descent line whose continiuity was traditionally a high priority for the Chinese. Moreover, the early years of the one-child policy in the countryside coincided with the substitution of the household responsibility system for collectivised agriculture. Foreign analysts and Chinese commentators have for the most part concurred that the reform made fertility reduction more difficult. On the one hand as households became independent economic units, the economic value of children to peasants was reinforced, and on the other, it was much more difficult for the government to exercise control over peasant households (Davin 1985). The devolution of profit and loss to peasant households meant that it was no longer possible to dock their workpoint income for defiance of the one-child rule. New efforts to enforce the one-child rule were made on the basis of the so-called double-contract system (Banister 1987, 205). Peasants contracted not only to deliver grain quotas to the state in exchange for the right to farm a given area of land, but also to limit their reproduction. The original intention was that non-compliance would be met both by raised grain quotas and by a reduction in the land allocated to the household. Double contracts were partly undermined by the Central Committee's 'Document No 1' of 1984 which granted peasants tenure of their land for 15 years or more (Davin 1985, 64). Without regular redistribution of land, non-compliance could be punished only by raising the grain quota or substituting a fine. Perhaps because it created less tension than a penalty levied year by year for fourteen years or so, most penalties in the rural areas seem in the end to have been exacted in the form of a lump-sum payment.

When the single-child programme was introduced in 1979, the rural areas were told to aim for a 50 per cent compliance rate. But in February 1980, Chen Muhua, then the Director of the State Comission for Family Planning, asked for 90 per cent (Davin 1985, 38). It is hardly surprising given this suddenly raised target, and the difficulties arising from agricultural reform, that implementation of the policy became more insistent up to 1983. Report of coercion peaked in 1983, the year in which calls were issued for mandatory sterilisation for women with two children, IUD insertion for those with one and abortions of unauthorised pregnancies. Banister (1987) details many instances of coercion which she regards as characterising the whole one-child campaign. Wolf (1986) offers a more even-handed consideration of the ethical aspects of the policy. Many reports of female infanticide appeared in the press (e.g. Yang 1982; Guangming Ribao 1982). These are difficult to evaluate. There is no doubt that female infanticide occurred, but equally, some reports, possibly emanating from people anxious to see the policy modified, were probably exaggerated. Whatever the truth, reports of infanticide put the Chinese Government under strong internal and external pressure to act, if necessary by relaxing the policy. At the same time some foreign scholars, whose increasing co-operation with their Chinese counterparts meant that their opinions would not go unnoticed, began to challenge the idea that the one-child policy was the only way to achieve China's goal of limiting her population to 1.2 billion in the year 2000 (Bongaarts and Greenhalgh 1985), or even that this goal was desirable given the costs it would entail (Banister 1987, ch. 10).

In spring 1984 the Central Committee acted to reduce growing tension with the issue of 'Document No. 7' (discussed in Greenhalgh 1986). This condemned coercion, urged voluntarism and persuasion, and advised a flexibility of approach which would allow more copules to have second children. The new policy used the slogan, 'open a small hole but close up the large one'. The idea was that an over-restrictive limit on second births made large numbers of second births outside the plan inevitable. Once such defiance was widespread, it was difficult to get anyone to toe the line, and even third and subsequent parity births could not be controlled.

Provincial regulations had always contained lists of conditions under which exceptions to the one-child rule could be authorised, and after the appearance of Document 7 these began to widen. Broadly they recognised the economic value of children by allowing exceptions in cases where a parent or the first child was handicapped, or where the family lived in a poor mountainous area or had special economic difficulties. Exceptions for overseas Chinese, national minorities and those in hazardous occupations, made the right to have a second child part of generally privileged treatment. Other exceptions, made for couples of whom both were themselves only children, or for men whose brothers were all infertile, seem to show concern, despite the need to reduce current cohorts, that the family tree should not be narrowed down in any one family for too long. The biggest of the 'little holes' opened in this time was the waiver, found in both the Guanxi and the Liaoning provincial regulations, that a rural couple experiencing real difficulties because the first child was a girl, could have a second, providing the births were spaced (Greenhalgh 1986, 496). At first this seemed an isolated case. Well-informed western scholars even argued that the authorities would presumably be uneasy with such an exception, given its implicit gender discrimination. But by 1988, many provinces were allowing second births to all rural couples whose first child was a girl, and in that year this relaxation was confirmed as national policy for the rural areas in general, although a few areas, including the Sichuan and Anhui and the rural areas around Shanghai and Beijing have maintained more restrictive rules (People 1989, 11-12.).

Public hostility to the one-child policy and official unease at some of the problems its implementation involved, appear to have persuaded the Central Commitee to issue 'Document No 7' which urged some modifications to birth control work. The provincial authorities were probably inspired to relax the rules both by this document, and by encouraging data about rates of fertility, natural growth and reductions in higher order births in all localities in 1984 and 1985 (Greenhalgh 1986). It is possible that these trends were influenced by the fact that 1984 was, according to the Chinese calendar, an extremely inauspicious year in which to be born and that they should therefore have been recognised as short-term (Wang Jiachuan 1988). Whatever the truth of this, all these rates showed sharp rises in 1986 and 1987. (Hardee-Cleaveland and Banister 1988, 248). Responding both to these rises and to the marriage boom projected to begin in the late 1980s and to continue until it peaks in 1993, official statements once more underscored the importance of maintaining a tight control on birth planning (Wan Li 1986). Those who had ceased to bother with the restrictions were castigated. Some western observers claimed that this might herald 'shifting back to a harder line' (Hardee-Cleaveland and Banister 1988), but semiofficial statements have since denied such a shift (Zeng Yi 1989). In fact, tightening up and relaxation seemed to have been combined. The regulations are to be enforced, yet the most important of all the modifications to the one-child rule - permission to have a second child for those whose first is a girl - has, as we have seen, been approved at national level, and as of 1989, with certain important exceptions, is being applied throughout China (Zeng Yi 1989).

Gender implications of the one-child policy and its modifications

As I have already argued, the one-child policy in its original form had various negative consequences for females. Most prominent among these were the re-emergence of female infanticide and differential care for girl babies, phenomena which appear to have been serious enough to distort the sex ratio in the youngest age groups. Nationally the 1982 census reported 108.5 male to every 100 female births (Aird 1983). These figures are not easy to interpret. There has always been under-registration of females in China, and in the present situation some peasants may try to avoid conflict by failing to report female births and continuing to try for a son. However most analysts find the data disturbing. The national average masked marked regional differences, for example between the reassuringly low 105.4:100 in Shanghai an area where female labour is in demand and where for socio-economic reasons one would expect son preference to be weak, and alarmingly high figures such as those for Guangxi and Anhui, which produced figures of 110.7 and 112.5 respectively. Both are provinces where son preference is strong. (For discussions of regional differences in son preference in different provinces see Arnold and Liu 1986 and Peng 1989).

In the past the majority of Chinese women probably went into their first labour hoping for a boy, but the birth of a daughter would not have been greeted with despair. Her arrival was at least welcome proof that her parents were capable of having children. Survey data from both the People's Republic (Whyte and Gu 1987) and Taiwan (Freeman 1986) seem to indicate that most parents would welcome a daugthter in a family of three children and many would prefer a boy and a girl to two sons. The problem arises when the state insist that the first child should also be the last.

If they know that they will only be allowed one child, women must endure considerable stress throughout their pregnancy and labour wondering what the sex of their child will be. Women were traditionally held to be responsible for the sex of their infants, and despite attempts at scientific education, this notion persists. There have been widespread reports of the ill-treatment of the mothers of baby girls, ranging from a refusal to give them the special foods traditionally offered to parturient women, through to persistent abuse, violent beatings and even murder (e.g. Renmin Ribao 1983).

To comply with Government policy, each couple must control their fertility. Women carry a disproportionate share of this burden. Prior to the one-child policy, sterilisation was a common method of birth control, especially in the countryside, and even now, although for obvious reasons the parents of single children prefer to rely on reversible contraception, sterilisation remains the norm for those who have a second child. Except in Sichuan, female sterilisations far outnumber vasectomies, despite the relative simplicity of the latter procedure. The IUD is the most commonly used contraceptive in China with especially high user rates in the countryside—3 per cent of all contracepting couples as opposed to 8 per cent for the pill. (Qian and Xiao 1983). The Chinese IUD has no tail and cannot be safely removed by the user or by any unskilled person. IUDs are not supposed to be forced on women, but removals which have not been officially sanctioned are referred to as 'illegal removals', even if they have been sought by the woman herself (Sichuan Regulations, article 28). Those who perform them are subject to imprisonment and the fees they have charged can be confiscated. Other methods of contraception are little used in the villages. China is to the forefront in research to develop a satisfactory male contraceptive, and the Women's Federation has resolved that 'men should also be urged to take contraceptive measures'. (Fifth Women's Congress 1983). Nonetheless the responsibility for contraception still falls mainly on women and they suffer when it fails.

The media now carry fewer complaints about forced abortions and it seems probable that the level of coercion has been reduced by the official emphasis on voluntarism. However there is a sense in which the authorities are pulling both ways. The system under which cadres responsible for family planning receive bonuses for success, and can be penalised for failing to keep birth rates in their areas sufficiently low, is clearly one of the factors which has produced coercion (Chen and Kols 1982, 199). Moreover many women abort much-wanted pregnancies even though they are not *physically* coerced to do so. Overwhelming moral, social and economic pressure is covered by the word 'persuasion'. Fluctuations in implentation have sometimes led to women getting pregnant in the belief that they will get away with it, only to find themselves caught up in an enforcement campaign. They may then have to undergo abortions in the second or even in the third trimester. Women who are trying to carry through an unauthorised pregnancy sometimes hide with relatives in other villages or in the city. If caught, such women are escorted back to their homes by officials of the public security bureau as if they were criminals and persuaded to abort. The pressure on unmarried women who become pregnant is probably even greater. For example the current regulations for Sichuan Province state that no children must be born to unmarried women (Sichuan Regulations article 7). This seems to imply mandatory abortion which is also prescribed for the mentally deficient or those with other serious heridity conditions (Sichuan Regulations article 13). Great vigilance is required to prevent 'out-of-plan' births. Birth control workers are supposed to watch constantly for out-of-plan pregnancies, and in the best-organised areas, women of child-bearing age are supposed to undergo monthly checkups (Hardee-Cleaveland and Banister 1988).

The power which the whole system of planned birth gives to officials is of course open to abuse. In his study of a Sichuan village, Endicott describes the way in which, even before the advent of the single child policy, the party secretary had harrassed a young woman against whom he had a grudge (Endicott 1988, 188-189). At the time she was pregnant with her second child and he demanded that to stay within the local plan, she get an abortion and get pregnant the following year. She protested that she had already left a four-year gap and went ahead and had the child. He refused to register it, a serious matter as without registration she could not receive a grain ration or a private plot allocation for the child. A year later, he agreed to register the child on condition that her husband, a soldier posted near Beijing thousand miles away from his wife at that time, had a vasectomy. The husband complied but the party secretary still managed to delay the child's registration by another year.

It could be argued that birth control work empowers some women, for at the grass-roots levels, most birth-control workers are female. Indeed their tasks, which include keeping records of the menstrual cycles of women under their charge, urging them and their families to accept the one-child certificate, advising on contraception, arranging abortions, IUD insertions and sterilisations and handing out permissions to get pregnant, would no doubt be regarded as inappropriate for a man. However this work, far from being empowering, seems to make women the scapegoats for an unpopular policy (Banister 1987, 365; Davin 1987, 124). In many cases such women have already had experience of working with the Women's Federation, or as cadres with special responsibility for helping abused women and protecting women's rights. The unpopularity which they suffer for their birth control activities can impair their effectiveness in other fields. In rural China, where there is a shortage of women with confidence, education and determination to work as cadres, this is a very real loss from which women's interests will suffer.

In the community studied by Endicott, Zhong, the head of the women's association, was a woman with two children. Like other female cadres and party members she had a responsibility for birth control work, and again in common with other activists of her age, she had two children, born before the introduction of the one-child limit. In 1983, tensions were running high over the one-child policy and threats were made by villagers against this woman's son. When she appealed to the party commitee for support, the result was a shock. In a decision opposed by all six of the women party members, the party committee decided that Zhong should resign and that her post should be given to a younger woman who was not an activist but who had only one child. Endicott's interpretation was that the male-dominated comittee took advantage of the situation to get rid of a strong women's leader and replace her with someone who would be more compliant (Endicott 1988, 185-193).

It is clear that there can be real physical danger to not only the cadres involved in birth control work but to the medical workers who are also frequently female. Article 27 of the Sichuan provincial regulations reflects the problem when it affirms that those who insult, threaten or beat doctors, nurses and other personnel in charge of birth control work will be punished.

It seems only fair to observe that the single-child policy has also had some beneficial effects for females. Where a couple's only child is female, once the firm decision is taken to rear her, resources will be concentrated on her as they would not have been if she had had brothers. Differential treatment in the past has resulted in women being depressingly disadvantaged in educational terms. Among Chinese over 12 years old in 1982, 45 per cent females were illiterate compared to 19 per cent males (Arnold and Liu 1986, 225). The demand for child labour which has accompanied the introduction of contract systems affected girls' school enrollment much more adversely than that of boys. In time-honoured fashion, peasant parents invest in their sons who will stay with them, not in daughters who will marry out. Of 2.73 million school-age children not enrolled in school, 83 per cent are girls. (Women of China 1989, 5). In some areas teachers make special arrangements such as night classes for female child labourers, but often the girls miss school altogether, attend only sporadically or leave early. Where a girl is an only child, her treatment will surely be different and more effort will be made to send her to school.

Another positive side-effect of the policy is the attention given to child health. It is recognised that infant mortality must be reduced to give peasants the confidence to restrict their families so serverely. Single children are offered special health check-ups without charge. A veritable advice industry has developed to offer instruction in such matters as child care and nutrition to an audience which seems remarkably receptive (Davin 1990). At a time when the rural medical health system has seen lamentable decline, the protection and fostering of child health is especially fortunate, and the same is true of gynaecological and maternity care, also seen as essential to the success of population policy. Regular monitoring of women's menstrual cycles has probably facilitated the diagnosis and treatment of various gynaecological disorders, while the possibility of lowering both maternal and infant mortality must arise from improved facilities and the reduction in high parity births.

Problems in implementing the one-child policy have highlighted the persistence of gender inequality in the countryside decades after the revolution. It is no longer possible to argue that this is simply a remnant of pre-revolutionary society which will die a natural death. To some extent, the Women's Federation has been able to take advantage of the concern with the status of women which has arisen both from revulsion at infanticide and from an understanding of the relationship between female status and fertility levels. While the Federation has not recovered the militant image it had in revolutionary years, its efforts to help women have considerably stepped up in the past decade. It has run campaigns against violence against women, organised training classes at all levels for women to work on women's issues, and has generally been more visible in support of women's rights.

Table 1. Percentage distribution of family size preferences by number and sex of children preferred, reported in surveys in Danjiang County, Hubei, rural and urban areas, 1986

Preference	Rural	Urban	Total
One, either sex	3.7	7.2	4.8
One girl	0.7	2.2	1.2
One boy	0.8	0.8	0.8
Two, either sex	24.3	24.4	24.3
Two girls	1.6	0.3	1.2
Two boys	0.3	0.3	0.3
One girl, one boy	50.2	62.5	54.1
Three either sex	6.3	0.8	4.6
Two boys, one girl	6.2	0.6	4.4
Two girls, one boy	1.4	0.6	1.1
More than three	4.3	0.3	3.0
Total, per cent	100	100	100
Number	750	350	1100[1]

1. 661 married women and 469 men of childbearing age (15-49)

Source: Martin King Whyte and S. Z. Gu, Popular Response to China's Fertility Transition (*Population and Development Review*, September 1987, 476)

Having presented a generalised picture of the implications of the single-child policy in its original form for the female population of the rural areas, I will now turn finally to the specific implications of the recent relaxation on second births in the countryside. There are some exceptional rural areas where permission to have a second child does not depend on the sex of the first. These do not concern me here. My discussion focusses on the concession which is being applied nationally with the exception of Sichuan and Anhui provinces and the municipalities of Beijing and Shanghai, that parents in rural areas whose first child is a girl can now get permission to have a second child. Spacing is still of course demanded - in general a gap between four and eight years is compulsory—but nonetheless this means in effect that the one-child policy now applies only to about half the rural population, while the other half are asked to limit their families to two.

The application of the new norms to peasant couples will mean that of about three quarters of them will eventually have a son and only one quarter (those whose second child is also a daughter) will be asked to accept that they cannot have one. It is expected, probably correctly, that this relaxation will make policy easier to implement. In the past the parents of only daughters were less willing than those with only sons to take out one child certificates thus undertaking to have no more children (Arnold and Liu 1986). However such indications of preferred family size and composition in China as available, consistently show that very few peasants would choose to 'stop at one'. Indeed, despite all that is said about son preference, a survey carried out in rural Hubei found that among those questioned, a family of two girls was actually much more popular than one of one boy (see table 1 below). Obviously the results of one small-scale investigation cannot be assumed to hold good for China as a whole, but the survey indicates the possibility that the group with one son may be more resistant to the one-child limit than the policy-makers hope. Just over half those parents allowed a second birth may be expected to produce a son, and with a family of one boy and one girl, will presumably consider themselves luckier than those who had a boy first time. The remainder, about a quarter of the total, will have to content themselves with two daughters. These couples may present a problem, for they will still face the elimination of the male descent line, the loss of their youthful labour power on the marriage of their daugthers, and a difficult old age without co-resident children. Well-off households may be able to attract marrying-in sons-in-law from poorer families or less prosperous areas (see Ji 1988), but the scope for this, the traditional strategy of families without sons, must be limited in cohorts shaped by regulations under which no ordinary family will be authorised to give birth to more than one healthy boy (Whyte and Gu 1987, 478). However, the significant reduction in the number of families likely to be highly resistant to population policy will certainly make the work of birth control cadres less difficult.

Some of the negative consequences of the one-child policy for rural females will be mitigated by the opening of this so called 'small hole'. For example, although the *second* girl, and the mother who gives birth to her, remain vulnerable to resentment and ill-treatment, the incidence of infanticide and abandonment and ill-treatment should drop significantly with the decrease in the number of families denied a son.

Less positively, the new regulations, if effective, will create two major groupings of peasant families, those with a single child on whom family resources are concentrated, and those with two children between whom the resources must be split. Children in the first group must be expected to grow up better nourished, healthier and better educated than those in the second. The vast majority of privileged only children will be boys, and approximately two thirds of the all boys will belong to single-child families, while almost all girls will belong to families with two children. Where families defy the regulations to have more than two children, it is likely that the majority of their children will be girls. The implication of this can be fully captured if one remembers that a primary determinant of poverty and prosperity in individual peasant families is the dependency ratio. Families with only one child, already advantaged by a low dependency ratio, also receive various subsidies to reward their single-child state. The great majority of girls will grow up in families which are poorer, have less to spend on their children and must divide what there is between more than one child. A girl in a sibling set of two sisters who are treated equally, may be expected to do better than a girl with a brother who gets preferential treatment. Most importantly, girls as a whole will grow up significantly less privileged than boys as a whole.

The new modification will also presumably have an effect on the differential character development of boys and girls. A lot has been written in China about the new generation of only children, much of it in my opinion rather exaggerated.[1] But it is probably true that only children will grow up more assertive and demanding whereas those socialised in a two-child family must learn to defer and compromise. Given the probable distribution of male and female children between one and two-child families, the effect will be to exacerbate gender difference in the division of these characteristics, a division which already tends to support male dominance.

Last but not least, the modification not only recognises son preference, in trying to deal with the problems to which this social phenomenon gives rise, it panders to it. While the early propaganda for the single child proclaimed 'a girl is as good as a boy' the new regulations implicitly accept that, at least for peasant parents, she is not as good. The posters which show beaming parents holding their only child nearly always portray the baby as a girl, but in real life such parents, if they live in rural areas, are now told, 'never mind you can try again'. The authorities can hardly be blamed for the *existence* of son preference in China, it has survived all the challenges they have been able to make to it. In this context to recognise and allow for son preference is probably the lesser of two evils, especially as it can be expected to save female lives. At the same time, this recognition makes the government's line on equality less clear and, as I have shown, will result in most peasant girls growing up in poorer families than most peasant boys. It thus raises further obstacles to the progress of sexual equality in rural China.

Note

1.   One Chinese social scientist listed the following characteristics for single children: 'wilfulness, finicality, selfishness, jealousy, complacency, timidity, pettiness, obstinacy, vanity, aloofness, conceitedness and unscrupulousness' (Bian 1987).

References

Aird 1983: John S. Aird, 'The Preliminary Results of China's 1982 Census'. *China Quarterly* 96 1983 613-640.

Arnold and Liu 1986: F. Arnold and Liu Zhaoxiang, 'Sex Preference, Fertility and Family Planning in China'. *Population and Development Review*, 12:2, June 1986, 221-46.

Banister 1987: Judith Banister, *China's Changing Population*. Stanford: Stanford U.P. 1987.

Bian 1987: Bian Yanjie, 'A Preliminary Analysis of the Basic Features of the Life Styles of China's Single-Child Families'. *Social Sciences in China*, 8:3, September 1987.

Bongaarts and Greenhalgh 1985: Johan Bongaarts and Susan Greenhalgh, 'An Alternative to the One-Child Policy in China'. *Population and Development Review*, 11:4, December 1985, 585-617.

Chen and Kols 1982: Chen Pi-chao and Adrienne Kols, 'Population and Birth Planning in the People's Republic of China'. *Population Reports* 10:1, January-Februray 1982.

Chen and Tyler 1982: Charles Chen and Carl W. Tyler, 'Demographic Implications of Family Size Alternatives in the People's Republic of China'. *China Quarterly*, No. 89, December 1982, 65-73.

Croll 1985: Elisabeth Croll, Delia Davin and Penny Kane (eds.), *China's One Child Family Policy*, London: Macmillan.

Crane and Finkle 1989: Barbara B. Crane and Jason L. Finkle, 'The United States, China, and the United Nations Population Fund: Dynamics of US policymaking'. *Population and Development Review*, 15:1, March 1989, 23-60.

Davin 1985: 'The Single-Child Policy in the Countryside', in Croll E., Davin D and Kane P. (eds.), *China's One Child Family Policy*. London: Macmillan.

Davin 1987: Delia Davin, 'Gender and Population Control in the People's Republic of China'. In Haleh Afshar (ed.), *Women, State and Ideology*. London: Macmillan.

Davin 1990: Delia Davin, 'Early Childhood Education in the Age of the One-Child Family'. In I. Epstein (ed.), *Chinese Education: Problems, Policies and Prospects*. New York: Garland.

Endicott 1988: Stephen Endicott, *Red Earth: Revolution in a Sichuan Village*. London: I.B. Tauris.

Fifth Women's Congress: 'Report of the Fifth Chinese Women's National Congress, September 1983'. *Summary of World Broadcasts*, 12 November 1983.

Freeman 1986: Ronald Freeman, 'Policy Options After the Demographic Transition: The Case of Taiwan'. *Population and Development Review*, 12:1, March 1986, 77-100.

Greenhalgh 1986: Susan Greenhalgh, 'Shifts in China's Population Policy 1984-6: Views from the Central, Provincial and Local Levels'. *Population and Development Review*, 12:3, September 1986, 491-515.

Guangming Ribao 1982: 'On the Protection of Baby Girls'. *Guangming Ribao*, 30 December 1982.

Hardee-Cleaveland and Banister 1988: Karen Hardee-Cleaveland and Judith Banister, 'Fertility Policy and Implementation in China, 1986-88'. *Population and Development Review*, 14:2, June 1988, 245-286.

Ji 1988: Ji Ping, Zhang Kaidi and Liu Dawei, 'An analysis of marital migration among residents of Beijing's suburbs'. *Chinese Sociology and Anthropology*, Winter 1988-1989.

Peng 1989: Peng Yizhe, 'Major Determinants of China's Fertility Transition'. *China Quarterly*, No. 117, March 1989, 1-37.

People 1989: *People*. The journal of the International Planned Parenthood Federation, 16:1, January 1989.

Qian and Xiao 1983: Qian Xinzhong and Xiao Zhenyu, *An Analysis of the One in One Thousand Fertility Survey*. Beijing: Beijing Economics College.

Renmin Ribao 1983: 'Resolutely Oppose Discrimination Against Women', *Renmin Ribao*, 3 March 1983.

Sichuan regulations 1988: 'Sichuan Birth Planning Provincial Regulations', *Population and Development Review*, 14:2, June 1988, 369-375.

Wan Li 1986: Vice-Premier Wan Li's speech to a national birth control conference. In *Renmin Ribao* 3 March 1986. Translated in *Population and Development Review*, 12:3, September 1986, 603-606.

Wang 1988: Wang Jiachuan, 'Determinants of Fertility Increase in Sichuan 1981-86'. *Population and Development Review*, 14:3, September 1988, 482-487.

Whyte and Gu 1987: Martin King Whyte and S. Z. Gu, 'Popular Response to China's Fertility Transition'. *Population and Development Review*, 12:1, March 1986, 101-117.

Women of China 1989: 'Primary Education for Girls', 'Night School Girls', 'Education for Daughters of the Ethnic Minorities'. *Women of China*, March 1989.

Yang 1982: Yang Fan, 'Save the Baby Girls'. *Zhongguo Qingnian Bao*, 9 November 1982.

Zeng Yi 1989: Zeng Yi, 'A Policy in Transition', *People*, 16:1, 1989, 20.

Zhang and Sang 1989: 'Planning her Family', in Zhang Xinxin and Sang Ye, *Chinese Lives*. Edited by W.J.F. Jenner and D. Davin, Harmondsworth: Penguin.

LABOUR, ENTERPRISE, AND REDISTRIBUTION

The Ambiguities of Labour and Market in Periurban Communities in China During the Reform Decade

Flemming Christiansen

Rural communities on the fringes of China's large cities have experienced great changes during the Reform Decade 1979-89. These communities are unique in the sense that they form the borderline between the urban and the rural economies. Rural and urban China have been divided into two distinct sectors, following their own paths of development and being governed by very different political and economic systems. Placed at the junction between these systems, periurban areas[1] have been exposed to conflicting trends of the reform policies that started after the Third Plenum in December 1978. Not depending on agricultural production for the major part of economic activities, they have been able to profit from the liberalisation of private entrepreneurship in the country-side when the collective frameworks for production were gradually broken down during the early 1980s. At the same time they have been increasingly integrated into the urban economy as a result of urban expansion. This has created an ambiguous economic, social and political configuration, which is partly collective in nature, but which also reflects, perhaps in the most radical form, the formation of a quasi-market economy, and at the same time increasing interaction with the distributional economy dominating the urban economy. The rural-urban dichotomy has, due to changes in both rural and urban economy, begun to crumble, but the two sectors have not yet been integrated into one system. Bureaucratic and political divisions proliferate and have, as will be described in more detail below taken new forms in the course of development during the 1980s.

Rural periurban communities, therefore, reflect the dual nature of Chinese economy as it evolved during the Reforms. This duality is not merely a theoretical phenomenon. It manifests itself in the daily life of the peasants inhabiting periurban districts to the extent that the borderline between rural and urban society divides households. To understand the reforms, both theoretically and practically, it is illuminating to look at their impacts on periurban households since they span both the rural and the urban sectors. Such an approach may render insights in the new social structures that have come about during the reforms.

The discussion shall focus on the labour opportunities that present themselves to the households and will move on to a critical assessment of some of the basic characteristics of periurban economy. One of the main problems in Chinese rural development is the surplus of labour. The policy of accumulating funds for investing in and sustaining an urban industrial sector has been pursued at the cost of agriculture. Agriculture has, in spite of apparent successes since 1949, never become a modernised, effective production sector; rather than operating on a rational scale, using skilled labour, agriculture is forced to absorb the surplus work force. Even after the post-1978 reforms brought about a huge expansion of off-farm labour opportunities, virtually tripling the number of employees in rural non-farm sectors, the total labour force in agriculture has been constantly growing except for a small net decline in 1983-84 (Statistical Yearbook 1988, 172 and 293). Hence, the reforms have only partly succeeded in solving the problem of irrational, small scale agriculture. We must see the peri-urban labour situation against this background.

Social Divisions During the Reforms

The rural-urban division lines in China are based on several bureaucratically imposed systems which were designed in the 1950s to control population mobility, economic interchange (trade, investment) and political administration *within an economic system based on state controlled resource allocation*. The three main systems to be analysed here are the *hukou* system, the administrative division between rural and urban areas and the rural collective ownership system. These systems and the changes that have taken place in them especially since 1978 form the framework for the rural dwellers' labour opportunities.

The *hukou* system (Zhang 1988, Potter 1983, Goldstein and Goldstein 1985, Christiansen 1990) divides Chinese citizens into 'agricultural' and 'urban resident' population (*nongye renkou, chengshi jumin renkou*). Every citizen belongs to either of these classifications, which are registered with local police offices and are entered in household registration books (*hukou dengji bu*) held by every family. The *hukou* registration forms the basis for public resource allocation. Urban residents are entitled to a number of rationed goods at subsidised prices, job allocation through the Labour Administration Bureaus and concomitant to their occupation in state-owned enterprises to free or low-fee schooling for their children, medicare, housing and fuel. People with 'agricultural' registration do not share these privileges. 'Agricultural' *hukou* is linked with the collective ownership of the means of production, and the *hukou* registration is bound to a specific administrative village (*cun*, formerly production brigade), but *de facto* to a production team. Each person with an 'agricultural' *hukou* in a production team is a member of that team and shares its collective assets with the other members, including land and collective enterprises. Food grain distribution, work allocation and social security are managed directly within the production team or the administrative village. Transfer of *hukou* status is very difficult, both across the classification and between localities. The rationale of the *hukou* system was to prevent migration from the countryside to the cities, and it appears to have been very successful in doing so between 1958 when it was instituted and the start of the reforms. It was sustained by the state trade monopoly, which interdicted private trade in most commodities. The supplies on food in the cities was based on very elaborate rationing systems, and the only way of obtaining grain in the cities was to present rationing coupons issued locally. For these reasons people without urban resident *hukou* were not able to stay for a long time in the cities.

When the markets for agricultural products were gradually liberalised in the late 1970s and early 1980s, free market trade made it possible for non-residents to obtain the most important commodities to stay in the cities for longer periods. At the same time, the emerging urban markets for rural commodities and services supplied by individual entrepreneurs (often originating in the countryside) opened up new avenues for earning an income in the cities. In this way the household registration system has lost much of it practical function. However, it still functions as a tool for distribution of subsidised goods and privileges.

The second division line is the administrative division between rural and urban China.[2] At the basic level, townships are subdivided in villagers' committees, while towns are subdivided in residents' committees and villagers' committees. Counties are subdivided in townships and/or towns, while city districts are subdivided in residents' committees or townships and/or towns. Cities are subdivided in counties and city districts. Provinces are subdivided in cities. However, this administrative division was instituted in the 1980s after the 1982 Constitution was introduced. Before, in the 1970s, provinces were divided in cities and districts (*diqu*), districts being subdivided in counties. The administration of cities and their surrounding counties, accordingly, converged at the provincial level. The reform of the administrative system has aimed at putting rural (county) and urban (city) planning and administration under a unified jurisdiction in the so called 'central cities' (*zhongdian chengshi*), but in practical administration the difference between the rural and urban sector is maintained under the new structures.[3] In Jiangsu province and probably also in other provinces, there has been an effort to unify rural and urban administration at lower levels. Towns and townships merged to become larger town jurisdictions; this was the case in Qixia District of Nanjing City, where October People's Commune merged with Qixia Town to form a new Qixia Town. This integration has undoubtedly furthered comprehensive planning and a convergence of rural and urban economy. The rural-urban dichotomy as reflected in jurisdiction boundaries is not, and has never been, a simple division line, but is an intricate, convoluted structure. As seen from the political center, the most important division is that between counties and city districts which have different governmental structures, while the individual citizens perceive of the difference between administrative village and residents' committees as the most important one.

Jurisdiction and *hukou* do not totally overlap. In a township there may be a large number of inhabitants with urban *hukou* status. They do not belong to the community in the economic sense, even though they are fully integrated socially. In the 1980s, this has become an increasingly important trend.

The third borderline between rural and urban areas is that of ownership. Rural areas are dominated by collective ownership, i. e. community ownership of the major means of production. Each member of a production team is a co-owner of the land and the local township and village enterprises. Urban areas are dominated by state ownership, officially called 'the ownership by the whole people' (*quanmin suoyouzhi*), and urban collective ownership. These differ in that all Chinese citizens own the assets belonging to the state, which administrates them on their behalf, while the urban collective assets are owned by the workers in a system of workers' cooperatives. Rural ownership is integrated in the local political structures, which represent the peasants vis-à-vis the state, while the urban economy is integrated in various levels of state administration. Political and economic control with the country-side, due to the difference in ownership is intermediate as opposed to the more direct bureaucratic control within the urban economy. Rural collective ownership also differs from urban forms of ownership in that it is comprehensive, covering a wide range of economic activities, integrating them with civil affairs and communal services within distinct geo-graphical boundaries, while urban forms of ownership divides different economic activities in various types of 'work units' (*danwei*). These work units, as compared to enterprises in other countries, have a wider range of social functions, but they represent a much more sophisticated form of 'division of labour' than China's rural communities. During the reforms, rural collective ownership has been challenged by the introduction of private ownership in various forms, and the apportionment of land under the responsibility system as well as the greater independence of village and township enterprises have changed the nature of rural collective ownership from a unitary distributional system to a complicated system of economic exchange within the rural communities. This will be discussed later.

As already mentioned, rural collective ownership is intimately linked with the *hukou* system, membership of the rural community depending directly on *hukou* status.

These very concrete division lines initially made it possible for the Chinese leadership to allow the rural reforms to develop at a different pace than the urban reforms, but the reforms entailed an erosion of rural-urban divisions which has made it difficult or even impossible to assert the key role of the state in inter-sectoral exchange. This change first came about in periurban districts. The main aspects were the opening up of the markets and the increasing independence of enterprises.

Changing Labour Opportunities and Social Stratification

The periurban communities are rural by all above-mentioned standards. Most inhabitants were, at least before the reforms started, classified as 'agricultural' *hukou*, the communities were organised within the framework of rural collective ownership, and they were organised as people's communes with subordinate production brigades (in the 1980s these were changed into townships or towns with subordinate administrative villages). The only aspect where they differed from genuinely rural communities, was the fact that they were subordinated to city districts rather than counties.

When the rural reforms started in the late 1970s periurban communities were deeply affected. The labour opportunities of the peasants increased, and deep-going changes occurred in the social structures of the communities.

When the responsibility system for agricultural production was introduced in the early 1980s, land was apportioned to the individual households on production contracts. Many peri-urban districts were exempt from state procurement quotas on grain or had rather small quotas because these areas were classified as '*ren duo di shao*', indicating that they were densely populated and lacked sufficient land resources to produce grain for the market. In such cases the land was divided amongst the households on an equitable basis for food-grain consumption with no or few contract obligations (e. g. insignificant quotas on part of the second annual crop which is often wheat). During the 1970s most periurban communities had started a huge variety of non-agricultural enterprises, most of which were managed by the people's communes or the production brigades; most of these enterprises remained in the possession of the communities as collective assets, while small enterprises, often those based on seasonal or irregular operation were dissolved, in which case their machines and other implements were sold off to individual members of the communities or were divided among members on a contract basis. Accordingly, from the outset of the reforms agricultural pro-duction had very little significance for these communities, only covering the basic need for self-supply with grain. Some communities had, of course, specialised in the production of tea, vegetables, fruits, silk, tobacco, milk and other non-grain products. The land for such purposes was divided among major producers (so-called 'specialised households', *zhuanyehu*) on contracts. Cash incomes from agriculture were, therefore, generally limited to specialised production of this type. All other cash incomes had to be derived from rural collective enterprises and private entrepreneurship.

The consequences of this for households in periurban districts was an increasing occupational diversification. Families would often encompass members earning incomes from various sources, including for example tea production, work as cadres in local governments, wage labour in collective enterprises, wage labour in private or individual enterprises, private entrepreneurship locally or on a migratory basis.

During the reforms, urban expansion took an upswing. Construction of urban enterprises and urban housing created needs for construction workers. These were recruited in the countryside. New land was needed for expansion, especially on the outskirts of the large cities. Some land was requisitioned from rural communities. This was, for example, the case in Qixia Town (Nanjing City), where seven former production teams were dissolved between 1984 and 1987 to make place for *inter alia* an oil refinery (see Lu and Selden 1987 for other examples). As part of the agreement to yield the land, part of the rural labour force was transferred to work in state-owned enterprises and was reclassified as urban residents (Christiansen 1990). In some cases transfer to work in state-owned enterprises was impossible, so some rural labourers were reclassified as urban residents, but assigned work within rural collective enterprises, which received a lump sum of for example 10,000 yuan for employing them. This was the practice in Wangzhuang Township (Wuxi City), where approximately 400 people were assigned work in this way, constituting over three per cent of the total population. Their *hukou* classification is termed 'big collective' *hukou*.[4]

The need for workers in state-owned enterprises in some parts of the country increased and workers were recruited on temporary contracts, which gave them no right to *hukou* transfer.

In order to avoid cumbersome negotiations involving the Labour Bureau, the Land Administration Bureau, Ministries and City Governments (which are responsible for regional planning) to start land requisitioning procedures, and probably also to keep some of their production outside the state plan, urban industries have in the 1970s and 1980s established subsidiaries in rural areas, preferably in periurban districts, which were classified as rural collective and are managed by villagers' committees or township governments. The investments in these enterprises were shared on contract basis between the rural community and the mother enterprise, and the workers were recruited among the rural population. This type of urban expansion had the advantage for the urban enterprise and the city level state authorities that the initial investment per work force was smaller than for regular workers in the urban sector, and the state was not committed to all social privileges that would be liable if the workers were to obtain the urban household status. Such enterprises had the advantage for the village or the township that they constituted a stable source of income for communal purposes and facilitated labour transfer.

Occupation of members of rural communities in the urban sector, therefore, took very different forms. Some were selected to leave the 'agricultural' classification to work in state-owned enterprises, others, those who obtain 'big collective' *hukou* registration, work in village or township enterprises. Paradoxically, in contrast to their fellow villagers they are not co-owners of these enterprises, since the change of *hukou* status has dissociated them from collective ownership. Others were occupied in state enterprises without change of *hukou* status, including people working in construction gangs and as temporary workers (*linshigong*, also often referred to as 'contract workers', *hetonggong*). In 1984 the number of temporary workers, probably excluding those occupied in construction gangs, exceeded six million (Yearbook of Chinese Rural Statistics 1985, 230). Yet others were occupied in subsidiaries of large urban enterprises, without the privileges of urban workers.

In addition to the above-mentioned types there are rural migrant workers, people who are attracted from other parts of the countryside to work in a township or an administrative village. These include farmers, workers in township or village enterprises and workers in various types of private enterprises. A separate group are vendors and craftsmen who roam the countryside, taking up odd jobs on a private basis. In the Suburban District of Wuxi there are many examples of the former types. A large group of farmers were attracted to an administrative village in Wangzhuang Township to grow vegetables (NMRB 1986, Christiansen 1990). Wuxi City Government had, faced with shortages of vegetables in the urban market, forced Wangzhuang Township to make land available for vegetable production. Since there was no quota land left, land used for food grain for local consumption was confiscated and turned into vegetable fields. The afflicted peasants received grain coupons as a compensation (these were distributed through the administrative village). Having ample opportunities for other occupations, no locals were prepared to take upon them vegetable farming, which is considered dirty and tiresome work. The administrative village established an office for vegetable farming, which signed contracts with a small number of non-local managers who attracted workers on a contract basis. Most of the workers were recruited in rural communities in North Jiangsu, and they arrived as individuals or as whole families to undertake vegetable farming. Wangzhuang also had a severe lack of labourers for the rapidly expanding collective enterprises, and a large number of people were recruited in North Jiangsu and in nearby Yixing. By 1987, the total number of allochtonous workers in Wangzhuang including both vegetable growers and industrial workers was approximately 1,500, constituting 12.2 per cent of the total population. In Guzhuang, in Qixia Town under Nanjing City, many skilled workers from rural parts of Anhui Province and from Luhe County in North Jiangsu have been employed by private entrepreneurs. In all these cases, the workers retain their original *hukou* registration.

In all parts of the Chinese countryside, individual artisans cater for the market for rural house decoration and furnishing that has emerged as a result of soaring demands for dowry outfit. Before a marriage is agreed upon, the groom is required to have a new house or at least one big room in his parents' house at his exclusive disposal. The room or the house must be furnished and decorated at a certain standard, including linoleum floors, carpets, wall paper, new furniture, mirrors, and, of course, refrigerators, radio-cassettes, television sets etc.

This indicates that the labour opportunities have increased much during the reform era, creating a very complicated structure in the rural labour market. The newly emerged labour market is not an open market in any sense. Depending on the different forms of *hukou* registration (in regard to classification and to locality), and the different types of ownership of the means of production, the labourers have different rights and privileges. As opposed to the pre-reform situation, the *labour market transcends village and township boundaries*, but is restricted by administrative divisions and ownership-based distinctions. These phenomena are manifest in periurban communities, which are more directly than other parts of the countryside exposed to urban growth, but they exert their influence on the whole of the countryside, especially in the form of migration of labour. The labour market, if we continue to use this term to describe the quasi-market structures depicted above, is essentially *fragmented*, i. e. the *formal* and *informal* status of the labourers within their communities and with regard to official classification, determine their actual opportunities and they restrict labour mobility. This means that wages and other income opportunities are not weighed against each other in open competition of skills, qualifications and remuneration. The value of a *hukou* registration cannot be measured in economic terms, and career opportunities are not open to everybody on identical terms.

Allocation of work in state owned enterprises is subject to bureaucratic decisions, and although applications are, according to rules introduced in 1986 (GWYGB 1986, 744-747), solicited from prospect workers, people with 'agricultural' *hukou* are *de facto* excluded from this 'market' segment. When peasants are, occasionally, recruited for regular work in state owned enterprises (e. g. when rural land is requisitioned), a very selective distributional apparatus is in force. The villagers' committee is given the task of selecting candidates for the jobs. This is ideally done by equalizing favours among the members of the administrative village. In one team where the author carried out field research, 13 members had been transferred during the 1980s, representing 11 households; the rules for selecting candidates were formulated so as to favour families in dire straits and households carrying heavy social burdens (families of revolutionary martyrs and families of active servicemen) etc. The selection must be endorsed by the township government and the labour bureau. Distribution of jobs within the township and village enterprises in principle also follow rules of community 'justice'. In reality, of course, it should not be excluded that such favours, being distributed by political elites dominating villagers' committees and township governments which have innumerable personal and family ties in the communities, are subject to favouritism and nepotism.

Licensing of private entrepreneurs and credits for their enterprise operation are also decided upon politically within the communities. Labour recruitment in the private sectors is relatively free, but depends on patronage ties (*guanxi*).

What superficially looks like an open rural labour market, therefore, cannot be considered in such terms, market-like conditions are only created in marginal situations. If, for example, there exists an acute, local need for labourers, like in Wangzhuang, or if special skills are not available locally, as in Guzhuang, market mechanisms appear to be in force. However, in my interviews with people who have been recruited for work outside their home village, I have never come across any person who had not been introduced to his employer through *guanxi* channels. This might not so much be a result of defective market competition as of badly functioning public information channels.

Social Stratification

The periurban households are subject to a labour market, which is limited by and to a certain degree replicates egalitarian structures which were in existence before the reforms started (e. g. the idea of social 'justice' in work allocation). At the same time, occupational diversification under the present system generates social inequality. Those persons who were in a good starting position when the responsibility system was introduced were able to make a headstart into private entrepreneurship. There are several aspects involved here, but I shall mention the three, perhaps most important ones:

(a) When collective assets were sold or put under a contract, including trucks, tractors, tea fields, chicken farms etc. those who had a say in the community were able to reserve the best parts for themselves, in most cases because they had the skills to operate them;[5] there being no public market for these assets, their value was extremely difficult to calculate. The change from collective operation implied that the former uses for the assets suggested lower future returns than later proved to be the case. Under-used or irrationally utilized equipment in a stagnating, collective economy could yield much higher returns if operated privately in a quasi-market economy. Therefore, most of the assets sold off in the early 1980s were underestimated in price. Since they were, in most cases, to be sold within the community, and since all contracts on tea fields and similar side-line productions were to be held within the community, the prices were probably also influenced by the villagers' actual purchasing power or ability to raise credits for operating funds.

(b) Those families who, at the specific time when the collective spoils were divided, had the right composition of able-bodied adult workers, skills and *guanxi*, were able to undertake private business, while others were not. People who started private enterprises later were disfavoured by competition from the enterprises that had started earlier and by greater restrictions on credits and licensing. An example of this is that the persons buying trucks in 1983 when private possession of large motor vehicles was legalised could obtain credits to this end. In 1985, credits for motor vehicles were not available any more due to national policies. Private entrepreneurship, therefore, originates in very advantageous circumstances for a relatively small group of people.

(c) Other people who have started individual and private enterprises have done so because they were not able to be occupied in other types of off-farm pursuits. The author has, in his investigations, come across a number of people who started or planned to start small businesses due to very unfortunate circumstances, including failure to be employed on a permanent basis in collective enterprises and lacking proper *guanxi*. Such people have difficulty in collecting sufficient operating funds for their activities and they tend to be limited to a very small scale of operation with little prospect of expanding their activities.

Some families in periurban villages have very few members in work. In some cases married women did not get the opportunity to work, and in some cases young men and women were not able to find jobs. This means that the living standard in these families is very low.

Social stratification is perhaps most obvious in relation to matrimony. For reasons obscure to the author, villagers relate social status with marriage. The patrilocal marriage pattern dictates that the son must raise a 'dowry capital' to be able to marry. This 'capital' consists, as already mentioned, of separate living quarters for the young couple and a number of durable consumer items for their exclusive use. The bride is seen as an asset for her in-law family, and her quality is expressed in the size of the 'dowry capital'. Marriage often takes place within a network of brokerage, involving go-betweens who mediate the terms for the marriage. Brokerage is often internalised, reducing the actual negotiations to a minimum, in extreme cases brokerage is left to the young couple themselves. However, it appears from the author's observations that the terms are, in such cases, still based on a socially accepted norm within the community.

Those families which are able to make the highest 'dowry investments' acclaim the highest social esteem and are, through marriage, able to expand their *guanxi* networks. For rich entrepreneurial families this is not a problem. For periurban families basing their incomes on wage earnings, the incomes from all adult children are used toward the marriage of the oldest son. This means that full occupation is essential for all adult members of the family beneath retirement age. In 1987 and 1988, 'dowry capital' in Guzhuang was in a range between 5,000 and 10,000 yuan. The need for an average 'dowry capital' can thus be covered by full employment of the son who is going to marry between his 16th and 24th year of age, earning a high annual income averaging 1,000 yuan. Family property will normally not be split (*fenjia*) before all sons are married, thus obliging the oldest son to contribute with part of his income to the marriage of his younger brothers.

Social stratification can be identified by looking at the age of marriage and the size of 'dowry capital'. Families that are, for one or another reason, not able to secure sufficient funds for marriage, will loose out, and the sons will end up as bachelors or will marry late with the lest attractive women, who may turn out to be bad earners. Low social status will lead to low incomes and will press such families into a downward social spiral.

Market and labour in a wider perspective

It has been argued by Kornai (1986) that socialist economies tend to create scarcity of goods and services. Although I shall not analyse Chinese economy in terms of a 'socialist firm', some of Kornai's observations appear to be useful for examining the conflict between market and allocational economy in China. Egalitarian distribution of key goods at subsidised prices creates an unsatiable demand for these goods. The supply of these key goods is constrained by the availability of resources to produce them and not by the consumers' spending power, since prices are kept low. In Kornai's opinion this is the classical state of affairs in socialist economy (Kornai, 1986, 10). The rural-urban dichotomy and its institutions as they existed in China before the reforms started were able to regulate demand through rationing systems and collective redistribution, thereby preventing scarcity of goods from becoming obvious. The demand for agricultural products in urban communities could basically be covered, since plan targets were harmonised with urban demand. However, a number of factors put a constraint on this system: (a) The productive capacity of agriculture was limited by the retention of the population in the countryside, which restrained effectiveness and impeded technological development. (b) The negative terms of trade between rural and urban China restricted funds for technological development.

The development policies for China which were set out in the 1950s aimed at transferring funds from agriculture to develop industry, i. e. *primitive accumulation*. Industry was then supposed to supply the technological base for developing agriculture, thus creating the foundation for further industrialisation which could absorb the surplus labour force. However, the development of industry was cut off from rural economy to the extent that exchange of goods was not linked to an expansion of labour opportunities that could absorb the growing labour population. Urban economy was barely able to absorb the natural increase in the urban labour population, only occupying about 20 million workers from the countryside in the 1960s and 1970s. In the period 1966 - 1976 about 13 or 14 million people were transferred from the rural to the urban sector and in 1978-1986 an additional 10.1 million peasants became regular workers and urban residents (Taylor 1988:742-743). In the 1970s a policy of promoting rural industrialisation was initiated, which aimed at creating a structurally different type of *primitive accumulation* within the existing rural frameworks. In this way, rural-urban recirculation was supplemented by rural-rural recirculation of funds between rural enterprises and agriculture.

The latter form of recirculation was kept within the individual communities, and the returns from rural industry could be more directly invested for communal purposes and could be used for promoting agricultural production. Under the work-point systems then in force, all members of the communities would profit directly from greater incomes. When household based operation was introduced with the responsibility system and the markets were opened at the beginning of the reforms, the situation changed radically.

The main outcome of the change was that the redistributional character of the rural communities vanished when production was privatized. However, as Ole Odgaard observes in his contribution to this volume, the collectives still perform a crucial function in collective redistribution, albeit on other terms than before the reforms started. They are partly forced to subsidize agricultural production with surpluses from industrial and trade activities under 'compensate agriculture with industry' (*yi gong bu nong*) programmes, since the state procurement prices are so low that farmers are worse off than fellow-villagers working in other sectors.

Chinese economy is, accordingly, divided into a number of spheres, (a) the state redistributive economy, (b) the community redistributive economy, and (c) the private commodity economy. These three spheres operate according to different internal rules; the competition between them being unequal, there has arisen demands to protect vested interests. Urban workers are not inclined to give up their privileges and are opposed to price increases, thereby reinforcing the division lines in Chinese society. The private commodity economy is both marginal (or complementary to the state and collective redistributive systems) and a prime equaliser between the systems. It is marginal since it covers only a small fragment of total production, but it is the only field where prices are fixed without state intervention. The price differentials existing between the systems and between the systems and the free domestic market are—illegally—skimmed off by dubious go-betweens or corrupt cadres (Oi 1986).

Conclusion

The free market and private initiative were designed to solve the problems of lack of goods or the threat of declining production. The inherent scarcity of goods in socialist economy was at the outset of the reforms regarded as a problem that could be resolved by mobilising the peasantry by means of individual economic incentives, imbuing upon them the need for private entrepreneurship. Private production for the market would, it appears to have been thought, fill in the gap of scarcity and thereby relative unemployment. The growth in private commodity production could presumably only progress at the high rates seen in the 1980s due to the perpetuation of *scarcity*, constantly generated by the state distribution economy, which created a relative competitiveness and demand in an inequal market. This has been of crucial advantage for periurban communities and other land deficient areas, which have increasingly been forced to rely on off-farm production for their incomes due to their demographic growth and the structural restrictions on migration.

This situation constitutes an intriguing paradox. The quasi-market structures have been promoted by the persistence of the state redistribution system. In the political arena, they have also been seen to *reinforce* the bureaucratic divisions. The competition from the rural labour force and the long term equalisation of average incomes and living standards between the sectors, which are likely to emerge under expanding market structures, challenge the vested economic and political interests of the urban working class. So far, the Chinese authorities have upheld the most important barriers which protect urban workers from the rural peril, *inter alia* the *hukou* system and the state subsidies on core consumer goods for the urban population.

The situation in periurban districts indicate that the extant problems of Chinese economy cannot be solved within the framework of state redistribution. The emerging market forces, which are up till today fragmented and marginal, have been strongly promoted by the existing redistributive system and have generated a political situation which does not promise a rapid dismantling of rural-urban barriers. The ambiguity of periurban labour markets can only be expected to persist.

Notes

The research presented in this article is part of a larger project, financed by the Danish Research Council for Development Research (1986-1989). The author wants to thank Jørgen Delman for his critical comments on an earlier draft.

1. In this article, (rural) periurban areas are defined as the part of the countryside which is not under county (*xian*) jurisdiction, but is under the jurisdiction of city districts (shiqu) and is subdivided into towns (*zhen*) and townships (*xiang*). In common Chinese usage these city districts are referred to as 'suburban districts' (*jiaoqu*). The author is aware that many of the characteristics discussed below also manifest themselves in the most developed counties, especially in the coastal regions and in Sichuan. However, it is considered important to limit the analysis to a distinct and manageable type of community. Many of the findings are derived from the author's field work in the Suburban District of Wuxi and Qixia District of Nanjing, both in Jiangsu Province.

2. The following discussion does not reflect the administrative structures in autonomous regions and in sub-provincial national minority areas.

3. For a compelling analysis of the political and macro-economic context of this scheme, see Unger (1987). See also Cabestan (1986, 882).

4. 'Big collective' *hukou* is a category of the urban registration, which is normally used to signify workers in urban collective enterprises. The Labour Bureau and the police departments use the procedures for registration of workers in urban collective enterprises by analogy to register workers in rural enterprises.

5. The author's own field work suggests that the initial division of the communal assets was to the favour of local elites.

References

Cabestan (1986): Jean-Pierre Cabestan, "La réforme de l'administration chinoise et ses limites". *Revue Tiers Monde* XXVII:108, Octobre-Décembre 1986, 877-895.

Christiansen (1990): Flemming Christiansen, "Social Divisions and Peasant Mobility in the People's Republic: The Implications of the Hukou System'. *Issues and Studies*, 26:4 (April 1990), 23-42.

Goldstein and Goldstein (1985): Sidney Goldstein and Alice Goldstein, *Population Mobility in the People's Republic of China*. Honolulu: East-West Center (*Papers of the East-West Population Center*, no. 95).

GWYGB (1986): "Guoying qiye zhaoyong gongren zanxing guiding". *Zhonghua Renmin Gongheguo Guowuyuan Gongbao* 1986:25, 744-745.

Kornai (1986): János Kornai, *Contradictions and Dilemmas. Studies on the Socialist Economy and Society*. Cambridge (Mass.) etc.: The MIT Press.

Lu and Selden (1987): Aiguo Lu and Mark Selden (1987), "The Reform of Land Ownership and the Political Economy of Contemporary China". *Peasant Studies* XIV:4, Summer 1987, 229-249.

NMRB (1986): "Wangzhuang zhao waixiang laoli fazhan benxiang jingji". *Nongmin Ribao* 30 August 1986, p. 1.

Oi (1986): Jean C. Oi, "Peasant Households between Plan and Market". *Modern China* XII:2, April 1986, 230-251.

Potter (1983): Sulamith Heins Potter, "The Position of Peasants in Modern China's Social Order". *Modern China* 9:4, October 1983, 465-499.

Statistical Yearbook (1988): *Zhongguo tongji nianjian 1988*. Beijing: Zhongguo Tongji Chubanshe

Taylor (1988): Jeffrey R. Taylor, "Rural Employment Trends and the Legacy of Surplus Labour 1978-86". *The China Quarterly* 116, December 1988, 736-766.

Unger (1987): Jonathan Unger, "Local Power and Economic Reform: The Chinese Leadership's Present Dilemmas". *China Information* II:2, Autumn 1987, 1-15.

Zhang (1988): Zhang Qingwu, *Basic Facts on the Household Registration System*. Edited and translated by Michael Dutton. Armonk: M. E. Sharpe Inc. (*Chinese Economic Studies* XXII:1).

Collective Control of Income Distribution:
A Case Study of Private Enterprises in Sichuan Province

Ole Odgaard

This article aims to analyze how private enterprises have affected three particular aspects of rural development: Firstly, income levels and income distribution. Secondly, local economic development via income redistribution. Thirdly, collective control of the local community. In other words, I will examine how private enterprises affect income distribution and how the local government attempts to control and redistribute parts of the income of private enterprises.

I shall concentrate on the small private enterprises - the so-called individual enterprises - since they are by far the most common and represent the first step towards 'leaving the land but not the countryside, entering the factory but not the city' (*litu bu lixiang, jinchang bu jincheng*).

As will be shown, the development of private enterprise has led to a rapidly growing income differentiation. Apart from specialized households, the high income groups in the agricultural sector derive almost entirely from private enterprise. Interestingly, it would appear that part of the profit of private enterprises is - to a larger extent than might have been expected - redistributed to the local community's benefit. This case study concludes that collective redistribution via taxes and local levies raises substantial sums to finance local welfare, productive accumulation, and agricultural aid.

This redistribution is the result of intervention by the local government. This case study concludes that administrative control has not been dismantled, even though increased autonomy has been granted. State intervention in private enterprise seems to take place increasingly more direct than in the agricultural sector.

It will be suggested that this aspect of rural institutional reform ought to attract more attention. The impact of private enterprises on local community development can only be understood in relation to their institutional setting. This is highly relevant when analyzing their role in financing local irrigation schemes, schools, clinics, agricultural aid etc.. The funds extracted through local taxation and the imposition of fees on private enterprises substitute for the declining state investments in agriculture. This aspect has so far been neglected in the foreign China-watchers' economic reform debate.

The household-based enterprises in rural China have given impetus to far-reaching changes. They started mushrooming in 1981, and by the end of 1988 engaged twelve per cent of the rural labour force, producing 18 per cent of the total rural product.[1] Since these official figures are probably underreported[2], it is abundantly clear that private enterprise has become a major factor in China's rural transformation.

The development of private enterprises constitutes a significant shift in Chinese development strategy. The collectively owned enterprises are no longer in the forefront of China's rural transformation; their previous role of developing non-agricultural occupations and incomes has now been taken over by private enterprises.[3] Given the existing highly intensified agricultural production on very small plots (averaging only 0.1 ha. per capita), the development of private enterprises is now the most important means of raising the rural living standard and expanding the growth of the secondary and tertiary sectors.

In this article 'private enterprise' comprises what are officially termed individual enterprises (employing seven or less workers, called *geti qiye*), private enterprises (employing more than seven workers, called *siying qiye*)(GWYGB 1988, 483-491; Young 1988; Christiansen 1989) and joint enterprises involving several households (called *lianhu qiye*). Unless necessary, no distinction will be made between these three types of private enterprises. As mentioned, most research findings referred to in this article concern what are officially called individual enterprises, the dominant type of private enterprise in China.

Income Distribution

Few analyses have been made so far of the effects of private enterprises on income distribution. Those available focus primarily on the income differences between agriculture and other sectors. They all show a similar trend: there are substantial income increases to be gained by switching from agricultural to rural non-agricultural activities.

An income survey of a village in Hebei showed that farmers earned 240 yuan per year, while rural factory workers earned 600 yuan (NMRB, 23 March 1985). A more detailed survey from Sichuan showed that the daily individual gross income earned in animal husbandry and agriculture was on average 4.4 and 4.9 yuan respectively. In contrast, processing of agricultural by-products and commerce/catering yielded incomes of 8.4 yuan and 8.6 yuan respectively. A very high daily income of 15 yuan was earned in industrial processing and transport (NMRB, 13 May 1986).

These surveys did not correlate these incomes to local income differentiation between families, nor was it their intention to do so. It was my aim to analyze income differences between families to see how high income occupations were distributed among local families, and their resultant impact on local income distribution. To do this incomes must be analyzed in relation to both occupational pattern and distribution of high-income activities among families. As a member of a research team I undertook such an in-depth study in the village of Xincun, Wenjiang county. Detailed information on, e.g., income distribution was compiled for each of the 320 families in the village.[4] The income distribution trend was very clear: The 320 families had all gained substantial increases in income from higher crop yields during the last ten years. Differences in income, however, were attributable to involvement in non-cultivation activities, such as animal husbandry and especially commerce, industry and transport. This is particularly clear in the breakdown of income types according to family income level shown for 1987 in table 1.

In general the larger families counted more non-agricultural workers. The high incomes correlated closely to the number of workers in non-farming occupations, a clear indication of the contradiction between the economic reforms and the one child-policy. Since there is a close correlation between number of family members and high incomes, a per capita cal-

Table 1. Gross Income Distribution for all 320 families in Xincun (A)

(1987, yuan)	*Poorest 25 pct.*	*Second poorest 25 pct.*	*Second richest 25 pct.*	*Richest 25 pct.*	*Gini coef- ficient of quartiles (B)*
Gross Income	205,840	248,306	305,770	447,492	0.16
Of this (C):					
* farming	96,287	108,546	120,308	113,495	0.04
* animal husbandry	68,719	86,527	113,429	144,272	0.15
* industry	8,950	17,300	21,200	43,030	0.50
* commerce/service	2,950	7,900	14,250	59,000	0.52
* transport	3,100	1,050	3,800	40,500	0.59

320 families: 1377 persons, labour force: 849 persons.
Gross income: includes grain etc. for personal consumption. Taxes and levies are included.

A. The formation of quartiles is done from information on each of the 320 households in Xincun.
B. A Gini coefficient is the most precise measure of relative income distribution, since the middle income-groups as well as poor and rich income groups are included in the figure. The Gini coefficient has a max. value of 1 (absolute inequality, and a min. value of 0 (absolute equality).
C. The minor incomes from fishery, sideline and construction are, though not listed in the table, included in the total gross income figure above.

Table 2. The Net Income Distribution for the Richest and Poorest Families in Xincun

Net income per family member (1987, yuan)(A):	*Less than 450 yuan*	*Over 1400 yuan*
Share of total income (B):		
* farming	62 pct.	16 pct.
* animal husbandry	30 pct.	17 pct.
* construction	3 pct.	5 pct.
* industry	0 pct.	18 pct.
* commerce/service	0 pct.	16 pct.
* transport	0 pct.	26 pct.
Number of families	16	17
per cent of total	5 pct.	5 pct.
Average number of family members	3.4	4.6

Net income: Includes grain etc. for personal consumption. Expenses of purchased inputs as well as taxes and levies have been deducted.

A. The average net per capita income for all families in 1987 was 806 yuan.
B. The share of the less important activities of fishery and sidelines is included in the income figure.

culation of each family income is a more precise indication of the inter-household differentiation. This is illustrated in table 2, where the income distribution is specified for the most affluent and the poorest families.

17 of the 320 families had a net per capita income in 1987 of more than 1,400 yuan. The income from crops and animal husbandry amounted to a mere 33 per cent of the total income for these households, as compared to 71 per cent for all families in Xincun. The richest family specialized in transport, and only 3.6 per cent of its total income of 20,756 yuan came from agriculture. 16 households had a net income of less than 450 yuan per person, and their income from cultivation and animal husbandry made up 92 per cent of the total.

Interestingly, there was almost no difference between the richest and poorest households in per capita income from farming. Thus, the local income differentiation was due to the unequal inter-family distribution of high income occupations, especially in transport, industry, commerce and service.[5] The 17 richest households earned an average 59 per cent of their income in these sectors (64 per cent when construction is included). The 16 poorest households only earned three per cent of their total income from such activities.

It is thus evident that the unequal inter-family income distribution is primarily due to occupational factors. It would be even more unequal if it were possible to distinguish between the incomes of private enterprise proprietors and those of collective enterprise labourers or employees in private enterprises. The income figures gathered for each family listed one figure only; e.g. for industry the figure did not list the source of the industrial income - be it enterprise ownership or wage labour. The very high incomes were attained by private enterprise *proprietors* in sausage processing, transportation, commerce etc. - not by the employees, although their incomes were higher than those of farmers or agricultural labourers.

This need to distinguish between enterprise proprietors and employees is further accentuated by the official statistical method, where rural incomes are never simultaneously divided into branches and types of ownership. However, such information was acquired through a case study of private enterprises in Renshou County.[6]

In 1987 the average net income in Renshou County was 287 yuan per person - or 1,197 yuan per family. The average net income is significantly lower than that of the private entrepreneur families in the area, i.e. 2,788 yuan. Some of the basic data from the survey is summarized in table 3.

As table 3 shows, income from private enterprises constitute the major reason for the unequal distribution of family incomes. Thus the lowest net household income of private entrepreneurs was found in commerce and service, which nevertheless was 1.6 times higher than the average household income. The households engaged in handicraft/industry and food processing had a net income between 2.2 and 2.6 times higher. The highest incomes were found in construction and transport, where net household incomes were 3.5 and 4.5 fold higher than average.[7]

The general income level of all private enterprises is even higher than the figures in table 3 indicate. One reason is that the majority of the 40 surveyed enterprises consisted of individual enterprises (*geti qiye*) employing less than eight workers, since I was especially interested in this type of private enterprise.

Table 3. Average Income Level of Private Enterprises:
Enterprise and Township Survey from Renshou County (1987, yuan)

	Household Net income	*Of this:* Private Enterprise Net income	
* Commerce and service	1,657	1,257	(76 pct.)
* Handicraft/Industry	2,273	1,986	(87 pct.)
* Food processing	2,739	2,340	(85 pct.)
* Construction	3,593	3,293	(92 pct.)
* Transport	4,621	4,150	(90 pct.)
Average of 38 surveyed Private Enterprises (A)	2,788	2,410	(86 pct.)
Average of all Households in 10 surveyed Townships in Renshou (B)	1,034	93(C)	(9 pct.)
Official figure for whole of Renshou	1,197	-	-

A.   Only the individual type of private enterprises (*geti qiye*)
B.   From 8 townships and 18 villages
C.   Estimate based on reported figures

Furthermore, the figures quoted are mostly official data. These figures, however, do not reflect actual incomes, since they are negotiated between the officials of the Tax Bureau and the private entrepreneurs. Based on 30 interviews with enterprise owners, I estimate that these officially reported incomes are underestimated by 30 to 40 pct., in some cases even more, since the local cadres have difficulties in estimating the actual turnover if products are marketed outside the local market. Some locals told me about an entrepreneur who was 'stupid enough' to state his real income to the cadre from the tax bureau. In consequence he was charged a tax substantially higher than for other entrepreneurs, because the cadre automatically assumed that the figure was understated. Some enterprise proprietors had much higher incomes than officially registered. For example, a semi-skilled hairdresser in a permanent shop admitted to me that her yearly net income was 6,000 yuan - or six times the average net household income, and substantially more than officialy registered.

The incomes earned in the private enterprise sector are remarkably high. Possession of the necessary qualifications and initiative can yield substantial incomes. Surprisingly, few cadres in Renshou were engaged in private enterprises. Only thirteen per cent of all entrepreneurs surveyed were (ex)party or P.L.A. members, while as many as 43 per cent had acquired their skills from previous employment in collective and private enterprises. This was clearly a much more important factor than cadre background. Jean Oi has argued that cadres who initially resisted private enterprise became actively involved when it became clear that the reforms were here to stay, as personal risk was then minimal (Oi 1986). As will be argued in the following section, I do not believe that the small degree of cadre involvement in Renshou indicated personal apprehension or resistance, though conflicting interests obviously exist. On the contrary, I found that many cadres interviewed regarded private enterprises as beneficial to the local community, since the revenues from the private enterprises were redistributed in the society at large. Also, as will be argued in the final section, no uniform pattern of cadre attitudes to private enterprise can be found. On the contrary, a diversified pattern of cadre attitudes exists due to the different economic and social impacts of the three types of private enterprise on social stability, income distribution and community welfare.

Redistribution of Enterprise Revenue

Redistribution largely takes the form of taxes (*shui*), levies (*fei*), and supplementary financial aid to poor households. The importance of private enterprises in financing local amenities, welfare, public accumulation etc. via taxes and levies has increased considerably during the last five years. It is, however, impossible to extract such information from official statistics, which only cover central state taxes and levies collected at the county level and above.[8] The bulk of private enterprise tax payments is appropriated by local authorities and does not figure in official statistics.

In order to gather information on the size of both local and central taxes and levies, questionnaires were sent to several township governments. The compiled results are summarized in table 4.

Table 4. Public Payments from Private Enterprises (A): Survey of 3 Townships in Renshou County

	1984	*1987*
Number of private enterprises	167	521
Per cent. contributed by private enterprises of:		
* Total labour force	4.6	
* Total gross income	2.5	19.9
* Total central and local taxes + levies	5.3	40.6
Public Productive Accumulation Fund (1,000 yuan)	220	326
Public Common Fund (1,000 yuan)	297	450

A. Only the individual type of private enterprises (*geti qiye*).

As illustrated in table 4, the private enterprises make remarkably high contributions to the public treasury via local taxes and levies. Thus, private enterprises, while employing a mere five per cent of the officially registered labour force, produced fully one-fifth of the total gross income and contributed as much as 40 per cent of the total tax and levy payment in 1987.

The total payment per private enterprise (*geti qiye*) increased from 110 yuan in 1984 to 402 yuan in 1987. This increase is not due to a heavier tax burden—the total payment ranges from between 3.5 and 4.8 per cent of the gross income—but is the result of expanding production and higher incomes in most private enterprises.

The central state tax may amount to one half of the total taxes and levies paid. This was confirmed by figures from the county tax bureau, which on the average received 205 yuan per private enterprise (my survey of the township governments registered an average total payment of 402 yuan to both local and central authorities. Thus approximately 200 yuan was retained by the local authorities. The real amount may well be much higher).

A survey of private enterprises for example, revealed much higher payments (many rural enterprise proprietors had kept tax receipts). The questionnaires demonstrated that substantially higher taxes and levies were paid than officially stated, and that additional fees existed, though they were not registered as such. This is summarized in table 5.

Table 5. Public Payments by Private Enterprises: Enterprise Survey from Renshou County

(1987, yuan)	Taxes + Levies (A)	Support to Poor HH (B)	Total Payment	Total as pct of Turnover
* Commerce/service	464	418	882	11.4 pct.
* Handicraft/industry	1,060	500	1,560	7.2 pct.
* Food processing	900	561	1,461	14.1 pct.
* Construction	2,237	1,500	3,737	15.7 pct.
* Transport	3,846	214	4,060	21.1 pct.
Average of 38 surveyed (C)	1,479	534	2,013	13.4 pct.
Average amount of central tax per private enterprise	205	-	205	3.9 pct.

A. Both central and local taxies and levies.

B. Support to poor households and 5 guarantee households for purchase of chemical fertilizer and pesticides.

C. Only the individual type of private enterprises (*geti qiye*)

The survey shows that each private enterprise contributed nearly 1,500 yuan to local and central authorities in 1987. Although not officially registered as a levy, an additional average fee of more than 500 yuan was paid as a subsidy to poor families earmarked for the purchase of farm inputs. Hence, as a result of the combined interest of central and local governments, rural enterprises were requested to support agriculture. The contract between the local government and a private enterprise had in some cases stipulated that the private enterprise should supply services free of charge to the poor families. E.g. a private medical clinic was to supply certain services free of charge to the poor households - besides their assigned task of carrying out public hygiene campaigns in the Township.

There was a progressive tax rate ranging from seven to 11 per cent of the turnover in the low income branches to 21 per cent in the high income branch of transportation. Such tax rates may not seem excessive, but due to high costs of production, the tax rate reveals a much higher percentage when calculated as a part of the net income. This is illustrated in table 6.

Table 6. Re-distribution of Private Enterprise Incomes:
Enterprise Survey from Renshou County

(Yuan per enterprise, 1987) (A)	*Total Public Payment (B)*	*Net income (C)*	*Tax rate of income*
* Commerce/Service	882	2,139	41.2 pct.
* Handicraft/Industry	1,560	3,546	44.0 pct.
* Food Processing	1,461	3,801	38.4 pct.
* Construction	3,737	7,030	53.2 pct.
* Transport	4,060	8,210	49.5 pct.
Average of 38 surveyed enterprises	4,013	4,423	45.5 pct.

A. Only the individual type of private enterprises (*geti qiye*).
B. Taxes, levies and non-registered fee.
C. Net income before public payments.

As shown in the table, the actual income tax rate amounted to almost 50 per cent Since enterprise owners have an obvious interest in reporting their actual tax burden but not their actual income, the real tax rate is probably less than that listed in the table. However, this survey focused mainly on the small, private enterprises, thus the average tax payment for all private enterprises in Renshou may well exceed the average figure found in this survey. The findings cast an interesting light on the actual redistribution of private enterprise income.

If each of the 19,763 registered private enterprises in Renshou county contributed as much to the public treasury as the 38 surveyed (the amount is probably higher due to the several large enterprises in Renshou), it may be calculated that a total amount of 39.8 mill. yuan was redistributed in 1988. This amounts to 10.3 per cent of the total rural net income in Renshou - or 123 yuan per rural household.

The considerable public payments and the de facto progressive tax rate are due in particular to the many cumulative local levies. Officially, local levies serve to finance local administration and public expenses associated with private enterprises. A registration levy (paid to the Bureau of Industry and Commerce) of a mere four yuan was raised to 20 yuan in July 1988. A city construction levy of one per cent of the turnover is allocated to financing the building of market sites etc. A marketing and management levy of one per cent is to finance the public administration. A host of similar levies could be listed.

But a myriad of other levies exist, as it was termed, 'according to specific local needs'. These are, of course, impossible for the higher level authorities to control. Thus several entrepreneurs complained of these levies which they were not legally obliged to pay. E.g.

pedlars are not subject to central taxes. The private sector was burdened with so many levies that entrepreneurs could not distinguish the purpose of one levy from another. They often complained of being milked via local taxes to finance construction of schools, clinics etc., and indeed the local community supports such practices. The different types of public payment ascertained during my field study are listed in table 7.

Table 7. Public Payments made by Private Enterprises in Renshou County, 1988

Central taxes	*Local levies*
* Business and product tax	* Registration levy
	* City construction levy
* Personal income tax	* Marketing and management levy
	* Education levy
	* Street outlet levy
	* Road levy
	* Transportation levy
	* Repair levy
	* Hygiene levy
	* Health certificate levy
	* Timber levy
	* Individual Business Association levy
	* Public security levy
	* Contract levy
	* Township and Village levy

As shown in table 7, a vast variety of levies in Renshou were supposed to finance local administration as well as local public amenities. Another case study also reported a high number of different levies imposed on private enterprises (JJCK, 17 Oct. 1988). Often the purpose of such levies is to extract funds to finance local projects. Although this practice does not fully comply with current legislation, it seems difficult to label it as corruption or illegal. Most people in the local community as well as cadres at higher levels are well aware of this practice, and a cadre called it 'fulfilment of social obligations'.

The transfer of revenues from private enterprises to public funds occurs not merely through formal taxes and levies. The price of inputs purchased from state units or supply-and-marketing cooperatives may for private enterprises be twice the price paid by collective enterprises. In some cases it may be quite difficult to obtain rationed inputs such as cement or timber without resorting to corruption. This has given rise to a vast number of middlemen who exploit those supplementing their household income with a small private enterprise. This was especially the case for carpenters in chronically short supply of timber.

Thus, local redistribution of private enterprise revenue via local levies and higher input prices etc. seems extremely high in relation to average tax payments. It is my impression that this is common practice in many localities. If so, this certainly warrants further study, since the impact of local rural enterprises on the financing of social amenities, agricultural inputs, the rural infrastructure, etc. deserves much more attention when discussing declining state investments in agriculture. The decreased state investments are apparently being substituted by funds collected locally. Money is extracted from local activities with a high value-adding effect and/or from high income groups. In this perspective, the redistribution of revenues from private enterprises is crucial for financing the rural infrastructure. As shown in table 4, these revenues are now a major source of finance for local productive investments. In 1988 in the whole of Renshou county, five million yuan were invested in agriculture. 2.5 million yuan of these public investments were specific payments to agriculture from rural enterprises[9]—the major source being private enterprises.

The falling state investments, especially in the agricultural sector, have for many China-watchers largely explained the lack of funds available to the collective rural infrastructure. This ought not to be the case when local investments have at the same time increased substantially. Even official estimates claim that rural enterprise levies to be invested in agricultural infrastructure in the period 1980-1984 were three times as high as the state investments (Stettner and Oram 1987, 50). Adding the finances from unregistered local redistribution such as those indicated above, the importance of (private) rural enterprise deserves much more thorough investigation if the reform problems confronting the agricultural sector are to be adequately explained.

The reports of the deterioration of rural infrastructure (Watson 1987; Fewsmith 1988) are indeed alarming. But the reasons for these problems might rather be that local finances from rural enterprises are not being channeled into agricultural investments but into collective enterprises, which are much more profitable than agriculture. However, I was not in a position to verify this assumption.

It is nevertheless obvious that very considerable financial resources from private enterprises have created a new interdependence in many communities between local authorities and private enterprises. The community benefits from the redistribution of private enterprise profits, while the enterprises depend on the goodwill of and favorable treatment by the local cadres in terms of obtaining permits, supplies of inputs, making transport arrangements, obtaining information, conducting tax negotiations, and utilizing guanxi.

Local Society - Private Enterprise Relations

The questionnaires and interviews indicated that cadres in Renshou held different attitudes towards the various types of local private enterprises. Three distinct attitudes could be discerned:[10]

Joint Family Enterprises

Joint family enterprises (*lianhu qiye*) receive support from most cadres. Sincere hopes were voiced that they would develop faster and better, since they are capable of spreading the wealth to most families in the villages. As one cadre said: 'Their creation of wealth is of benefit to individuals as well as society'. Also, they are easier to control due to their greater dependence on public support for inputs and supplies. Moreover, all joint enterprises are required to keep accounts and expenditure records. Tax evasion and corruption etc. are rare in jointly managed enterprises consisting of perhaps ten families, due to mutual control. As their income is equally distributed and because they have a higher level of social organization, they generate less social conflict in the local community.

The Individual Enterprises

The individual enterprises (*geti qiye*) have fairly broad cadre support. They can develop production and service with limited resources, which the collectives cannot. Also, private enterprises have the advantage of being subject to less rigid administrative procedures, and are more flexible due to their less standardized production and management. Some of the collective enterprises are for example unable to offer the newest product designs, adapt to new fashions, or rapidly improve quality levels (though fake brands and copies appear as negative side effects of the private sector) etc.

Evidently these small enterprises seem to be able to develop new types of production while providing the local community with benefits from revenue redistribution. But they also generate social tension, since their high incomes contribute to more unequal consumption patterns. However, their benefits outweigh their disadvantages.

The Large Private Enterprises

The large private enterprises (*siying qiye*) are subject to severe criticism. They compete with collective enterprises to a much higher extent, they aggravate unequal income distribution, and in particular their extremely high incomes generate social conflict in the villages. Their business success is founded in guanxi and 'unsocial behaviour', it is said, not in 'honest work'. The scale of their marketing outside local markets makes their profits harder to estimate. Thus, *some* cadres impose heavy levies on these unpopular enterprises - often in accordance with local opinion.

Other cadres criticize the management of large scale enterprises, which often continue to use traditional, antiquated management methods in new, more technological settings, too rigid to shift to more formalized but still flexible forms of production. There is, indeed, a large difference between (a) a small-scale enterprise using simple technology and having ad-hoc financial management, and (b) a large enterprise (employing maybe 50 labourers) which requires production planning, substantial investments, more formalized procedures in obtaining bank loans and input supplies, etc.

If the managers of these enterprises are untrained and have no experience from previous work in collective enterprises, they will inevitably face difficulties overcoming such management problems. Some of them fail and go bankrupt. Thus, many expressed the attitude: 'why not pick the orange, before the tree withers'.

Although the local township governments and village committees fully supported the joint family enterprises, these ventures often faced the same problem as the large private enterprises: they were unable to handle the shift to a more advanced, large-scale type of production. Problems of expansion had worsened in Renshou to such an extent that the local branch of the Agricultural Bank of China had stipulated that no loans or credits should be granted to a number of joint enterprises, which according to regulations were entitled to receive loans. To alleviate the situation local cadres had begun to resort to illegal means to convert successful large private enterprises (or small joint enterprises) into collective enterprises; or simply to confiscate their business license. They did so because large private enterprises had aggravated social tensions by their very high incomes, or because of bad management.

Thus, a very successful entrepreneur producing bamboo furniture for export was ordered to convert his large enterprise into a collectively owned enterprise. He strongly objected and threatened to take the case to court. After some time a compromise was reached: the entrepreneur could keep his factory if he conducted a training program to pass on his special skills to technicians in collective enterprises.

Another entrepreneur faced a similar threat of expropriation. The village committee intended to take over his profitable cotton mill. He was less fortunate and, eventually, his business license was revoked - officially because of a shortage of electric power. Instead, a village-operated cotton mill was constructed less than 50 miles away, using the same source of energy. The real motive for revoking the business license was, of course, different than that officially stated. The idea of opening such an enterprise on a collective basis had not occurred to the village committee until the entrepreneur suddenly demonstrated its potential to the local community. Subsequently, the competition from his factory was sabotaged by legal means.

Of course, more straightforward and legal means of controlling the major private enterprises were adopted as well. Though the Chinese press often stresses the use of indirect guidance via economic levers to control the private enterprises, my field results suggest that direct means of control are more common. This is especially true for large private enterprises employing many workers, which are controlled strictly by local authorities.

The laissez-faire attitude condoning certain practices not in full compliance with current legislation, is gradually being abandoned as far as large private enterprises are concerned. In Renshou County, such enterprises are now requested to join the Individual Business Association, which is made up of both enterprise owners and employees. Despite its name, the organization is directly controlled by the local government. The purpose is, among other things, to gain insight into and control the large enterprises so as to avoid malpractice. Supervised group evaluations are practised when discussing work conditions, safety, wages, tax payments, conditions for granting credit etc.. Also, labour contracts must now be utilized by such large enterprises, and each enterprise contract is subject to scrutiny and approval by the Individual Business Association.

Local authorities also stressed the importance of tax reforms, hoping to exert full economic control over the private enterprise in order to prevent tax evasion and bankruptcy. Enterprises were requested to keep accounts. In October 1988, 389 large private enterprises came under public administration. From then on, all accounting and bookkeeping was undertaken by public accountants stationed at the private enterprises. Their salary was paid by the private enterprise. In order to avoid corruption, the Tax Bureau at county level assigned an accountant to each enterprise. He was responsible for controlling this enterprise for a fixed period, after which he was rotated to another enterprise.[11] I am not yet aware, however, of the real effect of this intervention.

Thus, the market conditions for rural private enterprises can hardly be categorized as free in any liberal sense. The restrictions on circulation of goods, the lack of market information and scarcity of inputs allow middlemen and corrupt bureaucrats to exploit and control the quasi-market conditions. Institutional intervention often seems to be a more important factor in the development of enterprises than the market oriented activities of entrepreneurs.

Planning certainly persists in the reform era and may, as indicated in this article, transgress its legal limits in order to counter malpractice. But in the long term, the increased importance of family clans, political corruption and cadre-entrepreneurs may alter the local social structure and existing channels of state control (Odgaard 1988). It is noteworthy, however, that the extensive growth and importance of private enterprises apparently has not (yet) eroded state control. As described in this article, forceful social, political and economic means of intervention aim to enhance a new form of socialist controlled redistribution of part of the private enterprise incomes.

Summary
The private rural enterprises in Renshou started to mushroom in 1982 - 1983. Their impact on local income distribution is clear: the household income level of families engaged in private enterprise ranged between two and five times that of the average household income. The very high incomes are concentrated in particular in the private enterprise sectors of transport, construction and the processing industry.

The real incomes of private enterprises are probably much higher than officially stated. Interviews revealed much higher incomes than those registered by the Tax Bureau. Substantial income differences have arisen due to the expansion of private enterprises. Although some enterprises faced problems of increased taxes, scarcity of inputs, policy changes and insufficient management, most of them continue to expand their scope of business and increase their profits.

However, part of the incomes of private enterprises has been subject to public redistribution via taxes, levies etc. The official statistics are most unreliable. My survey of the township governments showed an average increase in public payments from 110 yuan in 1984 to 402 yuan in 1987 per private enterprise. This is due to the increasing multitude of local levies, many of which, including even important fees, go unregistered or are categorized differently. These revenues certainly do not figure in centrally registered statistics. The survey data revealed a total public payment of more than 2,000 yuan per private enterprise (13.4 per cent of turnover), much more than the official county government figure of 205 yuan (3.8 per cent of turnover).

Obviously, this matter was quite controversial for the local authorities, and much of the official data gathered on this topic was misleading. Information from only three townships, which nevertheless contained data on 521 private enterprises, could be applied to this particular aspect. In 1987 these enterprises engaged a mere five per cent of the labour force, but their share of local and central taxes and levies consisted of no less than 40 per cent.

There was a close correlation between the high income groups of private entrepreneurs and groups with a high educational level or with professional training via previous work in collective enterprises. The expected large group of (ex)cadres among the private enterprise owners was not found. However, this is not a sign of general cadre resistance towards private enterprises. Most cadres interviewed were well aware of the benefits to be gained from this blooming sector. Actually, many local communities had become more or less dependent on the financial contribution made by private enterprises—just as many entrepreneurs were highly dependent on the political goodwill and many services supplied by, or—more precisely—bought from local cadres, who acted as agents of the local community. This type of redistribution should be investigated further when evaluating the effects of decreasing state investments in agriculture.

The attitude of local authorities towards redistribution seemed to differentiate between the three types of private enterprises. The joint family enterprises (*lianhu qiye*) received support and paid less extortionate local levies. Their redistributional effect was optimal because their income was divided among many families. The individual enterprises (*geti qiye*) were recognized for their ability to develop production and service with limited resources, even though they also provoked social tension by yielding substantially higher incomes. The redistributive measures provided finances for local community development, relatively larger in size than that of the joint family enterprises.

The major private enterprises (*siying qiye*) were exposed to the most local redistributive intervention. Envy and social conflict had occasioned heavy local levies and attempts by local authorities to expropriate these enterprises in order to curb their so-called unsocial behaviour and derive a benefit from their profits. A more strict adherence to current legislation and new means of collective control (via the Individual Business Association and public accountancy companies) were imposed.

The planning system and collective control have not been abolished. Instead, attempts are made to integrate the benefits provided by private enterprise in the form of increased productivity and higher incomes with new forms of collective control. The outcome is a substantial redistribution of the profits made by private enterprises. This new form of socialist-controlled redistribution needs further investigation when evaluating income distribution and the effects of decollectivization and declining state investments in agriculture.

The impact of private enterprises on development may well be quite different in other localities. This is due to the many and varied forms of relations between local state and local society. Unfortunately this is not adequately reflected in the general literature on private enterprises. The assumption often prevails that most cadres are actively involved in private enterprises solely for their own benefit. As demonstrated in this article, such general assumptions cannot be made. The impact of private enterprises on economic and social development can only be ascertained by analyzing the specific relations between the local state and the private enterprises.

Notes

The author feels indebted to Jørgen Delman for his extremely useful comments on this article. My research on private rural enterprises in Renshou County has been associated with simultaneous research undertaken in Renshou by Jørgen Delman on local agricultural extension services. Our association has enabled us to share information as well as discuss findings and conclusions on our research in Renshou. Peter Druijven, Flemming Christiansen, Ole Hyldtoft, and Irene Nørlund have also contributed with helpful comments. However, the author takes full responsibility for the opinions expressed and any inaccuracies the article may contain.

1. 46.5 of 400.7 million rural labourers and 228.3 of 1253.5 billion yuan. (NYNJ 1989, 251, 340, 345.

2. Several types of private business are not required to register, e.g. pedlars and private units operating less than three months per year. In addition to these private units many private enterprises register as a collective township enterprise or simply avoid registration in order to avoid paying taxes. Hence, Wang Zhongming (Director of China's State Administration for Industry and Commerce Individual Economy Department) estimates that at least between four and six million private enterprises were not registered among the 11.6 million by the end of 1985 (De Rosario 1986).

3. Unlike the collective rural enterprises, the private enterprises are managed by single families or several families on a cooperative basis. Production is according to market demand, and profit is normally shared according to each family's share of investment. Investment is voluntary and may legally be withdrawn. They confront fewer geographical or administrative barriers, and there are also fewer political restrictions and less intervention than for collective enterprises. The new rural enterprises can also co-produce or trade with all kinds of organizations (JJRB, 27 June 1985).

4. The data on income was gathered during March 1988, and partly cross-checked by means of household interviews. For a detailed analysis of all collected data, of which only a minor part is presented here, see: Odgaard et. al, 1990.

5. Construction would undoubtedly also have been included but for the neighbouring village which had developed a large private construction enterprise catering to Xincun's needs.

6. The field study was conducted in September-November 1988 in cooperation with the Renshou County Department of Agriculture and Animal Husbandry. The field study consisted primarily of the following: 40 interviews were conducted with private enterprise owners, and 15 with cadres from county and township authorities in charge of private enterprises (e.g. tax bureau, Industrial and Commercial Bureau's department of private enterprises etc.); 50 questionnaires to selected, private enterprises, and of the 40 returned 38 were useful. Another type of questionnaire was sent to 8 selected township governments and 18 village committees having a total population of more than 110,000 inhabitants. Cross checks were done via the questionnaires' design and by means of comparing the two types of questionnaires, cross-checking with data obtained via interviews with authorities and enterprise-owners. In instances of miscorrelation, the data was deleted. The results from my second field study in Renshou, conducted in spring 1990, have not been included in this article.

7. The level of private enterprise incomes correlated closely with the educational level of the head of households surveyed. Participation in professional training courses proved an important factor - especially among the very high income groups who had received training during previous employment in collective enterprises. Furthermore, the income level increased with a high number of employees, with higher investments, guanxi and with a secure public input supply. Age was not a significant factor, since the number of young profit-minded entrepreneurs had expanded significantly in recent years.

8. In 1985 and 1986 central taxes and levies for the whole of China amounted to 2,863 and 3,680 billion yuan—or 3.8 and 3.4 pct. of the gross income of all types of private enterprises. (Cf. NTZL 1985, 214-215; NTZL 1986, 172-73). In Renshou County, a central three per cent business and product tax is imposed on all private enterprises, whose net income exceeds 120 yuan per month in commerce and service and 200 yuan per month in other branches. In addition, a personal net income tax is imposed where individual incomes from all activities exceed 400 yuan per month. The total taxes paid by private enterprises amounted to 3.9 per cent of total turnover in Renshou County in 1987. The tax laws and practices vary greatly from locality to locality. For the recent central tax laws, see Guojia Shuishou 1986, 330-345.

9. I am grateful to Jørgen Delman for bringing this figure to my attention. It was gathered during his field study (on agricultural extension service) in Renshou County in March-April 1989.
10. Three other types of private enterprises seem to be applicable in the more wealthy rural areas: (1) single family enterprises, (2) joint family enterprises, (3) share or stock enterprises formed by rural families and collective units in cooperation (Pan Zhouli and Xie Jianmin 1988). The share or stock enterprises present in rich areas were not observed in Renshou, where a more important distinction was between individual and private types of single family enterprises.
11. A similar practice has been suggested for the whole of Guangdong province (Mo Zhen 1986).

References

Christiansen (1989): Flemming Christiansen, 'The Justification and Legalization of Private Enterprises in China, 1983-1988'. *China Information*, 4:2, Autum 1989, 78-91.

De Rosario (1986): Louise De Rosario, 'The Private Dilemma'. *Far Eastern Economic Review,* 20 November 1986, 68-69.

Fewsmith (1988): Joseph Fewsmith, 'Agricultural Crisis in China'. *Problems of Communism*, vol. 37, November-December 1988, 78-93.

Guojia Shuishou (1986): *Guojia Shuishou*, Beijing: Zhongguo Falü Chubanshe.

GWYGB (1988): 'Zhonghua Renmin Gongheguo Siying Qiye Zanxing Tiaoli'. *Zhongguo Renmin Gongheguo Gouwuyuan Gongbao* No. 15.

JJCK: *Jingji Cankao*, Beijing.

JJRB: *Jingji Ribao*, Beijing.

Mo Zhen (1986): Mo Zhen, 'Tighten Control over Big Labour-Hiring Households in Rural Areas'. *Keji Guanli Yanjiu*. Translated in *Chinese Economic Studies*, 21:2, Winter 1987-88.

NMRB: *Nongmin Ribao*, Beijing.

NTZL (1985): *Zhongguo Nongmuyuye Tongji Ziliao - 1985*, Beijing: Nongye Chubanshe, 1986.

NTZL (1986): *Zhongguo Nongmuyuye Tongji Ziliao - 1986*, Beijing: Nongye Chubanshe, 1987.

NYNJ (1987): *Zhongguo Nongye Nianjian - 1987*, Beijing: Nongye Chubanshe, 1987.

Odgaard (1988): Ole Odgaard, 'The Succes of Rural Enterprises in China: Some Notes on Their Social and Economic Effects'. *China Information*, 3:2, Autum 1988, 63-76.

Odgaard (1990): Ole Odgaard et al., 'Occupational Pattern and Income Inequality in a Sichuan Village'. *Copenhagen Papers in East and Southeast Asian Studies*, No. 5, pp. 73-90.

Oi (1986): Jean C. Oi, 'Commercializing China's Rural Cadres'. *Problems of Communism*, vol. 35, September-October 1986, 1-15.

Pan Zhouli and Xie Jianmin (1988): Pan Zhouli and Xie Jianmin, 'Guanyu siying qiye ruogan wenti de tantao'. *Nongye Jingji Wenti*, No. 1, 43-45.

Stettner and Oram (1987): Nora Stettner and Bert Oram, *Changes in China - The Role of Cooperatives in the New Socialism*, Manchester: The Co-operative Press Ltd.

Watson (1987): Andrew Watson, 'The Family Farm, Land Use and Accumulation in Agriculture'. *The Australian Journal of Chinese Affairs* No. 17, 1-27.

Young (1989): Susan Young, 'Policy, Practice and the Private Sector' in *The Australian Journal of Chinese Affairs*, No. 21, 57-80.

POVERTY AND SECURITY
IN RURAL AREAS

On the Establishment of a Poverty-Oriented Rural Development Policy in China

Johannes Küchler

During the past decades China has received world-wide attention for its successes in eliminating rural poverty. Yet the post-Mao policy of opening and reform revealed that despite all efforts in the early 1980s more than ten per cent of the rural population, living in ecologically sensitive areas, were still confronted with a day-to-day fight for physical survival. The following notes present a brief introduction to a new regional development policy aimed at the abolition of persistent rural poverty and discuss its potential contribution to environmental rehabilitation.

The Historic Setting: From Relief to Development

Industrialization implies social polarization. Historically speaking, this became evident first within urban areas. In order to reduce tension and for better control of potential conflicts social politics and urban planning became established in the 19th century in Western Europe and the United States. It took several decades before it became fully evident that industrialization also leads to serious disparities within the nationstate as a whole. Persistent rural poverty was not perceived as a political problem before the decades after World War I. In these years countries like the USA, Great Britain, Austria, Switzerland, Sweden and Norway as well as Fascist Italy and Germany set up initial schemes for better control, economic exploitation and life improvement in the peripheral areas of their national territories as well as their backward and sensitive mountain areas. It was in this period and political setting that regional planning and regional development were formulated as distinct political tools.

These historic examples show that programs aiming at the abolition of rural poverty contain elements of social policy as well as regional planning: In contrast to social security schemes, they focus less on individuals (children, women, handicapped, old people) but rather on larger units of the rural population characterized by similar living circumstances. In contrast to regional planning the emphasis is on poverty areas within a region. Anti-poverty programs are less concerned with the total region as a natural or administrative entity, generally comprising all social segments and economic sectors with different degrees of wealth or levels of development. While social politics and regional planning are, in principle, concerned with continuous responsibilities and activies, poverty eradication schemes can be—though not always—accomplished within a limited span of time.

The results of the above-mentioned efforts as well as the resulting performance of the poverty areas in post-war Europe are well known. While specific support schemes for agriculture in remote areas continue to exist on a more and more elaborate scale, the general problem of persistent poverty in peripheral regions was mainly solved by emigration and by the expansion of tourism as an additional source of income. These two options hardly offer a way-out for poor Third World countries like India, Brazil or China, each of which has tens of millions of people in remote poverty regions.

Here solutions have to be found on the assumption that the poor rural population cannot be dislocated and development must be based on the existing limited local/regional resource potential.

In comparison to the historic examples of the highly industrialized countries it appears to be rather early for China to be setting up such a consistent development strategy after barely four decades of industrialization. It took less than ten years to establish a specific policy, organization and set of policy instruments to deal with areas of rural poverty. A detailed inquiry into the evolution of this new field of politics has yet to be written. The following remarks will illustrate some of its aspects and major events:

(a) In November 1978 the first articles about this issue appeared in Renmin Ribao by Tong Dalin, Shi Shan and Bao Tong (Tong Dalin and Bao Tong 1978).

(b) In December 1978 the famous Third Plenum of the Eleventh Central Committee proclaimed that the problems of food and clothing for the people of China as a whole should be solved by the end of the 1980s.

(c) The series of inventories for China's natural and human resources (i.e. soil survey, zoning of agricultural lands, population census) and the creation of a consistent system of national statistics in the first half of the 1980s produced further evidence on the extent of the problem.

(d) New laws and regulations (i.e. forestry, environmental protection, soil and water conservation) as well as economic reform (establishment of household responsibility system between 1981 and 1983) created favorable conditions for the implemention of this new policy (Betke and Küchler 1987, 98-99).

(e) A series of publications on poverty areas since 1984 reflects intensified research on questions such as the diversification of the local economy, ways to transfer capital, economic-ecological systems, the role of the state in poverty eradication, the relative importance of the primary, secondary and tertiary sector, the effects of labour migration, the importance of modern technologies, growth poles in regional development. In short - one has the impression that the full range of western academic discussion on development and underdevelopment is repeated within a few years.[1]

(f) Besides the various ministries and banks traditionally dealing with social security and disaster relief, the State Council has since 1983 supported a model scheme to improve conditions in the Northwest: The Sanxi Regions Agricultural Construction Fund.[2]

(g) The 'Announcement Concerning the Support of Poverty Areas Transforming their Conditions' issued by the Central Commitee and the State Council on September 9th 1984 (Central Committee 1984) marked an important step towards the new policy and a new organizational structure: Thus far anti-poverty actions had been of an ad-hoc-nature and economically inefficient. For the Western reader the outlined new perspective reads like a late Chinese rediscovery of 'integrated rural development'. Government Agencies are urged to support the poor regions in establishing self-sustained growth through diversification, increased division of labour and commodity production. All provinces and autonomous regions were urged to set up leading groups responsible for the support of poverty areas.

(h) The Seventh Five Year Plan (1986-1990), approved by the Fourth Conference of the

Sixth National People's Congress on April 12th 1986, devotes a specific chapter to the 'economic development of old revolutionary bases, areas of national minorities, boundary regions and poor areas' (Seventh Five Year Plan 1986, 101-103). 4.5 billion yuan annually were devoted as low-interest loans and grants for the development of these regions.

(i) Simultaneously in April 1986 the 'Leading Group for Poor Areas Development' (*Pinkun diqu jingji fazhan lingdao xiaozu*, hereafter LGPAD) of the State Council was founded as a central coordinating agency. It is attached to the Ministry of Agriculture, Animal Husbandry, and Fisheries and consists of representatives from 17 ministries as well as relevant bank and research organizations. Similar bodies were established at the provincial and county level.

Motives Behind the New Strategy
The target group consists of poorly educated peasant families living dispersed and isolated literally at the fringe of society. Thus unlike industrial workers they can hardly be considered a potential threat to political stability. Why then did the Chinese government launch this new anti-poverty drive at this specific time, only a few years after proclaiming the slogan 'let one part (of society) get rich first'? Moreover, had the economic reforms after 1978 not brought about an impressive result in poverty eradication? In order to assess whether this new development policy can contribute to environmental protection or at least can be combined with efforts in this direction, we have to ask about the motivation behind this new strategy. Since the answers to these questions provided by Chinese publications and interview partners are not very clear, one has to speculate about the relative importance of the following motives:

The Economic Aspect
Fund saving: One of the most frequent arguments for a new effort on poverty eradication was that the established relief schemes were costly and inefficient just like 'sprinkling pepper' (*sa hujiaomian*). It is constantly pointed out that unfolding the full range of local assets will not only create savings but, in the long run, new economic potentials too. Although for many areas this may be a justified expectation, in general - as we shall discuss later - it will prove a rather naive assumption. Officially decision makers have to uphold this position for the simple reason that there is no other way out. In principle the population of the poverty areas has to stay where it lives now. Emigration either to the overcrowded lowlands or overseas - one of the remedies for poverty areas in the highly industrialized countries - is impossible or unfeasible in the case of China.

The Moral Aspect
Egalitarianism: For many urban Chinese - now rather well-off - it was shocking to discover the full range of hard-core poverty. For years they had lived comfortably with the official statements that although the Chinese people are still living in a stage of 'decent poverty' the problem of hunger had been solved once and for all. After 1978 they had to learn that living conditions in many of the glorified old revolutionary base areas decades after 'liberation' were worse than before. Rural poverty was a major topic of the media in the liberal intellectual climate of the 1980s. Articles, novels and films described old cadres, who - after

years of absence - revisited the heroic battlefields of their youth. They were reported to have wept confronted with the miserable life of their old local comrades. For a Communist Party this deplorable performance of the old base areas posed a very serious political and ideological challenge indeed.

It is therefore not surprising that so far these revolutionary base areas received highest priority although living conditions in some of them were not as appalling as in other poor regions.

Foreign Policy

Pacification of border areas: In the light of the international detente following the decade of 'cultural revolution' it appears unnecessary to make great efforts *now* to improve living conditions in the border areas. Military conflicts on boundary issues have become increasingly unlikely. On the other hand this improvement seems to be even more urgent than in the period of closed boundaries because with eased international trade national minorities in boundary areas will fully realize the degree of their backwardness. Poverty, for example, is evidently a good breeding ground for Panturkism and Islamic fundamentalism as well as Tibetan nationalism. Political instability in border areas is also counter-productive for the development of international tourism, for which the scenic and historic sites of these areas were extremely attractive. Either way, the evidence from the published sources suggests that de facto poor border areas in general so far had low priority in development programmes.

Discovery of External Resources

Foreign aid: Deng's famous phrase, 'it doesn't matter whether the cat is black or white if only it catches mice', relates also to money—*pecunia non olet*. The new political leadership, putting aside national pride, realized rather late (at the end of the 1970s) that according to the United Nations and World Bank classification, China was a 'low income, food-deficient country'. Thus it was a entitled to apply for the usual low-interest loans and grants available to this type of Third World country. Foreign financial institutions, impressed by Chinas overall economic performance, were willing to render assistance. They showed high esteem for China's achievements in dealing with rural poverty. At the same time, the first detailed report by the World Bank laconically notes that 'a detailed antipoverty program has yet to be formulated' (World Bank 1981, 88). This was grist to the mills of those officials in China calling for speedy action. Thus the establishment of the new strategy can be interpreted as an essential precondition for tapping a potentially continuous flow of cheap or free-of-charge foreign currency funds. The rationalization of national administration in the early 80's which led to the creation of a new 'super-ministry', the 'Ministry of Foreign Economic Relations and Trade' in March 1982 greatly facilitated access to and acquisition of foreign funds and knowhow. In my view, the awareness of these new cheap or even free-of-charge sources of foreign currency was one of the strongest motives pushing for the elaboration of this new strategy. This new and powerful ministry, with its 'section for international relations' in charge, provided the necessary fund-raising expertise which all other ministries so far dealing with relief actions were lacking. Consequently, throughout the 1980s the engagement of the World Bank, UNDP, World Food Programe, NGOs and bilateral projects in anti-poverty schemes constantly increased.

Environmental Protection via Economic Diversification

Since its very beginning in 1978 the debate about the new strategy for poverty areas pointed out the ecological inadequacy of the old *yi liang wei gang* policy (i. e. to give absolute priority to grain production) which had led to disastrous social and environmental consequences. With the loess plateau as a well known example, the nationwide environmental implications of extreme rural poverty could be impressively illustrated. The way out of the crisis was seen in diversified production, taking fully into account the specific local resource potential (*yindi zhiyi*). The underlying assumption was, and still is, that an appropriate land use policy would automatically solve the problem of resource destruction. Once unambiguous and stable legal positions for land use rights (including water resources) had been established, state interference in economic affairs had been minimized, *both* economic growth *and* ecological rehabilitation would become just two sides of the same coin. We shall come back to this official position later.

The New Anti-Poverty Strategy of 1986

The Dimension of the Problem in the Mid-1980s

Although the material needs for survival vary considerably according to climate and geology in a country as vast as China, for the purpose of broad national estimates every rural inhabitant is classified as 'poor' whose net annual income (excluding external state and local transfer payments) is below 50 per cent of the national average. The upsurge in agriculture since 1978 went hand in hand with an impressive decline in absolute rural poverty.

'Correcting for inflation, the income distribution data indicate a decline in absolute poverty from about 27 per cent of the rural population in 1979 to 11.3 per cent in 1986 and a reduction in the number of rural absolute poor of more than 100 million people, from between 200 to 220 million in 1979 to 70 million in 1986' (World Bank 1988, 5).

Included in these 70 mio. rural absolute poor were approximately 27 mio. extremely destitute, for whom the problem of most elementary food and clothing (*wenbao*) had not yet been solved by 1986.

In 1986, 751 counties in 23 provinces and autonomous regions totally or partly (several *xiang*), were to be labelled as poverty areas (table 1).

They were characterized by at least one of the four attributes: (a) mountainous (*shan*); (b) old revolutionary base area (*lao*); (c) located in international or provincial border areas (*bian*); (d) inhabited by national minorities (*shao*).

These poverty areas are confronted with all conceivable sorts of natural disadvantages (high altitude, steep slopes, extreme meteorological risks, mineralized water etc.), which have a strong impact on human health and production as well as on communications. Thus, it is not surprising that in almost every aspect of life the people of these areas are worse off than the average rural Chinese, let alone urban residents. These deficits have
been well

Table 1. Numbers of Xian per province or autonomous region which in 1985 were partly or completely classified as 'poverty areas'

Province/Region	Number of xian	Pecentage of all xian
Hebei	49	35
Shanxi	35	35
Inner Mongolia	37	44
Liaoning	11	24
Anhui	17	23
Zhejiang	3	4
Fujian	16	25
Jiangxi	54	64
Shandong	14	13
Henan	24	21
Hubei	37	52
Hunan	38	29
Guangdong	30	30
Guangxi	48	59
Sichuan	46	25
Guizhou	31	38
Yunnan	41	33
Tibet	77	91
Shaanxi	46	49
Gansu	43	57
Ningxia	8	47
Quinghai	19	50
Xinjiang	27	32
Total	751	

Source: Office of the Leading Group (LGPAD), 3/1989.

elaborated in various sources (Jiang Dehua et al. 1987; Xu Yulong and Qiu Yuanjin 1988). Combined, they present a formidable set of obstacles to any long term development.

Targets

The basic target, proclaimed in 1986, is:

'to supply people in most poor areas with enough food and clothing, to help such areas to generate a self-development capability in developing a local commodity economy and to gradually wipe out the poverty and to become prosperous' (OLG 1989,8).

In a first stage until 1990, the *wenbao* problem is to be solved for 90 per cent of the people

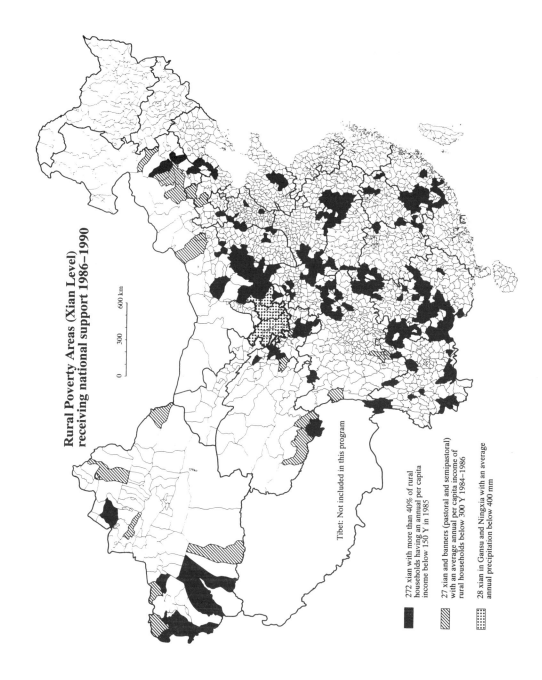

Rural Poverty Areas (Xian Level) receiving national support 1986–1990

0   300   600 km

Tibet: Not included in this program

272 xian with more than 40% of rural households having an annual per capita income below 150 Y in 1985

27 xian and banners (pastoral and semipastoral) with an average annual per capita income of rural households below 300 Y 1984–1986

28 xian in Gansu and Ningxia with an average annual precipitation below 400 mm

in poor areas (except for 'five guarantee' (*wubao)* households). In a further stage the emphasis should shift to regional economic development.

Categories of Aid Recipients
Funds are to be allocated according to the 'degree of poverty and special historical, economic and political factors in the poor regions' (OLG 1989, 9). This wording indicates the preferential treatment of old revolutionary base areas as well as the non-consideration of Tibet. Tibet does not fall under the competence of the LGPAD.[3]

Basically two categories of county units have to be distinguished, (a) those receiving national support and (b) those subject to provincial support schemes.[4]

State aid was granted to 327 xian consisting of these groups (See map: Rural Poverty Areas Receiving National Support 1986-1990, on facing page):

a) 28 counties of the Sanxi Scheme in Gansu and Ningxia, already in action since 1983;

b) 27 pastoral and semi-pastoral counties and banners with an average rural per capita income in 1984-1986 below 300 yuan.

c) By far the largest group consists of 272 counties, falling into following subcategories:

(i) Counties with an average rural per capita net income in 1985 below 150 yuan.
(ii) Old revolutionary bases and autonomous counties with an average rural per capita net income in 1985 below 200 yuan.
(iii) 'A few minority autonomous countries with special difficulties ... as well as some countries in major old revolutionary bases that had made great contributions to the Chinese revolution' (OLG 1989, 10). The annual average per capita net income in such countries in 1985 could range from 200 to 300 yuan.

The common denominator for these three subgroups was that at least 40 per cent of the total rural xian population had an annual per capita net income below 150 yuan. Many of these 'poor' counties were located isolated in rather well-off areas, i.e. in Zhejiang. Others form clusters. According to Peng Defu, Document No. 19 of the CCP Central Committee of 1984 distinguishes eleven large poverty areas (excluding Tibet and Xinjiang) with 6,194 townships in 225 counties/towns of 13 province-level units (Peng Defu 1986). Later research by the LGPAD led to distinguishing 18 large poverty areas (excluding the fringe areas of the Tarim basin in Xinjiang), totalling 523 counties/towns in 20 province-level units (Table 2). They can easily be localized on the map of China presenting the life-quality-index (see appendix) by comparing it with a physical map of China. So far, the most detailed and systematic typology of poverty areas has been presented by a team from the Geographical Research Institute under the Academic Sinica and the State Planning Commission (Jiang Dehua et al. 1987). It distinguishes 21 poverty regions in six physiographic regions of China with 751 counties involved.

The Institutional Framework for the New Policy

In accordance with the necessity of a multisectoral approach as a prerequisite for successful policy implementation, the new anti-poverty institutions were not designed as a quasi-ministerial structure. They are bodies at all administrative levels in which the representatives of various sector-institutions engaged in anti-poverty measures come together to guarantee an integrated approach. 'The main tasks of the leading group are: to organize, exercise leadership over, coordinate, supervise and examine the economic development in poor areas' (OLG 1989, 12). In early 1989 the LGPAD had 17 members from the following institutions on the national level: State Council; State Education Commission; State Nationalities Affairs Commission; Ministry of Finance; Ministry of Communications; Ministry of Water Conservancy; Ministry of Agriculture; Ministry of Forestry; Ministry of Commerce; Ministry of Material Equipment; Ministry of Public Health; Bank of China; Agricultural Bank of China; China Rural Development Research Center; Communist Youth League; All Chinese Federation of Trade Unions; Academy of Sciences; China Association for Science and Technology.

Surprisingly, some very important national institutions are not represented in LGPAD, i.e. the State Planning Commission and ministries such as the Ministry of Civil Affairs (reponsible for *wubao* questions), the Ministry for Construction (responsible for environmental protection) and the Ministry for Foreign Economic Relations and Trade (responsible for the allocation of foreign aid).

LGPAD is seconded by the Office of the Leading Group responsible for the regular executive work. It has four divisions for (a) policy research; (b) planning and coordination; (c) administrative affairs; (d) management of the Sanxi Area Project. Besides the Office LGPAD established three organs with special functions: A Cadre Training Center to improve the managerial skills of local cadres, a Development Foundation for Poor Regions in China for fund raising and distribution, and a Service Centre.

Although these organizational efforts may look very impressive, the general approach of LGPAD is a 'low profile' one. It aims primarily at the improvement and stronger integration of anti-poverty measures within the existing administrative structures. Thus, it is far removed from anything like the 'mass mobilization' campaigns of the Mao era.

Relying on the existing structures is not without pitfalls: The most important unit involved is the county, while poverty areas by their very nature tend to form contiguous areas at the periphery of several counties. Throughout Chinese history the county formed an 'independent kingdom' (*duli wangguo*). To assure an integrated approach for the development of one poverty area therefore implies a strong leadership at the next higher level of the prefecture (*diqu, shi*). How far this can really be established remains to be seen.

This problem is repeated at the higher levels. Poverty Areas exist as a contiguous zone along the boundaries of several prefectures or even provinces. How far can leading groups at these levels enforce a unified approach upon the administrations of different territorial units with diverging interests and different potentials?

Table 2. Officially acknowledged Major Poverty Regions in the Eastern, Central and Western Economic Zones

A: Classification of September 1984: 11 regions
B: Classification of LGPAD 1986: 18 regions

Region	Province/ autonomous region	A	B
Eastern Economic Zone			
Yimeng Shan	Shandong		9
Guangdong/Fujian boundary area			20
Central Economic Zone			
Nuluerhu Shan	Liaoning, Inner Mongolia, Hebei	14	18
Taihang Shan	Shanxi, Hebei	8	25
Luliang Shan	Shanxi	13	21
Qinling Daba Shan	Sichuan, Shaanxi, Hubei, Henan	67	68
Wuling Shan	Sichuan, Hunan, Hubei, Guizhou	33	40
Dabie Shan	Hubei, Henan, Anhui	14	27
Jinggang Shan	Jiangxi, Hunan		
Western Economic Zone			
Dingxi Region	Gansu		27
Xihaigu Region	Ningxia		8
Northern Shaanxi	Shaanxi, Gansu		27
Tibet			77
Southwest Yunnan	Yunnan	18	19
Hengduan Shan	Yunnan	19	19
Jiuwan Dashan	Guangxi, Guizhou	9	17
Wumeng Shan	Sichuan, Yunnan, Guizhou	23	32
Northwest Guizhou	Guizhou	7	29
Not included in either classification:			
Southern Xinjiang	Xinjiang		ca. 25

Source: Peng Defu 1986, 23; OLG 1989, 3.

Financing

The grants and credits devoted to poverty area development are funds managed by the Agricultural Bank of China, People's Bank of China, Ministry of Finance and the Industrial and Commercial Bank of China. Roughly three quarters of the four billion yuan annually are low interest loans. Furthermore (a) poor farmers were exempted from paying interest on old loans from the period of collective agriculture (*guazhang dingxi*); (b) poor areas were exempted from agricultural tax for three to five years after 1985; (c) in some provinces (i. e. Guizhou) poor areas were no longer obliged to sell grain to the state within the quota system; (d) in Guizhou primary school pupils were no longer charged tuition fees and text book expenses; (e) poor countries receiving state aid were exempted from taxes for the energy and transport construction funds; (f) State companies had to supply poor areas with certain amounts of chemical fertilizers, farmland plastic sheets, steel, timber and trucks at a 30 per cent discount (OLG 1989, 17-18).

State support for poverty areas in the past was inefficient mainly for two reasons: Firstly, most of the state subsidies had no immediate impact on rural production. They never reached the farmers but were used to finance the global county budget (water supply, industry, traffic and trade, culture, health and - last but not least - administration). As a remedy loans are now only to be granted on a contractual basis for specific approved projects, when good management as well as high economic efficiency is guaranteed. Secondly, banks in poor areas tradionally played only a very passive role. They were mere institutions for money transfer, acting by order of the local party leadership. It seems that banks before were not entitled to supervise and evaluate the economic efficiency of the projects which they were urged to finance. Moreover they had to distribute low interest credits designed for poverty alleviation without state compensation while giving high interest rates for savings. Thus a local bank as an individual enterprise could hardly make a profit. There were neither material incentives to increase savings nor to distribute credits. At the same time local banks were requested by their superior units to return available funds so that these were used as high interest loans in the relatively developed parts of the country (Tan Yueheng 1986). The new financing system designed in cooperation with LGPAD suggests a greater autonomy for local banks as individual economic enterprises. Not only are banks urged to participate in the design of contracts and project evaluation, it was also proposed that the loss of interest returns resulting from the distribution of low interest loans should be fully compensated by the state (Tan Yueheng 1986, 17).

Little is known about the actual state of the reform. Detailed information about the procedure and the conditions for the transfer of grants and credits are not yet available. Also, the scope of the projects supported as well as their regional distribution require further research.

LGPAD and its respective committees on all administrative echelons concerned do not exercise any direct budgetary power but funds will not be granted by the different financing institutions without its approval.

Other Means of Support
Besides management training for rural cadres and intensification of research LGPAD is also experimenting with two other instruments of non-financial support. Firstly, there are *bilateral partnerships*. In order to ease direct economic cooperation between production units in poverty areas and those in the urban-industrial centres LGPAD acts as a 'broker' by promoting bilateral partnerships. In spring 1989 27 such relations were established. Here are some examples: (a) State Planning Commission—Southwest and Northwest Fujian; (b) State Education Commission—Taihang Shan in Hebei; (c) State Science and Technology Commission—Dabie Shan in Henan, Hubei and Anhui; (d) Ministry of Civil Af-

fairs—Jinggang Shan in Jiangxi; (e) Ministry of Commerce—Yimeng Shan; (f) Ministry of Forestry—Jiuwandashan in Guangxi and Guizhou. Thus every poverty area is to have a partner institution at the national level as a liaison unit. At least some of these partnerships proved to be very fruitful for the allocation of new industrial investments in the poverty areas or for finding new markets for local products.

Secondly, there is *labour migration*. Although urban areas are confronted with a high rate of 'indigeneous' unemployment, labour exports from rural poverty areas were officially encouraged and even organized. The basic assumption is that each emigrated labourer is able to support one rural household. In 1987, Linyi Diqu in Shandong (covering the Yimeng Shan Poverty Region), for example, had 150.000 labourers from its six poor xian working outside the district boundaries. This amounts to between five and 20 per cent of the local village labour force. The average income of each individual labourer was 960 yuan (Linyi Party Committee 1987, 13).

Gansu province exported more than one million labourers into other parts of China in 1987. Young girls received special training to work as housemaids in cities like Beijing, Guangzhou and Xi'an (China Daily, 29 December 1987). Similar exports of female domestics from poor Anhui villages to Beijing have a long tradition.

Historic examples from Southern China and Europe suggest, that the positive effects of emigration (remittances, acquisition of know-how) are more than counterbalanced by the losses: migrants constitute the most active and innovative part of the village population. The other point is that emigration depends on the absorption capacity of the external labour market. Therefore its long term stability is not guaranted. In China, migration to urban areas was recently interrupted in spring 1989.

The Role of International Support

When projects of international cooperation began mushrooming in China, *technology transfer* was highest on the agenda due to the assumption, that the basic needs problem was already more or less solved. Thus throughout the 1980s only relatively few projects were directly concerned with poverty alleviation.

As mentioned before, the Loess Plateau received early attention. The World Bank massively supported the Sanxi-scheme in Gansu, financing the expansion of primary education as well as small scale rural industries. Four other World Bank projects of rural development were located in poor areas being concerned with the improvement of irrigation and drainage, complex agroforestry-systems and rural industries (World Bank 1988, 14-15). The biggest potential for anti-poverty actions can be generated by the World Food Programme and associated bilateral activities. From 1980 onwards, WFP indeed transferred large quantities of various types of food to China. Until 1987 the total value of food imports was in the range of 400-500 million US dollars.[5] But, although the projects supported were mainly located in rural areas only a minority was directly in support of the officially acknowledged poverty areas. This has changed during the last years. Recently the emphasis has shifted from the easily accessible eastern regions (coastal and central China) towards the larger hard-core poverty areas in the mountainous western parts of the country.

Once proper monitoring and evaluation is guaranteed, such internationally supported anti-poverty schemes can have a very positive impact:

(a) They have a mobilizing and stimulating effect on local bureaucracy. Provincial and xian cadres gain higher status by the acquisition of external funds. If the project proceeds successfully further funds may be expected.

(b) The participation of foreign experts and consultants can contribute to improved interaction and exchange of informations between the local representatives of different administrative sectors usually working very much isolated from each other.

(c) Foreign donors *can* influence the selection of the poverty area to be supported as well as the targets to be given priority.

(d) Foreign consultants *can* raise questions and introduce new proposals which so far local officials have not thought of.

In future two major problems have to be overcome: Firstly, Chinese officials and experts involved are very sensitive towards the world wide problem, that an aid-receiving-mentality may undermine local initiative. It is therefore indispensable to fit supports properly into the contract system. Secondly, so far - to my knowledge - LGPAD and its local units were little or not at all involved in project selection or fund acquisition. The fund-receiving counterpart is often a sector administration which naturally represents partial interests. To ensure a cross-sectoral approach, a greater participation of LGPAD institutions in the management of foreign funds is therefore highly desirable.

Environmental Considerations

It is certain that by the end of the Seventh Five Year Plan period the ongoing anti-poverty strategy will be officially presented as an almost unqualified success (Liang Chao 1990).

Certainly, significant contributions will have been made towards the elimination of the *wenbao* problem and rural drinking water shortage problem will have been achieved. But it is doubtful whether the official idea of establishing self-sustaining economic growth in the poverty regions after initial inputs can still be upheld. Too many disadvantages have to be overcome.

In a rather reflective article Hu Zhangwen (1987) raises this principal issue. He criticises those who consider the support of poverty regions as a unilateral action, a 'blood transfusion' (*shu xue*). He stresses that developing and backward regional systems have to be seen as historically and ecologically closely interdependant. He gives the example of mountain farmers, who have to move to poor sites to allow the construction of water reservoirs, while lowland farmers will profit from improved irrigation. For Hu the wide-spread opinion about the lack of sensitivity for ecological questions among poor village people is unjustified. He demands a partial transfer from the economic gains in the lowlands for protective investments in the mountain areas: 'Once such compensations would be granted, (mountain) farmers would not only not oppose but defend measures of soil and water conservation' (Hu Zhangwen 1987, 37).

Despite the fact that there is hardly any article or project design which does not include the aspects of 'energy' and 'ecology/environment', these two crucial points have—in my view —not yet received the attention they need. This is not a particular problem of the poor regions—although they are confronted with it most intimately—but one of China as a whole. Asian societies which are or have been understanding themselves as 'socialist', energy and environment have been low on the agenda with all the well documented implications. China's industrialization went hand in hand with a constant reduction of its natural reproduction capacity.

Countries like Austria and Switzerland have at least 30 per cent of their mountain areas covered by high quality forests, a considerable part of which is virtually untouchable as protective forest. In contrast with the Alps, China's mountain areas are not only larger in size but also exposed to even greater ecological extremes and risks. Yet despite continuous efforts for reforestation, China's forest (and grassland) resources have constantly been shrinking at an alarming rate. Chinese forests are usually of a very poor quality and protective forests (*baohu lin*) have not received sufficient attention (Dai 1990, 708; Betke 1989).

It is in this particular field that a genuine contribution of the poverty areas towards the national economy as a whole can be expected. The official position is, that local economic diversification will automatically bring about environmental improvement. This is wishful thinking because poor areas need immediate economic returns. They simply do not have the financial resources to take care of large-scale resource protection and rehabilitation.

In order to establish long term stable conditions for China's economy and society as a whole, a constant capital transfer into the poverty regions is inevitable to restore forest ecosystems. Besides local industrial and agricultural development, a large fraction of the poor regions' labour force should be trained for a national service function: preventive resource protection. Since this is in line with the global need to improve CO_2 absorbtion capacity, it is in the establishment of this new sector that future international aid will have to play a decisive role.

Notes

This report is based on (a) personal experiences with the establishment of a food for work scheme in Yimeng Shan, Shandong, supported by German funds; (b) informations supplied by Mr. Kong Candong and Gao Hongbing (Office of the Leading Group for Poor Areas Development), Prof. Ma Hongliang (Lanzhou University); (c) a preliminary study of published literature; (d) unpublished materials submitted to the 'Workshop on the Geo graphy of Poverty in China' in Beijing (April 1989), organized by the Office of the NGO China Group. The author gratefully acknowledges the valuable help of Ms. Li Jianming, Ms. Xia Fang, Ms. Sabine Rieß-Kramp, Zhu Xiaoxue, Christoph Peisert and Wolfgang Straub. A more extensive monograph is forthcoming.

1. A preliminary survey of available literature uncovered more than 60 articles dealing with various aspects of poverty region development. Some of the journals in which materials on poverty areas were published are: *Nongye Jingji Wenti* (Beijing); *Zhongguo Nongcun Jingji* (Beijing); *Fazzhan Yanjiu* (Fujian); *Neimenggu Jingji Tantao*; *Shehui Kexue Zhanxian* (Jilin); *Jiangxi Shehui Kexue*; *Guizhou Shehui Kexue*; *Shehui Kexue* (Lanzhou).

2. 'Sanxi' refers to poor areas in Dingxi, Hexi (Gansu) and Xihaigu in Ningxia. Further details on the scheme are presented by Delfs (1987, 83-86). See also Jia Youlin, Jin Yi, Feng Qiang (1988, 451-452).

3. No official explanation is known for the exclusion of the 77 poor counties of Tibet from the state-support coordinated by LGPAD. A separate 'Tibet Development Fund' was set up in 1987 as a potential partner for foreign NGOs willing to give support.

4. I shall not touch upon this huge second group with almost 500 counties involved, because the provincial conditions, criteria for support and programs differ widely and data are yet sparsely available.

5. WFP, Committee on food aid policies and programmes; unpublished project descriptions, 1981-1987, Rome.

References

Betke (1989): Dirk Betke, 'Die Umweltfrage'. In: E. Louven, (ed.), *Chinas Wirtschaft zu Beginn der 90er Jahre*, Hamburg, 54-82.

Betke and Küchler (1987): Dirk Betke and Johhannes Küchler, 'Shortage of Land Resources as a Factor in Development: The Example of The People's Republic of China'. In B. Gläser (ed.) *Learning from China?* London, 85-107.

Central Committee (1984): 'Guanyu bangzhu pinkun diqu jinkuai gaibian mianmaode tongzhi' (Circular on support to poor areas for a speedy change of their situation). *Renmin Ribao* 29 September 1984, 2.

Dai (1990): Dai Shifeng, 'Chinas Waldreserven nehmen ab'. *Allgemeine Forstzeitschrift* 27 (1990), 708.

Delfs (1978): Robert Delfs, 'A Model of Poverty'. *Far Eastern Economic Review* 10 September 1978, 83-86.

Hu Zhangwen (1987): Hu Zhangwen, 'Yanjiu kaifa pinkun diqu jingji bixu jianshe hongguan shengtai jingji guandian' (In studying poor region development one has to insist on an integral ecological-economical outlook). *Nongye Jingji Wenti* 1987:2, 34-37.

Jia Youlin, Jin Yi, Feng Qiang (1988): Jia Youlin, Jin Yi, Feng Qiang, 'Zai jianshe zhong qianjinde "Sanxi" diqu' (Advancing Sanxi Region under construction). In *Zhonguo nongye nianjian*, Beijing, 451-452.

Jiang Dehua (1987): Jiang Dehua, Zhang Yaoguang, Ho Shaofan, Yang Liu, *Zhongguo pinkun diqu leixing huafen yu kaifa yanjiu* (a study on the typology of China's poverty regions and their development). Beijing: Zhongguo Kexueyuan Dili Yanjiu Suo and Guojia Jiwei.

Liang Chao (1990): Liang Chao, '70m Rural People Lifted Above Poverty Line'. *China Daily* 30 June 1990.

Linyi Party Committee (1987): Zhonggong Shandongsheng Linyi Diwei, Shandongsheng Linyi Diquxingshu, *Tuchu zhongdian, qianghua cuoshi, jiakuai tuopin zhifu bufa* (Put more emphasis on accelerated poverty eradication). Unpublished report of the Party Committee of Linyi Prefecture, Shandong, for the national conference on the economic development of poverty regions.

OLG (1989): Office of the Leading Group of Economic Development in Poor Area under the State Council, *Outlines of Economic Development in China's Poor Areas*, Beijing 1 March 1989 (in English).

Peng Defu (1986): Peng Defu, 'Woguo shiyipian pinkun diqu qingkuang jianjie' (Introduction to the eleven poverty regions of our country). *Nongye Jingji Wenti*, 1986:8, 23-24, 14.

Seventh Five Year Plan (1986): *Zhonghua Remin Gongheguo, Guomin jingji he shehui fazhan diqige wunian jihua* (Seventh Five Year Plan for economic and social development). Beijing.

Tan Yueheng (1986): Tan Yueheng, 'Pinkun diqu zijin zhuru wenti tantao' (Discussing problems of capital transfer into poverty regions). *Nongye Jingji Wenti*, 1986:8, 15-17, 33.

Tong Dalin and Bao Tong (1978): Tong Dalin and Bao Tong, 'Guanyu xibei huangtu gaoyuan de jianshe fangzhen wenti' (Problems of the perspective for reconstruction of the Loess Plateau). *Renmin Ribao*, 26 November 1978, 2.

World Bank (1981): World Bank, *China: Socialist Agricultural Development. Annex C: Agricultural Development*, Report No. 3391-CHA.

World Bank (1988): World Bank, China Department, *China, a Poverty Profile, Issues and Bank Strategy*. Beijing 17 February 1988.

Xu Yulong and Qiu Yuanjin (1988): Xu Yulong, Qui Yuanjin, 'Pinkun diqude leixing, chanye jiegou tezheng yu zijin peizhi' (Types of poverty regions, characteristics of their production structure and methods of their financial support). *Shehui Kexue Zhanxian*, 1988:2, 25-31.

Rural Social Welfare in China

Athar Hussain

I take social security to cover various social mechanisms for preventing contingencies such as interruption of earnings, sickness and crop failures, or alleviating their effects, and measures to protect vulnerable social groups such as the elderly and the chronically poor. These social mechanisms need not take the form of social security programmes, but instead may be embedded in the economic organization or social relations. This is of particular importance in the case of rural China because, unlike urban areas, it lacks a comprehensive social security programme such as labour insurance. Moreover, the introduction of such a programme in the near future is highly unlikely. Thus the effect of the organization of the economy on the incidence and alleviation of deprivation assumes a central importance in the discussion of rural social security. So I first look briefly at the institutional transformations in rural areas since 1978, and then turn to other issues in the following order: (1) agricultural pricing and trading policies of the government; (2) social security programmes, including social relief, disaster relief and assistance to poor regions; (3) health provisions.

The rural social security system, narrowly defined, consists of the programmes under headings 2 and 3 above. Whilst social relief includes various income-maintenance programmes, disaster relief and health provisions cover specific contingencies. Assistance to poor regions overlaps with social relief and disaster relief. It is a programme to develop a coherent policy towards poor regions combining both relief and development assistance. Agricultural pricing and trading are included because of the important role they have played in determining real personal incomes and alleviating nutritional contingencies. China has been comparatively successful in preventing and alleviating deprivation in rural areas. Yet the rural social security system is, as we shall see, strikingly sparse. Social relief is contingent on a stringent means test, which is often concerned more with preventing the non-deserving from claiming relief than with ensuring a comprehensive coverage of all those in need. Although social security programmes in rural areas are by no means insignificant, on their own they do not seem weighty enough to account for China's comparative success in preventing deprivation in rural areas. The suggestion is that the success until now is due in large measure to the organization of the rural economy.

Transformations in the Rural Economy
From the point of view of social welfare, the most important attribute of the Chinese rural economy has been the absence of landlessness as the cause of destitution. There have been and still are in China rural poor with land. All rural households have had access to land either collectively or individually. Herein lies the crucial difference between the attributes of the rural poor in China and those in most other developing economies, where rural poverty and landlessness are bound together. There have been landless households in rural China, and

their numbers have grown rapidly in recent years with the economic reforms. But 'specialized households', as they are now termed, are not poor; on the contrary, they are landless by choice and are more likely to be among the more prosperous households.

Schematically, poverty in rural China is associated with two groups of factors. The first consists of natural factors such as poor soil, inhospitable climate and geographical isolation. These are the main attributes of poor regions, or causes of a low average income over an area. The second is the lack of sufficient labour power due to age, death and a large number of children, which is the main reason for why a household is poorer than the rest in the area. The map of rural poverty for China looks very different from those in other developing economies. Extreme poverty seems to be heavily concentrated in certain regions. This has had a profound effect in that rural poverty tends to be predominantly perceived in terms of regions rather than in terms of households, and, correspondingly, the focus of social security programmes is on regions rather than on households. The major exception to this rule is *wubao* which is directed towards the indigent elderly. Although the regional focus accords with the reality, it does create blind spots such as poor households in prosperous areas.

Broadly speaking, collectivization was marked out by two features: first, the centralized allocation of labour and, second, the collective disposal of income. Households had little discretion over the deployment of their own labour, and the centralized deployment of labour was marked by a heavy allocation of labour to infrastructural works. Aside from a relatively small income from the heavily constrained private activities, all income accrued initially to the collective. This gave the collective power to decide upon the disposal of income in cash and kind, which was done according partly to need and partly to work (see Parish and Whyte 1978, ch. 5; Croll 1982; Perkins and Yusuf 1984, ch. 5; Endicott 1988, 123-26). Remuneration for labour and income maintenance were intertwined; the relative weight assigned to each varied across units. Distribution according to needs reduced the risk of loss of income to households from the diminution of their labour force. Thus it addressed the principal cause of household poverty. To use an adage common in China, rural collectivization provided each rural family with an iron rice bowl - the bowl symbolises provision and iron the fact that the level of provision remains unaffected by everyday knocks and bumps, referring to variations in labour performed by a household.

The adverse effect of collectivization on incentives has been emphasised in the literature, but one may also keep in mind that the iron rice bowl provided a guaranteed income to not merely shirkers but also to households lacking sufficient labour due to sickness, old age and deaths. Under collectivization, financing social security, rural health insurance and infrastructural work posed no special problem. Local cadres decided upon the uses of income and the deployment of resources with or without the consent of households. However, coercion was not the sole prop of the system. Collective cultivation, it needs emphasizing, did engender a spirit of solidarity conducive to social security through local cooperation, albeit not to the same degree everywhere. The responsibility system has cut the ground from underneath social solidarity founded on collective cultivation (Hussain and Liu 1989).

The disposal of income by the collective and the centralized allocation of labour both had a special significance from the point of social insurance against natural disasters, which are recurrent events and have a strong bearing on rural incomes and consumption. That is, any diminution of income or damage to assets due to natural factors was automatically borne by all and not just a few households. By its very nature collectivization involved a pooling of risks; and as with most insurance systems, it also went together with adverse effects on incentives. Besides, during the collectivist era, there was a massive investment of resources and labour into infrastructure. Heroism rather than economic calculations guided much of that investment. The economic propriety of much of that investment is open to question. But, of that investment, one would single out massive investment in hydraulic construction as having a special significance for income maintenance in rural areas. At the end of the era of collective farming 45 per cent of the cultivable area in China was irrigated - which is an exceptionally high figure for a large and diverse country (see World Bank 1981, vol. 2, 23-24). Such a high proportion of irrigated area *prima facie* did help both to increase and stabilize yields.

Collective agriculture is now heavily discredited in China, and the speed with which it was displaced by family farming suggests that many of its features were strongly resented by the rural population. Assessed from the vantage point of what has happened in the rural economy since the decollectivization, there is little doubt that the collective rural economy stunted incentives, misallocated resources and held back personal incomes by putting household economic activites in a strait-jacket of collectivism. Yet it is also true that the shift to family farming has adversely affected communal social security arrangements and infrastructure, in particular irrigation systems.

In the wake of the reforms most of the restrictions on non-farming activities by rural households have been lifted. The pattern of distribution of collective land varies geographically, and so too the terms on which the land has been parcelled out. Predominantly, the land has been assigned to households in proportion to their size. Notwithstanding regional variations, implicit in the distribution of the cultivable land there remains a concern to provide each household with means to make a living. The living which households are able to make depends crucially on the locality. Since the land is still *de jure* collectively owned, there exists a possibility of changing the distribution of land to take account of the movement of the population from agricultural to non-agricultural activities, and demographic changes (for examples of re-adjustments in the distribution of land, see AYB 1986, 40-41). With the shift away from market oriented reforms since June 1989, such redistributions of land is likely to become more common.

The households in receipt of collectively-owned land have to pay the land tax, the local accumulation and welfare tax, and are obliged to sell to the government a portion of the produce. Taxes and the procurement quota obligation are divided pro rata to the land area. In effect, households are subject to a lump-sum tax. However, things are neither as orderly nor as uniform as this sparse description might suggest. The shift to family farming has cut the ground from underneath the local government in rural areas, which was intertwined with collective organization of economic activities. Generally speaking, the reorganization of local government has lagged behind economic changes. As a result, there is a problem of collection of accumulation and welfare taxes and the organization of public activities, at least in some rural areas. The important point is that under the responsibility system the diversity in the countryside is much greater than it was under collectivism.

Turning to its effects on social security, the responsibility system has undone many of the features associated with collectivization. Granting each household the power of disposal of income generated from the plot allocated to it reduces distribution according to needs, which is now limited by the size of the local welfare tax. This is intended, as the aim has been to 'smash the iron rice bowl'. *Ipso facto*, households have to bear individually the risk of the loss of income or assets due to a diminution of its labour force, and to damage from natural factors. The general point is that the reponsibility system has increased incentives, but it has also increased risks to be borne individually by rural households. The financing of social security programmes can no longer be decided by an administrative fiat; it depends on the willingness of households to contribute, and on the welfare tax the rural collective manages finally to collect. The parcelling out of the land, and giving households back the power to allocate their labour have unravelled the arrangements built around the collective deployment of income and resources. In particular, the rural health insurance system has, in most areas, been replaced with 'payment with service'. This means that in case of illness a household not only faces the risk of loss of income but also of larger expenditure. The general implication is that the rural social security system fashioned during the period of collective cultivation is increasingly out of alignment with the rural economy based around households. It requires a new financial foundation which takes into account the fact that increasingly income from activities accrues to households and not to the collective. It is also in need of a new framework for carrying out social welfare obligations, which increasingly cannot be left to benevolence and the spirit of solidarity in rural communities.

The responsibility system has also decreased the ability of rural collectives to mobilize labour for infrastructual works. In fact, the government has explicitly forbidden the use of labour and resources without adequate compensation (for a case study see Zweig 1989, ch. 7). The irrigated area declined steadily from 1978 to 1985, though since then the government has succeeded in partially reversing the trend (see ZTN 1988, 233). From the point of view of social security, the displacement of the collective economy by the household economy has to be coupled with the growth of either tax-financed social insurance or private insurance to cover the extra risks created by the displacement, but this is only beginning to happen on a significant scale.

When assessing the impact of the responsibility system on rural social security, one may bear in mind that rural incomes have risen at a record pace since the introduction of the system. Between 1978 and 1987, rural income per capita at current prices grew by 13 per cent per year (ZTN 1988, 799). Given that the rate of inflation over the period has averaged around six per cent per annum, the rate of growth of real incomes still comes to a high seven per cent. By doing away with restrictions on private activities, the economic reforms have provided rural households with wider and more varied opportunities for earning an income. Such opportunities, however, vary greatly with the locality.

Added to that, the economic reforms have given a fillip to rural industry. As most of it is collectively owned, collective economy in industrialized rural areas remains strong, with the difference that it is now anchored in industry rather than in agriculture. Employment in rural industry (township and village industry), which has increased very rapidly in recent years, occasionally brings with it occupational benefits such as old-age pensions and subsidized medical care, though not on the same scale as in urban areas. A portion of profits from collectively-owned industry is used for subsidizing agriculture and for financing rural social welfare. The rural industry's contribution to rural welfare in nominal terms has been growing at ten per cent per year over the ten years, 1978 - 1987 (see YRSES 1986, 168; ZTN 1988, 287). However, rural industry is very unevenly distributed. For example, in 1987 around 60 per cent of the national total of profits from rural industry accrued to only six out of 29 provinces, containing 28 per cent of the total rural population (ZTN 1988, 289; SYB 1987, 69). All these provinces are along the eastern seaboard of the country.

Pricing and Trading Policies of the Government

Although land tenure is the most important determinant of personal incomes in rural areas, trading arrangements have had a significant bearing on rural incomes. A part of the agricultural produce is sold to the government, voluntarily or not. In addition to that farmers purchase agricultural inputs such as fertilizers, manfactured consumer goods and also, in the case of a shortfall, staples such as grain. As government agencies have been by far the most important buyers of agricultural produce and the sellers of inputs to farmers, the price and trading policies of the government have had an important effect on the cash income of farmers. These policies have frequently been used for income-maintenance in rural areas, but on a piecemeal basis rather than as part of a concerted anti-poverty programme. The welfare impact of the pricing and trade policies of the government on rural areas is a large subject. Here I concentrate on two issues: first, the role of the state marketing network in alleviating nutritional contingencies in rural areas, and, second, the implications of the pricing policy for agricultural commodities on personal incomes.

I deal with the first issue in terms of how much grain is purchased from rural areas and the geographical pattern of sale of the purchased grain. On average, the government has purchased around a quarter of grain output, and resold around a third of its purchases back to rural areas - termed 'return sales' (*fan xiao*). Both these proportions have gone up since 1978, reflecting an increase in specialization in cropping patterns (see TPS 1987, 57). Until 1978, under the regime of 'taking grain as the key link' each rural locality, except a few permitted to specialize in cash crops were expected to devote enough of the cultivated area to grain to ensure self-sufficiency. With the relaxation, but not the disappearance, of the regime, there has been an increase in specialization, hence the increase in the proportion of return sales in recent years. The time-series of return sales make it clear that the state marketing network has not been used merely to siphon grain from rural to urban areas. It has also performed the important function of redistributing grain within rural areas. During the period of 'taking grain as the key link', *prima facie*, an overwhelming proportion of grain resold in rural areas was designed to alleviate nutritional contingencies.

Although the grain rationing system does not apply to rural areas, there has been in operation a system of 'guaranteed grain'. All rural inhabitants are supposed to have at least a certain amount of grain for own consumption. The minimum level, which has varied historically and regionally, is taken into account in setting procurement quotas. There is now a national standard for grain provision. Villages (or production teams or brigades) falling short of the minimum level are supplied grain from the state marketing network to make up the shortfall. The terms of supply are determined by a means test. Poor areas or areas struck with natural disasters are supplied grain either free or on loan (for details see Feuchtwang and Hussain 1988, 64-70). The provision of grain is the most important component of social relief and in disaster relief in rural areas. In the general outline, the system has not changed during the period of reforms, except that with the increase in personal incomes in rural areas, the government is less willing to supply grain on concessional terms.

Turning to the price policy of the government, since 1978 there has been a substantial increase in procurement prices for agricultural produce. Specifically, in the nine years between 1978 and 1986, the index of purchase prices of agricultural commodities rose by 77 per cent, which exceeds the total increase in the 26 years between 1952 - 1977 (TPS 1987, 115). In addition to that, the government has allowed farmers to sell their above-procurement quota output in private markets, where prices are higher than the procurement prices. These measures have helped to increase rural incomes, but they favour areas which have an agricultural surplus to sell. Very poor areas tend to have either little or no surplus to sell. The increase in procurement prices has been an important source of the increase in personal income in rural areas since 1978. However, the effect of procurement prices on the cash incomes of the farmers is complicated by changes in prices farmers pay for their input. In recent years the government has been cutting subsidies on agricultural inputs (see table 3 above; for a discussion see Sicular 1988). The net effect of the pricing policy of the government on the distribution of incomes in rural areas remains an issue for research.

Rural Social Security

For the purposes of discussion here one may divide rural social security programmes into two functional categories: (1) measures to maintain income and promote the development of poor regions; (2) public provisions for health, including cooperative rural insurance.

Income Maintenance and Income Promotion

This category covers three programmes: first, social relief (*shehui jiuji*), including *wubao*, second, disaster relief (*ziran zaihai jiuji*) and third, development assistance to poor regions. The main purpose of the first two is to provide a safety net to stop the rural population from slipping into the depths of deprivation. Social relief is subject to a stringent means test, and not meant to eliminate poverty in the sense of bringing everyone up to an adequate level. Thus, as we shall see, many who are officially recognized to be poor may not receive any assistance. Social relief is for the most part financed by the government. Rural collectives usually finance only the part of social relief provided to *wubao* households (explained below). Some rural collectives also have special programmes to help poor households in their locality. Development assistance to poor regions is not a separate programmes, it refers to a new initiative to develop a coherent policy towards poor areas combining relief and development assistance. This initiative is important because it marks the first beginnings of a nationwide programme to lift all rural inhabitants to an adequate standard of living.

Local social security programmes vary greatly between localities, and depend crucially on the initiative of the local leadership. It is these local programmes which have been heavily affected by the recent changes in the rural economy - adversely in some cases, and favourably in some others. However, social relief provided by the government seems to be better organized in the post-reform than in the pre-reform period.

Disaster Relief

In contrast to social relief, which is targeted towards the very poor, disaster relief is a much larger programme providing cover to the whole of the rural population against severe damage from natural causes. To give an idea of the relative sizes of the two programmes, in the four years (1983 - 1987), between 70 to 83 per cent of the combined expenditure on social relief and disaster relief has been devoted to disaster relief (see NTN 1986, 296; NTN 1987, 274; NTN 1988, 286). Around 60 per cent of disaster relief is provided to households in the form of living allowances consisting mainly of grain. Thus a significant part of the resale of grain to the countryside *(fanxiao)* consists of grain provided to households in disaster-affected areas. The eligibility for disaster relief has traditionally been assessed in terms of the shortfall in grain per capita from a minimum level. The usual practice has been to provide relief to all households in eligible areas regardless of means (for details see Hussain and Liu 1989, sec. 3, 9). Reports in the press seem to suggest that disaster relief have been marred by corruption and the diversion by local cadres of relief funds for other purposes.

In recent years, the government has tried to shift the emphasis of the programme from assistance after the incidence of disaster towards the prevention of damage from disaster, and there have been increasing criticisms of the 'grain test' to assess the extent of damage and eligibility for relief. The rural reforms have rendered the 'grain standard' increasingly obsolete. The cropping pattern has shifted away from grain, and an increasing proportion of income is derived from non-farming activities, which are less affected by natural disasters. There is a gradual, but still not a complete, switch from the 'grain standard' to the 'monetary standard' based on money income from all activities (for further discussion see Hussain and Liu 1989, Introduction and sec. 3). A benchmark of 150 yuan per capita per annum is commonly used in the headcount of those living in dire poverty. The shift to the monetary standard is hindered by the fact that in poor areas, an overwhelming proportion of consumption consists of non-marketed goods and household consumption and income surveys of rural areas are still very rare.

What is the extent of protection provided to the rural population against natural disasters, which is one of the main risks it faces? When assessing the extent of protection one needs to take into account not merely disaster relief provided by the government, which covers only severe damage, but also self-protection by rural communities. For rural inhabitants are expected to bear at least a part of damage from natural disasters. As pointed out earlier, collective cultivation involved a pooling of risks from crop loss. With the parcelling out of land under the responsibility system households have to bear the risk of damage to crops on their land indvidually, which on its own increases the risk of loss of income facing households. Thus from the point of view of social security against natural hazards, the growth of the household economy should be coupled with the growth of insurance, either private or social, to cover the extra risk.

A number of pilot cooperative insurance schemes have been initiated either by the Ministry of Civil Affairs or township or county governments. These insurance schemes cover damage to crops, dewellings and personal injury due to natural factors (or the acts of God as they are termed in the insurance industry). They are jointly financed by individual contributions and subsidies from the rural collective organizations, including rural industry, and from the government (for details see SBB: 30 December 1988; 14 Februrary 1989; 24 February 1989; 28 February 1989; 7 March 1989). They bear some resemblance to rural cooperative health insurance schemes of the collectivist era except that individual contributions cover a much larger proportion of costs, and the schemes are modelled on insurance policies. In some cases, these schemes co-insure with the People's Insurance Corportion. It seems likely that with the encouragement of provincial governments such schemes may spread to a large part of the countryside. However, the main problem with these schemes is that they are relatively expensive to establish, and unlikely to spread to poor areas without higher government subsidies. Poor areas are often poor because they are exposed to much higher incidence of natural disasters and households in such areas are less able to pay the levels of premia needed in such areas.

Social Relief

Social relief covers assistance to two types of households, as distinguished in the Chinese literature: 'five guarantees' households (*wubao hu*) and poor households (*pinkun hu* or *kunnan hu*). *Wubao*, which is a term dating from the 1950s, refers to the guarantee of food, health care, shelter, clothing and funeral for all citizens, hence the term five guarantees. However, over time the term has predominantly come to designate a special category of households or persons unable to earn a living and lacking relatives to depend on. Thus, as we shall see, the recipients of *wubao* relief are predominantly the elderly without family support. Although narrowly focused on people without support and, as we shall see, available to a relatively small number of people, *wubao* has a special significance in that it is linked to the tradition of looking after parents in old age. *Wubao* is seen as an obligation of rural collectives. In recent years, this obligation has been cited in birth control propaganda to demonstrate that couples without sons need not fear for support in old age, as the collective will be there ready to look after them. In contrast, poor households (*pinkun hu*) is a wider category, although distributed over the whole countryside, they are much more prevalent in underdeveloped areas often with poor soil and inhospitable climate.

The details of social relief for recent years are given in table 1.

Table 1. The Recipients of Social Relief

Year	No. of recipients (1)	pct. of rural population	pct. of poor assisted (2)	pct. of poor in rural population (3)
1978	30.2	4.0	n.a.	-
1980	46.4	6.0	54.3	11
1983	35.0	4.5	56.2	8
1984	38.0	5.4	46.9	11.5
1985	38.0	5.8	39.4	14.7
1986	40.0	6.4	39.0	16.4
1987	37.0	6.4	38.0	16.8

1. The figures for the number of recipients are in million, those for 1978-84 are from YRSES 1986, pp. 259 and 264; the rest are from ZTN 1988.

2. As provided in NTN 1986, 294; the figure for 1986 is from NTN 1987, 272; the figure for 1987 is NTN 1988, 284.

3. As implied by the percentage of the poor who are assisted.

The figures in column 1 refer to the recipients of relief, predominantly in kind; they do not include the recipients of assistance in the form of employment or production subsidies. For a low income country, the percentage of the rural population receiving assistance seems to be strikingly small, and, more important, so too is the percentage of the poor in the rural population. As shown by column 3, only a fraction of those officially recognized as poor receive social relief, and this fraction has been falling since 1983 for reasons explained below. Yet the percentage of the recipients of social relief in the rural population has been rising due to the decrease in the rural population. The percentage of the poor, including both the recipients and the non-recipients, in the rural population, as shown by column 4, is an indirect estimate derived from the percentage of the rural poor receiving social relief. The data on income distribution, which is discussed later, seems to come up with even smaller percentages.

Considering the rapid and widespread rise in personal incomes over this period, there is no plausible explanation for this apparent rise in poverty other than a better identification of the poor due to a greater sensitivity to rural poverty on the part of the government. This brings home the point that the existing figures for the rural poor in China have to be treated with great caution because to my knowledge there is as yet no systematic attempt at estimation.

The decrease in the percentage of the recognised poor receiving social relief shown by column 3, I would suggest, does not represent an erosion of social security, but a steady shift from consumption subsidies to production subsidies and public works programmes. The recipients of the former are counted under social relief but the latter are not. In recent years, there has been a proliferation of employment provision schemes in rural areas. The numbers of such schemes increased from 20,000 in 1980 to 50,000 in 1986 (NTN 1986, 294; NTN 1987, 252; see also NTN 1988: 284). Such schemes have been commonly used in developing economies such as India to alleviate deprivation in rural areas. But until recently China has not used public works schemes for this purpose. This may seem surprising because China has long been famous for massive mobilizations of rural labour for infrastructural works. The reason for this apparent paradox lies in the method of mobilization of labour and resources for capital projects during the era of collectivism.

During the period of collective cultivation, labour and resources used for infrastructural projects were frequently not remunerated at all. This resembled the traditional Chinese practice of requiring rural communities to supply labour and resources for the construction and maintenance of monuments and economic infrastructure. On occasions when labour and resources were renumerated, more often than not the renumeration came from collective rather than government funds. Infrastructural works were seen and commended by the leadership as attempts by rural communities to lift themselves from poverty through their own efforts. They were not used by the government for making income transfers to poor areas. For raising current consumption in deprived areas, the government tended to use the state marketing system to supply grain and agricultural inputs on concessional terms. Trade rather than public works was used as the main instrument of assistance in rural areas.

There has been an important change in the government policy towards infrastructual works in rural areas. One of the first acts of the reform leadership in China was to ban unrequited exactions of labour and resources by rural collectives (for a case study see Zweig

1989, ch. 7). This together with the change in the ideological climate has cut the ground from underneath revolutionary mobilizations of labour for collective ends. A result of this is the neglect of irrigation works to which we referred earlier. Now that the deployment of labour is devolved from collectives to households, relieving rural poverty by providing employment on government funded public works schemes is gaining in favour. The centralized deployment of labour during the collectivist era like a sponge absorbed all available labour, preventing the appearance of rural unemployment. With the devolution of labour deployment to households, underemployment and unemployment are surfacing as problems in rural areas.

Broadly speaking, there has been an important difference between the methods for relieving rural poverty in China and in India. The Chinese government with its tight control of trade in agricultural produce and inputs, and with its relatively underdeveloped public finance system has tended to rely more on assistance through commerce than on assistance from the government budget. In contrast, the Indian government with its more developed public finance system and with its looser hold over trade in agricultural produce and inputs has tended to rely more on budgetary assistance than on assistance through commerce. This contrast still holds but not as starkly as it did in the pre-reform period. As the system of public finance still remains comparatively underdeveloped, the Chinese government is naturally disposed towards using trade as a policy instrument for a wide variety of purposes.

Wubao relief
Turning to the details of *wubao* relief, table 2 presents the available figures:

Table 2. Recipients of *Wubao* relief

Year	Persons in millions	Percentage supported by collectives
1978	3.0	85
1980	2.9	86
1981	2.9	90
1982	3.0	90
1983	3.0	96
1984	3.0	91
1985	3.0	74
1986	2.9	75
1987	2.9	76

Source: STZ 1987, 120; NTN 1987, 266; NTN 1988, 278. The figures are rounded.

As indicated earlier, the recipients of *wubao* relief are predominantly the elderly without relatives to depend on. For example, in 1985-1987, they constituted on average 83 per cent of the recipients; the rest were orphans and the disabled (NTN 1987, 266; NTN 1988, 278). In effect, *wubao* is a support scheme for the indigent elderly in rural areas. What proportion of the elderly in rural areas receive *wubao*? Taking the 1982 population census figure for over-65s in the countryside and assuming that 83 per cent of the recipients of *wubao* relief are elderly people, the estimate for 1982 comes to just over three per cent. The proportion for recent years would be lower because whilst the numbers of over-65s has increased, the number of recipients has since 1982 remained constant or slightly decreased. This percentage may seem derisory by the norms of a welfare state, but is exceptional for a developing economy. In most developing economies, public provisions for the indigent elderly in rural areas simply do not exist. For example, India has a large number of anti-poverty programmes, but none directed towards the elderly poor. Turning to column 3, there has been a sharp decrease in the percentage of *wubao* elderly supported by collective institutions. According to circumstantial evidence, this represents a centralization of *wubao* relief away from villages, which are collective institutions, to townships and counties (for case studies see Hussain and Liu 1989, sec. 3).

The essential feature of the *wubao* system is that it is local, founded upon solidarity in rural communities. The levels and methods of provision have not been uniform. They have varied greatly in time and space, as do the criteria of eligibility for assistance. *Wubao* relief, although grounded in the constitution, lacks a detailed legal and regulatory framework specifying the sources of funds, the range of coverage, the rights of recipients and the obligations of collectives. In organization, it ranges between charity, carrying social stigma, and a formal social security programme with codified details of provision. Wubao relief is predominantly non-residential: the recipients live on their own or with relatives. However, an increasing proportion of them are accomodated in 'Houses of Respect' (*jinglao yuan*), and they receive a higher level of support than those living at home. Some of the richer areas have gone a step further and have introduced old-age pensions for farmers. This is an important innovation, but as yet only small proportion of areas deemed capable of financing such schemes have introduced them. Pension provided by such schemes cover only a part of subsistence. The introduction of such schemes seem to depend entirely on local initiative, there is as yet no mechanism to ensure that all areas capable of supporting on old-age pension schemes in fact have them (for details see Hussain and Liu 1989, Introduction and sec. 1).

In recent years *wubao* relief has come under strain from two sources. Prior to the reforms, it was organized at the level of the village (production team) and was intertwined with collective cultivation. There is evidence that, following the introduction of the responsibility system, it has been neglected or has broken down completely in some rural areas (for examples see, World Bank 1985, 30, 92-93 and 164; Bernstein 1985; Hussain and Liu 1989, sec. 3). There is a trend towards the township government taking over the responsibility for *wubao* relief, which in the future may become a norm for the whole of the countryside and provide the basis for a formalization of the system. Associated with this trend are attempts at diversifying the sources of funds for *wubao* relief. Contributions from beneficiaries or their relatives and from village and township enterprises have increased in importance. In some poor areas *wubao* relief is entirely financed by the Ministry of Civil Affairs, which is increasingly assuming the role of the Ministry of Rural Social Security. There are discussions of extending the scope of *wubao* to include the non-indigent elderly and running the schemes as semi-contributory old-age pension schemes. This is feasible in prosperous areas but the main problem is an almost complete absence of persons with training in how to run a pension scheme.

The second source of strain is the changing age-structure of the population and the birth control policy. As pointed out earlier, the percentage of the elderly in the population has been increasing. Added to that, the percentage of the elderly is higher in the rural than in the urban areas (Hussain and Liu 1989, sec. 4, 2). The discrepancy between rural and urban areas is likely to increase with the increase in migration from the countryside, consisting mostly of the young. This raises the doubt whether the *wubao* system, informally organized as it is, would be able to cope with the mounting burden implied by the demographic trend. The *wubao* support is used to persuade couples to forego children. Yet, as presently organized, it does not have much power of persuasion. On the contrary, it provides an incentive to breach the one-child policy. For it is strictly restricted to the elderly without children or near relatives to depend on.

In most areas, *wubao* is still designed more towards preventing the 'non-deserving' elderly from claiming relief than ensuring that all the 'deserving' elderly in fact get relief. For example, the property of *wubao* recipients is inherited by the collective not by their relatives. Rural authorities police to prevent families from transferring the burden of supporting their elderly to the collective. And *wubao* is projected as no more than a safety net against destitution. For couples of child-bearing age, *wubao* is an inferior alternative to having a son who would support them in old-age. The general point is that a scheme which is expressly designed for the elderly without relatives cannot appeal to the couples who have the option of depending on their children in old age. This is increasingly realised in China, and the concern to decrease the rural birth rates is the main source of pressure for an improvement in public support for the elderly in rural areas. There are some attempts at formalizing *wubao* support. For example, 17 out of 29 provinces has promulgated regulations concerning *wubao* relief (SBB 7 March 1989). The principal weakness of the system is the high proportion of people entitled to relief not receiving relief. It is said that up to ten per cent entitled to relief do not receive it. In fact, the proportion would be much higher if one included the elderly who, although poor, do not claim relief because of social stigma.

The system of old-age support in rural China is in a state of flux. A tripartite system of old-age support seems to be emerging. Rich rural areas, usually with well-developed rural industry, have enough financial resources to establish an universal old-age pension system. As yet labour insurance regulations do not apply to industries below the county. An extension of labour insurance to rural industry would automatically provide a large proportion of the population in such areas with old-age pensions. In areas of average prosperity, the trend is towards improving both the level and the range of *wubao* relief. In poor areas there is a problem because local financial resources are not enough to establish a system of relief for all those who qualify. In some cases, but not all, the Ministry of Civil Affairs has established heavily subsidized pilot schemes. The Chinese literature is full of accounts of local experiments in improving old-age support, but as yet beyond persuasion there is no mechanism to ensure that successful schemes are adopted in other areas. A wide variation in the standards of old-age support is inevitable; thus the main problem is not so much variation as the boundary between levels of support guaranteed to all, and what is left to vary with local conditions.

Aid to Poor Regions

A refreshing aspect of the economic reforms is that the leadership has been candid in admitting the extent of poverty in China. In 1985 Deng Xiaoping admitted that around 100 million people or about ten per cent of the total population still did not have enough to eat or wear (BR 1985:5). In 1986 the government set up 'The Leading Group Office for Economic Development of Poor Areas' under the State Council. The group is responsible for coordinating policy towards poor areas and has organizations reaching down to the township level. Each province is supposed to have a similar group with the Vice-Governor of the province as the head. It may seem surprising that despite China's comparative success preventing the incidence of abject rural poverty and the concern of successive leadership with the problem of poverty, the establishment of the group is the first concerted attempt to eliminate poverty, combining relief and development assistance. The goal was to provide by 1990 adequate food and clothing to the 90 per cent of those who lack these presently. Rather than go into the details of what the Leading Group has done and its plans for the near future, let me look at the some of the estimates of rural poverty provided by the Group.

A coherent anti-poverty programme presupposes a reliable estimate of goods or income for adequate subsistence. Currently, a per capita income of 200 - 150 yuan per annum denotes poverty and a per capita income below 150 yuan signifies dire poverty: not having enough to eat or wear. The figures for income distribution provided by the Leading Group Office are as follows:

Table 3. Per Capita Income Distribution in Rural Areas (per cent)

Group	1978	1980	1983	1984	1985	1986	1987
Above 500 yuan	2.4	9.0	18.2	22.3	28.7	35.5	
300-500 yuan	-	11.5	34.5	38.6	39.8	38.2	38.55
200-300 yuan	15.0	25.3	32.9	29.2	25.6	21.8	17.51
150-200 yuan	17.6	27.1	13.1	9.4	7.9	7.0	4.99
Below 150 yuan	65.0	34.4	7.6	4.6	4.4	4.3	3.25

Although this distribution is a considerable improvement over the headcount of the number of poor, it suffers from some serious defects. It seems highly implausible that the same poverty bands apply to the whole of China. As the pattern of consumption and the price level vary widely, one would expect the bands to vary from area to area. Leaving aside regional variations, how these bands have been arrived at is not stated in the Chinese literature. The per capita annual income of 200 yuan is selected because it was about 50 per cent of average rural income in 1985. Apart from these, there are formidable problems in measuring the money equivalent of incomes in rural areas, as a large proportion of what is consumed consists of non-marketed goods. These are technical problems, but their solution is central to an anti-poverty policy. Taking 200 yuan as the poverty line, the above figures imply that in 1987 8.24 per cent of the rural population lived in poverty. Given that the rural population in 1987 was around 577 million, the total of the rural poor comes around 48.5 million.

Turning from the numbers of the rural poor to poor regions, in 1988, out of the total

1936 counties, 679 were classified as poor and received some form of national or provincial support. These counties are further sub-divided as follows: (1) Extremely poor: 326 (48 per cent); (2) poor: 319 (47 per cent); (3) borderline: 34 (5 per cent).

Of the 679 poor counties, 273 (40 per cent) are in the so-called *sanxi* region in the North-West, and the rest are distributed all over the country, including the relatively prosperous provinces along the eastern seaboard. This suggests that rural poverty is not confined to the North-West and the South-West as it is normally projected in China.

The interesting point is that the percentage of poor counties in the total is 35 per cent, which is surprisingly high in comparison to the percentage of the poor in the rural population. If 35 per cent of the counties are in fact poor, then the percentage of the poor in the rural population ought to be much higher than 8.24 implied by the income distribution figures. At the moment I do not have the answer to the puzzle. This reinforces the point made earlier: although the incidence of rural poverty *prima facie* seems to be lower in China than in, for example, India, the extent of rural poverty has yet to be fully fathomed.

The success of anti-poverty programmes in China is almost exclusively measured in terms of the numbers crossing the poverty line. This index of success automatically biases anti-poverty programmes towards households or areas near the poverty line, as that will show a much higher success rate, than programmes directed towards the very poor who are far away from the poverty line. Moreover, this index does not distinguish between the temporarily poor and permanently poor. In fact, the index would show an improvement even if anti-poverty programmes do nothing for the poor because left to themselves the temporarily poor would sooner or later cross the poverty line. The implication is that apart from a more reliable estimate of poverty, anti-poverty programmes in China also need a more discriminating index of success.

Public Provision for Health in Rural Areas

Aside from providing access to land to the rural population, the extension of health care to a vast majority of the rural population has been a major achievement of the Chinese economy in the field of social security. Thanks to the emphasis on public hygiene and preventive care on the one hand, and the provision of primary medical care at the grass roots level on the other, China managed to reduce drastically, if not eliminate, the incidence of common parasitic and infectious diseases. A testimony of their success is provided by the massive national mortality survey of 1973 - 1975, which revealed that the cause pattern of mortality in China was closer to that of middle-income than of low-income economies, where parasitic and infectious diseases rank high among the causes of death (on the details of the mortality survey, see Banister 1987, 96-98). Much of this success was due to health campaigns, which were similar to campaigns in others fields such as those for investment in infrastructure or politics. All involved a massive mobilization of the population through a mixture of propaganda and coercion, which the collective rural economy facilitated. From an economic point of view, their main feature was their very low financial cost, because labour was in most cases not remunerated at all, or at very low rates when it occasionally was.

The decollectivization of the rural economy has, as it were, weakened the social immune system (for an account see Endicott 1988, ch. 12). For example schistosomiasis, which was eradicated by the 1970s, has now reappeard, and the percentage of inoculated infants decreased in the 1980s. Health campaigns have continued, but they neither have the same appeal nor the same effect as they did in the pre-reform period. The economics of campaigns has changed radically. With the shift to household economy, the opportunity cost of labour to rural household has increased; they are neither willing nor can be easily coerced into performing free or low-paid labour for wider social ends as they did before. The basic problem is that campaigns can no longer be sustained by propaganda alone, they require an adequate remuneration of labour for their success. The maintenance of preventive health care and public hygiene in rural areas requires a system of public finance which has been slow in developing. The government has taken a few steps to arrest the decline in preventive health care. For example, alarmed by the evidence of rise in infant mortality (for a discussion see Hussain and Stern 1988), the government in conjunction with UNICEF has now embarked on a national plan to achieve inoculation of at least 90 per cent infants by 1991.

A major achievement of the period of the Cultural Revolution (1966 - 1976) was the extension of primary medical care to villages. This involved dispatching medical personnel from cities and county towns to villages, the establishment of village health stations, training a huge number of paramedics - 'barefoot doctors' and part time medical personnel - and developing cooperative health insurance in villages. The policy was a success because it addressed the two issues central to the provision of primary medical care in rural areas of developing economies. The first is how to train medical personnel in sufficient numbers and, more important, to deploy them in the countryside. The second is how to finance medical care. The barefoot doctors, who became famous throughout the world, were the main medical personnel at the village level. They were rural residents with elementary medical training, which was short, focused on a few tasks and did not presuppose a high level of education. They worked part- or full-time aided by medical workers whom they trained. They dispensed basic primary health care, referred patients with severe illnesses to commune and county hospitals. Notwithstanding their name they did wear shoes, especially when performing medical tasks. The use of paramedics for primary health care is not novel to China; earlier on the Soviet Union too relied on paramedics (known as feldshers) for the same purpose. China's main achievement was training a very large number within a very short period of time. For example, in 1979 there were around two barefoot doctors per 1,000 inhabitants. This had its negative side too in that their level of training was highly variable, and many of them were entrusted with tasks well beyond their competence (see Chen 1989, part 2). Further, barefoot doctors could not be the permanent mainstay of primary health care in rural areas. For their training, elementary and narrowly focused as it was, ran the risk of being made obsolete by the success in improving public hygiene and eliminating parasitic and infectious diseases.

Starting from 1965 there was a concerted attempt to develop cooperative health insurance in the countryside. On the eve of decollectivization in 1979, around 80 per cent of production brigades (the middle tier of the commune, now termed villages), or about 85 per cent of the rural population had some form of health insurance system - an unparalleled achievement for a large developing economy (see World Bank 1984). Brigade members paid an annual fee in return for the reimbursement of outpatient and hospital costs, including medicines. The extent of coverage varied widely. Contributions from brigade members only covered a part of the costs, villages (production teams and production brigades) paid the rest from collective funds. The cooperative health insurance system was founded on collective agriculture, and together with barefoot doctors it came to be closely identified with the discredited period of the Cultural Revolution. Thus it seems that the leadership made no attempt to retain the system as land was parcelled out to households. As a result, in 1985 the rural health insurance system survived in a mere five per cent of brigades or villages as compared to 80 per cent in 1979 (Shao 1988). The rural health insurance system did suffer from some major defects, but its almost total disappearance is due in large measure to its wilful neglect by the leadership.

The responsibility system has had a debilitating effect on the rural heath care system. Not only has health insurance been replaced with payment according to health care, including the inoculation of children, but there has also been a massive decrease in medical personnel in rural areas (for details see Hussain and Stern 1988). The government has decontrolled drug production without developing an effective system to monitor quality (see Chen 1989, part 2). Many village health stations are left unattended because of the lack of personnel. The main reason for the decline in the number of personnel is financial. Subsidies for health care from collective funds have decreased. And the government tried to keep medical fees under a tight control, while rural incomes were rising. As a result, many barefoot doctors and other part-time medical personnel have found it more profitable to engage in non-medical pursuits.

Nevertheless, there have been some attempts to develop an alternative health care system for rural areas. Following Deng Xiaoping's advice that barefoot doctors should start wearing straw sandals, if not leather shoes, a proportion of them have acquired further medical training and been upgraded to the status of 'rural doctors' who work full time. In fact, the term 'barefoot doctors' is no longer used. Further, the Ministry of Public Health has introduced pilot rural insurance schemes in a number of villages (for details, see Shao 1988; Ron, Abel-Smith and Tamburi 1990, 93-108). However, the cost per head of these schemes is much higher than that of previous schemes. While such schemes may be applicable to richer rural areas, their introduction in poorer areas would depend crucially on subsidies from the government. Given the pressure on the government to keep its expenditure on a tight rein, comprehensive health insurance in poorer areas is a distant possibility. But one may well witness a rapid spread of health insurance in richer areas.

Conclusions

Although China has been comparatively successful in preventing deprivation in rural areas, formal social security programmes are sparse, and ill-coordinated. The rural social security system is tiered consisting of programmes founded upon local finance and initiative, on the one hand, and government programmes to cater for specific contingencies such as natural disasters. On the other hand there is not one but a number of separate safety nets, but it seems that they leave wide gaps letting particular categories of the rural poor to slip through. The main problem with local programmes such as *wubao* is huge variation in the standards of provision and coverage. The variation is due partly to differences in per capita income and thus to funds available to support such programmes. But there are also wide variations in areas with similar per capita income. What local programmes need is a national framework specifying the minimum obligations of local communities, the rights of recipients and the sources of funds. The Civil Affairs bureaux monitor local programmes but they neither have the power nor finances to ensure that some minimum standards are met.

The post-Mao leadership has been candid in admitting that there is still a sizeable problem of poverty in rural areas, and seems serious about formulating a concerted policy to eliminate rural poverty. Until recently the assumption has been that rapid growth would solve the problems of rural poverty. The experience of other countries shows that economic growth by itself is not sufficient to solve the problem of poverty. The solution of the problem requires specific policies directed towards that end. But as pointed out earlier that technical preconditions for such a policy are still not there. Apart from that there is also the problem of financing an anti-poverty programme. Given the budgetary situation at present, it is not obvious that the government is able to finance a comprehensive anti-poverty programme.

A fundamental problem with the rural social security system is that despite the radical changes in the wake of the economic reforms, the system still remains tied to the pre-reform distinctions. Even though in recent years rural industry has developed very rapidly and a majority of the labour force in some rural areas is employed in non-agricultural activities there has been no systematic attempt to develop a labour insurance system for rural industry. Although population migration has increased very sharply, there has as yet been no attempt to take into account the implications of migration for social welfare. For example, migration from the countryside, which consists mainly of the young, is likely to increase the proportion of the elderly in the rural population. Temporary migrants from rural areas to cities also pose a huge potential problem. According to a government estimate there are 50 million of them. Sending them back to the countryside when they are no longer needed solves the problem of unemployment and destitution in urban areas, but there has been little or no discussion of the problem their return creates in the countryside. Apart from rural to urban migration there is now also a great deal of migration within rural areas.

Unemployment is no longer a purely urban phenomenon, there is now a problem of unemployment in rural areas which is likely to increase over time. In the wake of the reforms, there has been within rural areas a massive shift of the labour force from farming to other activities. In particular, recent years have witnessed an explosive growth of rural industry—the township and village enterprises. This shift has a particular significance for the incidence of unemployment in rural areas, because whilst self-employment is almost a universal norm in farming, formal employment is prevalent in the non-farming sector. The sectoral shift in the rural labour force creates a potential problem of unemployment in that the employed can be laid off. In fact, this has already happened. The curb on investment in township and village industries imposed since autumn 1988 has led to redundancies on a large scale.

The general implication is that employment guarantee for just the labour force with urban registration is increasingly insufficient for maintaining a low rate of unemployment in the economy as a whole. And providing the agricultural labour force with land is no longer adequate to provide means for earning a living to the whole of the rural labour force, which also includes the labour force in the non-farm sector. In fact, households which opt out of farming altogether, termed 'specialized households' surrender their claim to agricultural land. It is not easy for them to revert to farming when they cannot make a living out of their non-farming activities. China needs extensive employment schemes in rural areas and also special provisions for rural immigrants in cities if it is to maintain the level of economic security its citizens enjoyed in the past.

Bibliography

Note: For an annotated bibliography of the Chinese literature on social security, see Hussain and Liu (1989).

AYB (1986): *China Agricultural Yearbook 1986*. Beijing: Agricultural Publishing House, 1987.

Banister (1987): J. Banister, *China's Changing Population*. Stanford: Stanford University Press.

Bernstein (1985): T. Bernstein, 'Reforming Chinese Agriculture'. *The China Business Review*, March - April: 45-49.

BR: *Beijing Review*. Beijing.

Chen (1989): C. C. Chen, *Medicine in Rural China*. Berkeley: University of California Press.

Croll (1982): E. Croll, *The Family Rice Bowl*. London: Zed Press.

Endicott (1988): S. Endicott, *Red Earth: Revolution in a Sichuan Village*. London: I. B. Tauris.

Feuchtwang and Hussain(1988): S. Feuchtwang and A. Hussain, 'The People's Livelihood and the Incidence of Poverty'. In S. Feuchtwang et al. (eds), *Transforming China's Economy in the Eighties*. London: Zed Press, vol. 1, 36-76.

Hussain and Liu (1989): A. Hussain and Liu Hong, 'Compendium of Literature on the Chinese Social Security System'. *China Programme, Research Working Papers*, No 3, STICERD, London School of Economics.

Hussain and Stern (1989): A. Hussain and N. Stern, 'On the Recent Increase in Death Rates in China'. *China Programme, Research Working Papers*, No. 6, STICERD, London School of Economics.

NTN: *Nongcun Tongji Nianjian*. Beijing: Zhongguo Tongji Chubanshe.

Parish and Whyte (1978): W. L. Parish and M. K. Whyte, *Village and Family in Contemporary China*. Chicago: The University of Chicago Press.

Perkins and Yusuf (1984): D. Perkins and S. Yusuf, *Rural Development in China*. Baltimore: The Johns Hopkins University Press.

Ron, Abel-Smith and Tamburi (1990): A. Ron, B. Abel-Smith and G. Tamburi, *Health Insurance in Developing Countries*. Geneva, International Labour Office.

SBB: *Shehui Baozhang Bao*. Beijing.

Shao (1988): Shao Yinong, *Health Care in China*. London: Office of Health Economics.

Sicular (1988): T. Sicular, 'Plan and Market in China's Agricultural Commerce.' *Journal of Political Economy*, No. 2, 283-307.

SYB: *Statistical Year Book of China*. Beijing: State Statistical Bureau.

World Bank (1983): *Socialist Economic Development*, Vols 1 and 2. Washington D.C.: World Bank.

World Bank (1984): *China: The Health Sector*. Washington D.C.: World Bank.

World Bank (1985): *China: Long-Term Development Issues and Options*. Washington D.C.: World Bank.

YRSES 1986: *Yearbook of Rural Social and Economic Statistics 1986*. Beijing: State Statistical Bureau.

ZTN 1988: *Zhongguo Tongji Nianjian 1988*. Beijing: Zhongguo Tongji Chubanshe.

Zweig (1989): D. Zweig, *Agrarian Radicalism in China 1968-1981*. Cambridge Mass.: Harvard University Press.

THE FRAMEWORK
OF RESOURCE DEVELOPMENT:
LAND AND WATER

Land Reclamation in the Hills and Along the Coast of Fujian: Recent History and Present Situation

Eduard B. Vermeer

Introduction

The mountainous province of Fujian (Fukien) has known a shortage of farmland for several centuries. Its four small river deltas can produce only a limited supply of foodgrain. Yet, between 1750 and 1850, its population doubled to about 15 million. Because of population pressure, many Fujianese migrated to Southeast Asia and the virgin territories of Taiwan. Many of those who went into overseas trade, shipping, fishery, or mining, eventually returned home. These entrepreneurs and migrant labourers provided their native villages and towns with capital, know-how and foreign economic ties, and the mobility of labour and capital in coastal Fujian may have been unique for China. The mountain regions of Northwest Fujian had seen a rapid development of exploitation of the slopes and valleys for the cultivation of tea, in response to European demand. After 1900, however, the demand for, and production of Fujianese teas declined. Hit by the loss of Taiwan in 1895, the civil wars of the 1930s and the Japanese invasion, the economy declined and by 1949 the population had again gone down to about 12 million.

From the history of the province we can see that various options were open to government and private persons to generate local income and employment to alleviate the lack of farmland: (a) crop specialization; this presupposed a market for the agricultural produce, and cheap transport; (b) diversification of rural production, leading to greater value added to crops and industrial products. This would depend on know-how and capital, and a secure supply of raw materials; (c) expansion of the cultivated area. In mountain areas, building of terraces was required for rice cultivation, but many other crops could be cultivated on sloping land; (d) intensification of agricultural production, in order to achieve higher yields. Increased inputs of labour and fertilizer, improvement of water supply, and the use of superior varieties were the major means of raising unit yields; (e) leaving agriculture for other occupations, such as trade or for other relations. The relative income in agriculture versus other economic sectors was a most important factor in this decision. The push and pull for emigration, whether temporary or permanent, varied greatly over time. Apart from income opportunities, the organizational and financial capacities of the Chinese clans and families, and the receptiveness of foreign countries were major factors.

Thus, the creation of new farmland (point c above) was one out of several options. Yet, after 1949 land reclamation became a major area of government and village activity. In this article, I will elaborate on both positive and negative factors contributing to land reclamation. They were: (a) demographic factors (a rapid, wave-like growth of the rural population, reduction of emigration); (b) economic factors (a loss of alternative income opportunities in trade, loss of farmland to other uses, a quota and price system which favoured food grain crops over commercial crops, improved transportation); (c) socio-economic factors (the forceful organization of bonded peasantry in collectives under central leadership, the need to create employment for rural and urban youths); (d) technical factors (the introduction of earth-moving equipment, pumping machinery and new crop varieties, improved know-how); and (e) political factors (local government and party wishing to play a dominant role in large-scale mobilization of labour and exploitation of resources, preference for self-reliance and autarchy, allocation of government funds, tax measures).

However, in many cases these factors were intertwined or even indistinct. The over one hundred state farms in Fujian, which were set up as nuclei of modern socialist development, were meant to provide employment, reclaim wasteland, supply products to the state, popularize techniques and to provide some services to the villages. Thus, they combined many functions.

In the 1980s, in China as elsewhere, conservation of water and soil has become a most important political consideration. In a situation where the demands on land are still growing, and government and farmers have obtained the means for a ruthless exploitation of natural resources, legislation and education leading to a more careful use of land are imperative. The reduction of government control of the economy and society in the 1980s has not made this task any easier. The successes and failures of the Chinese government in the conservation and management of land resources must be an important yardstick in the evaluation of its past and present rural policies.

In the following history of half a century of land reclamation in Fujian, I will first discuss some of the factors mentioned above. Subsequently, I will go into the scope, organization, financing, methods, and economic results of land reclamation and the possibilities for future development. Some indications will be given of its environmental effects. While most of the first half is based on written source materials, the second half depends heavily on two field studies of eight counties in the south of Fujian, which I conducted in 1986 and 1987. The assistance of the Fujian Provincial State Farm and Land Reclamation Bureau, the Fujian Provincial Agricultural Bureau, and many local bureaus of agriculture and water and soil conservation is much appreciated.

Factors Contributing to Land Reclamation

Population Pressure and Grain Shortage
Population pressure in Fujian had varied according to place and time, but after 1949 it became very pronounced. The traditional outlet of overseas emigration was affected by the occupation of Taiwan by Japan in 1895, and in 1938 through 1945 by the Japanese occupation of the coast. Under the policies of the People's Republic, opportunities for trade and employment overseas, and emigration, were much reduced. There even was a roll-back, when around 1960 thousands of refugees from Indonesia had to be resettled (Yongchun 1984).

The traditional migration to the cities was reversed after the institution of the collective framework of the People's Commune. In the post-Leap crisis, Fujian's urban population dropped from 3.3 million in 1960 to 2.3 million in 1963 (FJN 1987, 33). In the period 1966-

1976, almost 20,000 urban youths were sent, more or less permanently, to rural areas, and they often engaged in farmland capital construction. Most of them managed to return to the cities in the years 1977-1980 (Zhang Linchi 1986, 64-69). Under the collective system, the peasant was tied to the soil of his village, and opportunities for work outside became rare. Between 1950 and 1982 Fujian's population more than doubled (urban 118 per cent, rural 97 per cent increase) because of a declining death rate and high birth rates, particularly in 1955 through 1958 and in the decade 1963 to 1973. Almost all new employment had to be created within the village, and within agriculture. Around 1985, 86 per cent of Fujian's population was still rural, a percentage which, in spite of industrialization, had hardly changed from the mid-1950s and mid-1960s. Of the rural labour force in 1985, 22 per cent was considered superfluous; in mountain areas, the figure was nine per cent higher than in the plains (Lai Shishuang and Lai Shiping 1988).

A permanent local shortage of foodgrain had made it necessary to import grain over sea, and cultivate tubers. Around 1890, 'all villages along the coast had ships going to Taiwan; at least 600 to 700 grain ships went there each year to fetch grain for Quanzhou. After Taiwan was cut off, the sailors lost their employment and there was a danger of famine. Subsequently, sweet potatoes became the easiest substitute for grain' (Wu Zeng 1937, 10-12). In the 1930s, rice imports averaged 75,000 tons (polished) per year, or five per cent of local production (Zhen Mingzhang 1943). After 1937, rice production declined by some ten per cent, possibly because of a decrease of rural labour during the war (Zhen Taoying 1946, 213-226).

Statistics on farmland and foodgrain output in Fujian Province since 1949 show a marked increase of unit yields; however, foodgrain output did not always keep up with population growth (see table 1).

Table 1. Fujian Province: Cultivated Area, Population, and Foodgrain Output, 1956 - 1986

Year	Farmland (1,000 ha)	Population (1,000)	Farmland % (ha)	Grain output (1,000 tons)	Output % (kg)
1956	1,488	14,004	0.106	4,435	317
1966	1,321	18,137	0.073	4,500	248
1971	1,309	21,061	0.062	5,855	278
1976	1,303	23,619	0.055	6,000	254
1980	1,291	25,178	0.051	8,020	318
1986	1,250	27,493	0.045	7,510	273

Source: FJN 1987, 76

Over the years 1953 through 1986, net imports of grain totalled six million tons, two million of which were in the years 1981 through 1984 (Zhen Guojin 1987). In the past decade, foodgrain output first went up, to 8.6 million tons in 1983 and again in 1984, but fell again subsequently. As a consequence, imports had to be increased. In 1987, state commercial organizations sold (net) 2.5 million tons of foodgrain in Fujian, but their local purchases only amounted to 1.6 million tons; the difference (apart from an unknown change in stocks) was made up by domestic and foreign imports (Ministry of Commerce 1988, 578-597). A similar shortage of 875,000 tons is expected for 1990; in the year 2,000, it might increase to 1.5 million tons (Yu Xuemao 1988). The grain situation is getting worse, because of a decrease of sown area, reduced investments, higher costs of inputs, and a deterioration of irrigation facilities (Zhen Guojin 1987). Because of the ideologically and bureaucratically motivated policy of self-reliance, over the past decades there has been and there still is a continuous pressure on local authorities and peasants to increase grain production by all means - one of them being reclamation of land for grain cultivation.

Yet, for a variety of reasons, Fujian has registered a net decrease of farmland by an average of 0.5 per cent per year (see Table I). The loss of farmland to other uses, such as housing, has been recognized as a nationwide problem for many years. Since 1949, China has lost about half a million ha. of farmland every year, through erosion, desertification, roads and other infrastructure, use for housing and industry et cetera. Recently, some farmland has been converted to orchards, fish ponds, or pastures (statistically, this is loss of farmland, too).

In 1986, out of a reported provincial total of 12,000 ha. of lost farmland, only 4,200 ha. had been lost to housing and construction; 5,300 ha. had been converted to fruit trees, 1,300 ha. to fish ponds and 840 ha. to forestry, tea, or pastures (FJN ,1987). Thus, farmland losses are less dramatic than they might seem, except from the perspective of grain production. Of course, in per capita terms, since 1949 the reduction of available farmland has been dramatic.

Regrettably, few statistics are collected about losses of mountain land originally planted to tea, fruit and other trees. This has been a most serious phenomenon in Fujian. Generally, only net changes in total agricultural area are reported at the county level, and there is no easy link with statistics and reports about water and soil conservation. Thus, it becomes difficult or even impossible to compare the gains and losses of land reclamation.

Reduced Sources of Capital Investment
During the Song and Yuan dynasties, capital from commercial sources had greatly contributed to the development of coastal land reclamation. During the Qing dynasty, much local and outside capital had been invested in tea plantations in mountain areas. Merchant families diverted their wealth gained from overseas trade to agricultural undertakings and local welfare. Under the People's Republic, private capital was confiscated. The sources for investments at a level higher than the household were limited to loans from state controlled banks and credit coops, state budgetary allocations, and allocations by the rural collectives. Undoubtedly, the collective system was conducive to the undertaking of and investment in comparatively large-scale local projects of agricultural capital construction, because investment decisions were taken by village leaders instead of by individual peasants. However, around 1980 a pent-up demand for consumptive spending was released after the introduction of the household responsibility system, as almost all collective controls over agricultural production and household consumption were abolished. The capital accumulation rate of peasant households rose, from a low of 7.9 per cent in 1980, to a high of 16.4 per cent in 1981, but thereafter it stabilized at about ten to 11 per cent of net income (Zhou

Jinfei 1987). Of total accumulated funds, the percentage used for productive purposes dropped dramatically, from 48.2 per cent in 1981 to 18.7 per cent in 1987 (Huang and Su 1989).

State budgetary investments in agriculture, forestry, and water conservation in Fujian Province reached their highest levels in the years 1979 and 1980, with investments of 163 million yuan and 153 million yuan, respectively. Thereafter, they declined to about 80 million yuan per year in 1982 through 1984. Only for water conservation did the state budget continue to be a major source of funding; agriculture and forestry now had to pay their own. Of the 1984 total, 30 million yuan went to agriculture and water conservation each, and 14 million yuan went to forestry. In the 1986 budget, investments in water conservation still amounted to 39 million, but only eight million yuan was put into agriculture and forestry each (FJN 1987, 497, 506, 886).

The coastal areas of Fujian have been exceptional because of their continued ties with overseas Chinese investors, who also might be big spenders in their local community. Some counties now claim that half of their population resides (more or less temporarily) in foreign countries. In reality, no more than ten or twenty per cent of the labour force of coastal villages in South Fujian were working overseas,[1] and since then the number has fallen considerably. Even so, Fujian's present six million or so Overseas Chinese have been able and willing to remit considerable amounts of money to their families in their native villages, and since 1980 overseas Chinese have been allowed, and even encouraged, to invest directly themselves, and on some scale.

Markets and Infrastructure

Over the centuries, a sophisticated trade network evolved within Fujian, and between Fujian and other provinces as well as with foreign countries on the basis of water transport. Today, the main access to Fujian is still by sea. Fujian has more than 100 bays, which provide natural harbours. During the Qing, the conquest of Taiwan and the huge European demand for tea gave new impulses to trade. Tea, paper and timber were the major export items of the mountain areas in the Minjiang basin (Dai Yifeng 1988).

However, land and river routes in Fujian have been difficult to develop. Apart from Fuzhou, its natural harbours have only very small river basins as hinterlands. Both hills and mountains are generally steep and eroded, and the mountain area spreads over hundreds of miles. Roads follow the river courses, and only close to the coast do they connect Fujian's four major alluvial deltas. Because of the monsoon climate, the rivers have an irregular flow which supports little transport. Furthermore, trade and investments in Fujian suffered from the continued separation of Taiwan under the People's Republic. It seems that the perceived threat of attacks or invasion made the Communist government decide not to invest in large-scale development of Fujian's infrastructure or industries. There still is only one, non-electrified, railway which connects Fujian with the rest of China.

The lack of commercial opportunities and of access to raw materials, which have been the result of this underdeveloped infrastructure of inland Fujian, may be considered to be the main cause of the past slow, small-scale exploitation of its mountain resources, e.g. its forests. Major commercial mountain crops, such as fruit, could only be grown profitably after dramatic price rises in recent years. Fruit and timber prices have been going up by 20 per cent or more during the past few years. Both production and exports of tea have doubled between 1978 and 1988, to 55,000 tons and 35 million US dollars.[2] The high cost of transportation is now paid by the consumer.

The more favourable commercial situation for the farmers in mountain areas, which stimulated reclamation of wasteland and planting tea and trees, has only ncreased efficiency.

Decentralisation is subject to overall planning: rural irrigation work is planned at the higher, county, level; water allocation to the farms is subject to overall plan. Also, some features of the former communes, like 'labour accumulation' and integrated use of funds for simultaneous development of industry and agriculture, have been retained, but with a large latitude for variations according to local circumstances.

A study of irrigation management has to include many dimensions: socio-economic planning, engineering, environment, development administration, legal framework etc; all these aspects have to be viewed in the context of scarcity of water as projected in long-term requirements. This modest note focusses only on irrigation water delivery in the context of the economic responsibility system. Some basic data and information are hard to come by: for instance, country-wide data on collective sector's fiscal operations and on 'labour accumulation'; sufficiently illustrative judicial decisions on contracts. Some broad indications of a qualitative nature are presented below on the aspects of decentralisation.

Management

Irrigation District
Irrihowever, was commercialization of labour. Labour had been very cheap, and at almost free disposal to county and commune authorities. Labour costs in the coastal areas are incomparably higher now, and organizing it is more difficult. Demands for economic results and return on investment have been raised.

New Crops
Experience with a wide range of (sub)tropical crops was a precious asset obtained through the Fujianese overseas trading activities and the return of so many people who had lived in Southeast Asia. New World crops such as potatoes and tobacco found an early way into China through the Fujianese, who brought the new crops from the Philippines and later also from Taiwan (Lin Gengsheng 1982). In the first half of this century, experimentation with and popularization of new crops were undertaken mainly by returned Overseas Chinese investors, who formed small reclamation companies or experimental farms.

State involvement in the introduction of new crops started in 1935, with the establishment of the Fujian Provincial Agricultural Advancement Office. At that time, the production of vegetables and fruits (mainly longans, citrus, lychees and peaches) was still very modest, comprising only 2.2 per cent and 0.5 per cent of total cultivated area (Dai Dajin 1946, 197-212). At first, this organization concentrated on forestry and tree crops. Every county was required to set up a tree sapling farm and an agricultural promotion station. Eucalyptus, masson pine, tong-oil, and other trees used for a variety of purposes were popularized this way, but the war interrupted the work (Su Qiutao 1983). The war-time proposals and efforts of the Guomindang government stressed increased foodgrain production.

After 1949, there was a renewed emphasis on introduction and popularization of sub-tropical crops. Factors such as reopening of trade, improved transportation, rural safety, educational efforts, and finally effective government organization brought a complete change in the government's impact on and control of agriculture. Collectivization created particularly advantageous conditions for agricultural specialization, popularization and extension work, as well as for the establishment of both small and large-scale experimental farms run by village collectives or local governments. However, contacts with foreign institutions involved in crop breeding were weak because of China's isolated position, and Fujian's links with Southeast Asia were almost severed in the 1960-1980 period. Thus, although the spread of superior local varieties was fast, Fujian did not follow foreign developments in, for example, tangerine and banana breeding (Zhao Zhaobing 1984, 412).

Factors Constraining Land Reclamation

Rural Instability

Most of the factors constraining land reclamation varied more widely, over time, than the contributing factors. We have already referred to the lack of rural safety, and war, which made farmers abandon their land. A 1936 investigation of three coastal counties concluded that: 'Because of disorders, droughts, and soldiers, not only there is nobody willing to undertake farmland reclamation work, but farmland is even being abandoned...Whether reclamation can be profitable, has much to do with law and order' (Zhen Xicheng 1936, 113).

Statistics in 1940 showed that there was as much 'mature wasteland' (meaning abandoned farmland) as virgin wasteland. However, this concerned only government-designated wasteland for reclamation, in 21 counties, its total being almost 10,000 ha. (Fujian Nongkenzhi 1943?). Even after World War II was over, law and order was the prime problem for peasants who had settled in reclamation areas. In North Fujian, Guomindang soldiers plundered the crops of one of the government-supported reclamation districts, which was dissolved as a consequence. As the saying went: 'Army and people cooperate: You grow the crops and I harvest them!' (Wang Qigui 1946).

The Flight of Private Capital and Loss of Expertise

As a result of the war and the communist takeover, many rural entrepreneurs fled or had to retire from business, and the entire economy was severely affected. First in 1949, and again in the late 1950s, the communist government and the People's Communes nationalized or confiscated landholdings belonging to clans or landlords, temple properties and overseas Chinese properties and capital. Almost all mountain fruit farms and many tea farms fell into this category. Many large landholdings became state farms or commune experimentation farms, but in the process of transition to state or collective ownership valuable expertise and capital was lost. The misuse of capital and misguided management appeared most clearly during the Great Leap Forward, when local authorities mobilized the peasantry for large-scale opening up of mountain wasteland. Without proper preparation and economic planning, it became a giant failure, and in 1961 there was starvation in many counties. In 1962, Fujian foodgrain output was lower by one-fifth than in 1957, output of commercial crops had dropped by about one-half, and fruit and sugar cane even by two-thirds (FJN 1985, 82).

Natural Calamities

Rainstorms brought in by the monsoon cause serious damage to crops, properties and even life every few years. The most serious disaster in Fujianese history may have been the floods along the upper reaches of the Minjiang in 1609, when about 100,000 people drowned. In 1948, half a million ha. were flooded in the North, and 2,000 people killed or injured. After 1949, the protective sea and river dikes of Fujian have been greatly strengthened and extended, from 800 kilometers to 1,800 kilometers in 1969 and to 4,500 kilometers in 1984. Yet, in 1962 and again in 1968, about 75,000 ha. of farmland were flooded. After serious floods in 1973, all the dikes of the Jinjiang were raised to 1.5 meters above the historical highest water levels (Dianliju 1960, 5, 35, 84). Since then, continuous silting, man-made obstructions in the river bed, a narrowed river bed because of reclamation of land, and sugar cane cultivation along its banks have again increased vulnerability to floods (FJN 1986, 82-83).

Droughts mainly occur in March to June. In recent decades, the most serious ones were in 1946, 1954, 1957, 1965 and 1971. They extended over several hundreds of thousands of ha. and lasted for three months or more, reducing rice output by several hundreds of thousands tons. Large-scale building of reservoirs and the introduction of electrical pump irrigation since the 1960s have played a major role here. By 1984, 72 per cent of Fujian's cultivated area had irrigation facilities, two-thirds of which had an adequate guarantee against drought (Shuiliju 1985).

Ineffective and Unpredictable Policies, and a Lack of Secure Land Rights

A weak legal protection of land rights has been a major impediment for rational land use in China, both before and after the establishment of the People's Republic. The first official land survey was conducted from 1935 onward, and served taxation and planning purposes. Revisions resulting from it varied widely. As a rule, land taxes were revised upwards. It was only after the adoption of the 'Fujian Provincial Rules for Land Investigation' in 1937, that a strict set of land categories and rules could be applied (Su Zongwen 1937). However, the war made these efforts more difficult. In any case, the government lacked the apparatus to make sure that the rights of public and private land were respected (Lai Jiapan 1940, 7).

In Fujian, an elaborate system of land ownership rights had developed during the Qing. Distinctions were made between temporary and permanent tenancy rights, ownership of the surface, and ownership of the bottom. Part of the land was communal property, or of a dual private-communal character, such as temple land, school land, or it belonged to clans rather than to individuals. Like elsewhere in China on poor and mountain farmland, the availability of agricultural labour was the paramount factor. Therefore, the tenant position was strong. In dry land farming areas along the coast, almost all farmers were owners of their land (Nongye Gaikuang 1942). According to a 1942 survey of several counties in North Fujian, only about ten per cent of the reclaimable wasteland was state property. In Jianyang and Nanping Counties, most wasteland was owned by large landowners, but in four other counties, mostly by small landowners (Wang Qigui 1946). Thus, the degree of land redistribution under the 1950 Land Reform varied a great deal between areas. For the first time in history, Land Reform provided local government with systematic data on land ownership and use.

In the 1950s, all farmland, but also forest, wasteland and water bodies were either nationalized or privatized, and communal rights virtually disappeared. With collectivization, however, most land in use became collective property. In the Great Leap Forward, People's Communes grabbed as many local resources as they could, to the detriment both of the state and of private farmers. There was much felling and reclamation of slopes, and unprecedented damage to the environment. After three years, land ownership was returned to Production Brigades, and its use further delegated to production teams. In mountain areas, it meant that the natural village became the unit of ownership and production.

In the early 1980s, mountain and wasteland were distributed or sold to individual households again, the socalled *ziliushan*. Of the 73 per cent of Fujian's surface which is somewhat euphemistically designated as 'in use for forestry', around 1980 about half (4.5 million ha) was actually forested. 737,000 ha., or 9.4 per cent of the collectively-owned forest area were given to individual households, 1,910,000 ha. were contracted for by specialized households, 700,000 ha. remained under village collective enterprises, and 1,300,000 ha. were contracted for by forestry share companies. The state continued to manage its 110 state forestry farms (Ministry of Forestry 1987, 424). Thus, a variety of ownership forms has been recreated, and the previous system of overlapping and diffuse authority abolished. Even so, under the new laws, uncertainty and imprecise rules continue to exist, because government planning or (sometimes contradictory) policies may also take the place of law.

Each time during the past decades that ownership rights were changed, the resulting insecurity with the old and new owners would lead them to try and make a maximal profit within the shortest possible time. For long-term investment in land improvement and conservation of resources, a stable legal and political climate is vital. In the past 50 years, the upheavals of World War II, Land Reform, the Great Leap Forward, the Cultural Revolution, and decollectivization have all had extremely negative effects on proper land use.

Policies and Organization During the People's Republic

The Early Years
For the first few years after the communist takeover, there was no policy on reclamation of farmland. The concentration of army units along the Taiwan strait must have had some impact, but we lack all data. On the basis of the Land Reform Law of 1950, large landholdings were distributed, and communal land rights were privatized. Large tracts of mountain land, forests or wasteland were declared closed by communist authorities, for reasons of protection of resources (mainly against wanton felling of trees) or for military control. However, the peasants in the vicinity might still be allowed to cut grass and gather fuel.[3]

During this period, most localities concentrated on recovery of farmland which had gone to waste during the war years. According to an investigation conducted in eight different communities *(xiang)* in Fujian, agricultural production could be raised, firstly, by achieving higher unit yields, secondly, by multicropping, thirdly, by large-scale development of wasteland in mountain areas, much of which consisted of abandoned farmland. Between 1950 and 1954, however, the farmland area only increased by 2.3 per cent, and there still was some wasteland left (Ministry of Finance 1957).

In wasteland areas, reclamation farms were founded for and by demobilized soldiers and inmates of reform through labour camps. Most of the camps were dissolved in 1956, and their labour was replaced by rural youths. In the same year, the establishment of collectives, the Higher Agricultural Producers' Cooperatives, made it possible for villages to create specialized labour teams for development of wasteland, planting trees, water conservation projects and the like. Thus, from that year, not only the state farm system, but also capital construction on collective farmland received a boost. In Fujian a total of 98 state farms were founded between 1951 and 1958, and the existing seven state farms founded during the war were expanded. Most of these farms were located in hilly areas, some 15 in the mountains, and about 20 along the coast. Eight of the coastal farms were engaged in reclamation of coastal silt flats, and the other ones in animal husbandry and in fixing a 50,000 ha. sand and dune area through afforestation and other means (Lian Yuqing 1986). Most of these farms were located on poor soils, and lack of fertilizer made it difficult to improve soils and raise yields.

Large-Scale Irrigation Projects in the 1950s
After 1956, soils and yields in many newly reclaimed areas could be improved because of irrigation. Investments in water conservation went up rapidly, with the lion's share provided by the agricultural collectives in the form of labour. The state which had invested about four million yuan per year in the mid-1950s, increased its investment to ten million yuan in 1957, 24 million yuan in 1958, 35 million yuan in 1959 and 55 million yuan (planned) in 1960. This was the 'high tide of water conservancy construction'.

Since the early 1950s, the state repaired and strengthened the sea dikes and river dikes. Local communities dredged and repaired existing irrigation canals and spills, and constructed additional ones. In the late 1950s, construction of reservoirs became the main focus of attention (Dianliju 1960). The state helped in the surveying work and paid for materials such as cement and steel, and might supply mechanized transport. The collectives cut stones, dug earth, constructed roads, transported the necesssary materials to the project site, and built the project.

Initiatives Under the Great Leap Forward
The large-scale farmland capital construction projects of the Great Leap Forward 1958-1960 had a profound effect on local land reclamation efforts. Ideologically, natural resources such as water, mountain forests and coastal silt flats were now presented to the peasantry as reclaimable, through collective organization and action. One might distinguish at least five areas of action: (1) the felling of trees for fuel (for newly established backyard industries) and for timber (for construction projects, in Fujian but also for other provinces); (2) the building of new terraces on hills and mountain slopes. The felling of trees and construction of terraces on steep slopes is uniformly condemned nowadays, for its waste of resources and harm to the environment. The remnants of such terraces, long since abandoned in the case of rice paddies, or with very poor stands of tea, can be seen in most areas of Fujian; (3) the

introduction of new crops or new cropping systems (for instance, tea in Anxi and other counties in southern Fujian, sugar cane in counties north of Putian). This was a time of local experimentation, the record of which is rather incomplete, because only successful experiments have survived; (4) reclamation of land from the sea, by building dikes and constructing polders. Under the Great Leap Forward, construction of polders was not undertaken on a large scale, possibly because of the industrial orientation and consequent shortage of labour in coastal areas and the long gestation period; (5) construction of natural-flow irrigation systems, with reservoirs, impounding dams, diversion weirs, feeder canals et cetera. This large-scale construction of irrigation facilities is still vividly remembered, and usually condemned. A very large, often too large, number of natural-flow irrigation systems were constructed, on the basis of small- and medium-scale mountain reservoirs. Some projects were ill-advised, undertaken in haste and in a sloppy way, and were abandoned. Most required an extraordinary amount of labour or took up much valuable land. However, many of these projects became the backbone of irrigation systems which greatly increased yields and continue to do so today. Some projects lost most of their value in the 1970s, when electric pump irrigation became available, and most reservoirs (none of which were very large, usually having a capacity of several tens of million cubic meters) now have a reduced capacity, because of gradual siltation (Vermeer 1977). Examples of each may be noted in any county in Fujian.

These projects could have several immediate effects on land reclamation projects: (1) irrigation works increased the value of reclaimed farmland, particularly along the coast, by supplying fresh water to the crops. Without fresh water, reclamation of coastal wasteland was uneconomic. Salts had to be flushed out, and cultivation of dry crops such as peanuts or sweet potatoes was not very rewarding; (2) the loss of farmland occupied by reservoirs or canals (although in mountainous and water-rich Fujian, this came nowhere near the losses suffered in China's dry plain areas) created an acute local need for farmland to resettle displaced farmers. After the post-Leap crisis forced the temporary labourers in the cities and in industry to go back to farming, this problem became much more serious, and many were forced to go up the hill; (3) the construction of roads to quarries and project sites laid many areas open to exploitation, first for felling of trees and thereafter for cultivation of crops.

The Expansion of the State Farm System

The retrenchment of the early 1960s reduced Fujian's farmland acreage by 11 per cent to a temporary low of 1,283,000 ha. (FJN 1986, 80-81). However, it strengthened the state farm system. In 1961, a provincial state farm and Land Reclamation Bureau was founded, which controlled all aspects of its farms. It bought from the People's Communes all reclamation areas, which had been abandoned for lack of seeds, of pig manure (almost all pigs having been killed), labour strength or enthusiasm, or had been swept away by floods. Compensation was given for labour costs, nothing else. The Bureau also acquired all remaining Overseas Chinese plantations (which before had been under control of the regional and local Bureaus of Overseas Chinese Affairs). By 1965, it operated 143 state farms, throughout Fujian, with a total area of 180,000 ha., one tenth of which was cultivated to grain and other annual crops (FJN 1985, 116). However, during this period both government officials and local communities sobered up about the possibilities of reclamation of farmland, and scientists started to voice their concern about water and soil erosion (Zhao Zhaobing 1965). Later, it was reported that by autumn 1961, the area subject to serious water and soil erosion had jumped by 3,500 square kilometers over 1957, to 8,200 square kilometers (Nongye Weiyuanhui 1983 and FJN 1986, 83).[4] Water and soil erosion work, which had been under the Water Conservancy Bureau, was brought under an independent Water and Soil Erosion Committee in 1963. However, until the early 1980s, this committee had little power, and its activities concerned mainly (often aerial) sowing of grass and planting trees.

Polder Boom During the Cultural Revolution
The Cultural Revolution brought a new campaign for opening up wasteland. In that way, the post-war generation of youths could be put to work. Farmland capital construction projects were organized by state farms or county governments for the youths, who had been 'sent down'. Rural youths were organized in shock brigades, and following the Dazhai example and the Old Man Who Moved The Mountain, they went to build terraces on mountain slopes and to construct plains in the mountains. At first, there was little coordination, each city and each department making arrangements for its own youths. Many state farms had been closed down, and their goods stolen. The Land Reclamation Bureau, the Fujian Military District (which founded a Production and Construction Militia, which was abolished again in 1974 (Zhang Linchi 1986, 63), the Ministry of Light Industry, the Overseas Chinese Committee, the People's Liberation Army and the Water Conservancy Bureau each undertook sea polder projects. In 1973, the Fujian government decided that the Water Conservation Bureau should regain its responsibility for planning, execution, and management of all these projects.

If the 1950s marked the high tide of water conservation project construction, the Cultural Revolution years added a high tide of construction of polders from the sea to this. There were several causes. At the time, a great stress was laid on grain production, and commercial hill crops such as tea and fruit still fetched low prices and could not be sold freely. The urban youths lived concentrated in the coastal areas, and were likely to encounter language and other adaptation problems when sent to the mountains in the interior. The coastal counties and villages were somewhat less poor and more accessible; thus, the youths were better received, fed and controlled. Also, conquering the open space of the wasteland along the coast required large-scale organization of labour, boats for bringing in sand and stones, construction of spillgates and canals, and long-term planning for soil improvement and crops. The amount of labour involved was tremendous, especially when the sandy stretches were covered with a new layer of top soil fetched from elsewhere, by pushcarts or carts on rails. It had much appeal, it was promising, heroic and visible as an effort. Like Doctor Faustus, cadres could see 'how thousands at my bidding speed'.

Thus, in this period, all along the coast many dozens of polders were created. The People's Communes did not need permission for those smaller than 67 ha.; but for larger ones, the county government had to first give approval. Standards for the new dikes did not differ from those for existing ones: i.e. for inhabited areas, the capability to withstand a once-in-20-years flood, and for agricultural areas, a five-year standard was (and is) acceptable. With these requirements, and because most polders have been built on silt flats well above low tide level, dikes generally are only three to five meters high, about two meters wide at the top, but with a very gentle slope and a stone facing at the foot adding to their safety.[5] On average, about half of the total investment in construction was provided by the state, and the other half (mostly in the form of labour and locally available materials) by the communes or brigades. Moreover, for the first few years, loans were provided, which had to be repaid after the land had become productive, which might take two to five years, depending on the quality of the soil and the availability of irrigation water. A capacity of one cubic meter of water per second would generally suffice for one thousand ha. of two-crop rice. New land was planted to reeds for a year or two, then to sweet potatoes or beans for two more years, and finally to rice, once fresh water supply had been secured.

Unlike Holland, where new polders remain state property for the first seven years or more of their existence, in Fujian the new land used to be distributed almost immediately. According to local cadres, allocation of the new land was usually to adjacent villages, but sometimes also in part to state farms, or to 'sent-down' youths who had settled permanently. Allocation was based on three principles: the existing shortage of farmland available per capita, the average per capita grain output, and the absence of alternative employment opportunities. It was also on the basis of these criteria and planned allocation of land, that labour was drawn from the various villages or state farms for a reclamation project.

In the 1980s, polder construction has come to a virtual standstill, for several obvious reasons. A general shortage of irrigation water has affected even the existing polders, because upstream users, rightly or wrongly, can always claim irrigation water first. Grain production has become less rewarding than before, and many polders need comparatively large quantities of fertilizer for their sandy soils. Communes, which were capable of organizing cheap labour, have been abolished. The tidal flats are important breeding grounds for fish and other seafood, which may be financially more rewarding and are less labour-intensive than agriculture. Moreover, since 1984, permission has to be obtained from the provincial bureau of fish resources for all sea reclamation projects larger than 33 ha., because they might have an effect on fish breeding grounds. The state has invested less and less in agricultural projects, and as far as bank loans or private investments are concerned, the increase in interest rates has had a very negative effect on all farmland capital construction projects, because they usually take many years to complete and become productive.

The Economic Benefits of Polders

Statistics for Fujian over the 25 year period 1949 through 1984 showed that a total of 862 polders had been reclaimed from the sea, with a total surface of 70,000 ha. 60,000 ha. of this was land, of which 49,000 ha. had been planted to crops; part of the remaining land was in use for salt production. Of the water surface, 53 per cent was used for production of seafood.[6] Of the 60,000 ha. of new land, 37,000 ha. were created before 1975, 18,000 ha. were created between 1976 and 1980, and only 5,000 ha. from 1981 till 1985. Between 1973 and 1984, the state invested 102 million yuan in these projects through the Water Conservation Bureau, and the Land Reclamation Bureau added another 17 million yuan. From 1981 through 1985 state investments were less than half those of 1976 through 1980. Taking inflation into account, the decrease is much larger (FJN 1986, 163).

If we take a sample of 14 polders in the Putian-Quanzhou section as an example, state investments averaged about 5,000 yuan per ha. of farmland in the 1970s, and villages may have invested an equal amount. Of course, not all of the investment should be charged to agriculture. A new polder provided additional space for housing, roads, industrial activities, raising ducks, fishery, grazing and grass cutting, and sometimes salt pans. It might also save future expenses and add to security against floods by shortening the coast line and strengthening the dikes. In some cases, it connected an islet and its inhabitants to the mainland, thus solving their problems of communications and water and electricity supply. Even the direct economic returns of polder projects can not be evaluated easily, because of the complexity of inputs and rapid changes in prices of their products. Below, I will illustrate this with two examples: a collective polder project, and a state reclamation farm with salt panning.

The Ganjiang polder in Jinjiang County was built in 1970-1973 by the people's communes of Ganjiang and Shishi. There were already two small polders of 15 and 50 ha in existence, built in 1958 and 1965 by adjacent villages. These old polders were integrated, and their dikes demolished. The County Water Conservation Bureau had drawn up a plan, at the request of Ganjiang People's Commune. The County Government paid for all materials, and gave an additional subsidy of one to 1.5 yuan per day to the construction labourers (who were also awarded with workpoints from their collective). The county investment, totalling 1.1 million yuan, was retrieved by the allocation of 80 ha (out of a newly added total of 215 ha.) to the county, to be used for duck raising. The county, in turn, gave 15 ha to Shishi township. The collective villages devoted most of their new land to rice. Economic results were satisfactory; yields reached from six to nine tons per ha., which gave an average annual output of 13 to 14 tons. In the first decade, costs were low because little chemical fertilizer had to be applied, but subsequently larger and larger quantities were needed: by 1987 500 kg (46 per cent N) per ha., and at higher prices. In addition, manure and phosporous fertilizer had to be applied. To cut costs, many farmers had returned to ploughing with oxen. Water charges were raised in 1987, too, doubling from 30 yuan to 60 yuan per ha Local cadres confessed that agricultural use of the polder had become uneconomical, if compared with alternative uses for production of shrimps, seaslugs, fish, or ducks.

The July 1 polder in Huian County was built in 1970-1972, at a total investment of 7,140,000 yuan. The area had several advantages: it was originally a bay with two islets which facilitated its closure with dikes, irrigation water was available from two brooks, and there had already been salt pans before World War II. In the five year period of 1979-1983, total output value from all activities was 6.6 million yuan, net income from which amounted to 3.2 million yuan. As for the farmland area, in 1983 salt levels were still rather high. Thus, only 400 ha were cultivated, with sweet potatoes, peanuts, and soybeans, which gave an output during that year of 1,273 tons, valued at 458,000 yuan. The 240 ha of salt fields produced 15.1 tons of salt with a value of 1,404,000 yuan, i.e. 6,000 yuan per ha or over five times as much as the agricultural crops did. Shrimps, animal husbandry and 230 ha of trees added little to income. Of the total output value of 1,887,000 yuan in 1983, 889,000 yuan were left as net income. Thus, the original investment had been recovered in about ten years. This was considered a good return. By 1987, the farmland area of the July 1 polder had been expanded to 500 ha The soil was still being improved, by adding drainage ditches, planting Mumahuang (Casuarina Spp., which serve as windbreaks) and growing green fertilizer (notably sesbania). Fertilizer was also applied, 70 per cent of which was organic; chemical fertilizer application levels were about 100 kg (46 per cent N) nitrogenous and 150 to 400 kg phosphorous fertilizer per ha. Good topsoil was still continuously carried from elsewhere, to be applied on sandy plots. The value of the farmland was rather low; farmers usually bid 150 yuan of annual rent at auction. However, most land had been allocated free of charge to the villages, and passed on to their farmers, with no other financial obligation than paying the agricultural tax. Local cadres recognized that the economic benefit from salt farming was much higher than from agriculture, but told me that the social benefit of farmland was higher, because it provided employment for farmers with too little land.

Up the Mountains

In the years 1978-1980, Fujian witnessed an unprecedented opening up of mountain slopes, for planting tea, fruit trees, and other economic crops. The reason for this was a radical turnabout of state economic policies for mountain areas, to which the terms 'liberalization', 'suit agriculture to local conditions' and 'household responsibility system' have usually been applied. Especially in low-income areas—and most of Fujian fell in this category - mountain villages were freed from many previous state and collective controls of labour organization, income distribution, crop choice, marketing and transport. The individualized rewards under the household responsibility system, higher prices, and for fruit entirely free prices, together with reduced state demands for cultivation of foodgrain, encouraged the mountain farmers to renew their efforts to exploit their environment.

The local agricultural and forestry departments in Fujian, and the state farms (all of which were brought under County Government control) played a major role in stimulating and guiding local communities and individual efforts. They provided most of the seedlings for tea, tangerines and other fruit, and timber at low prices, and gave the necessary technical advice about soil improvement, fertilization, spacing, selection and breeding, pruning, pest control, preservation et cetera.

The tea and fruit trees are planted on medium and steep slopes, which usually have been terraced more or less. The gentle slopes have already been converted into rice paddies decades or centuries ago. Although many villages started to plant their slopes without creating terraces, in the course of the 1980s government propaganda and incentives for buiding terraces have become more and more effective. Also, sanctions could be applied after the adoption of several related laws, and after household land lease contracts had been drawn up with guarantees for preservation of the quality of the soil.

The function of the terraces is to conserve water, soil and fertilizer. Most terrace banks are made from overturned sods, but stone embankments are much more durable. On very steep slopes, which for fruit and tea may be up to 60 degrees, it is generally considered that the construction of terraces is environmentally and economically unviable. Soil erosion may be extremely serious there.

On average, the creation of stone terraces required an investment of about 15,000 yuan per ha (net cultivation area, but field roads included) in the early 1980s, and about 22,000 yuan by 1987. Of this, 20 per cent went into shaping of the terrain, 40 to 50 per cent into building the embankment, and 30 to 40 per cent into filling with topsoil. Earth terraces would cost about half this amount. Advised standards were: a top soil layer of at least 50 centimeters, a level (or, in case of tea, slightly inclining) terrace, adequate drainage ditches, and roads of access with a slope of no more than ten degrees (for tractor roads 16 degrees). Some counties gave a subsidy for good performance.

A smaller, second wave of reclamation of hills occurred in 1983-1984, with the contracting out of farmland and wasteland to private households for terms of 15 years or more. Generally speaking, individual farmers could not receive more than 0.6 to one ha of irrigated paddy fields, and not more than 0.3 to 0.5 ha of tea or fruit trees. If organized in collectives, however, each might receive considerably more. Two more factors stimulated fruit and tea cultivation in these years: the record grain harvests of 1983 and 1984, which reduced government pressure on farmers to cultivate grain, and brought grain prices down, and the price increases of fruits. Within a few years, wholesale prices of tangerines had gone up from a few fen to 1.30 yuan and more per kg., and tea reached eight to 20 yuan and more per kg. Belatedly and reluctantly, after 1985 the state agreed to raise timber sales' prices, while maintaining its price control. The extremely low prices for timber in the previous years had made cultivation of trees for timber very unattractive and felling greatly surpassed reforestation rates.

Various forms of organization were applied in the mountains. After 1980, mountain slopes were allocated by the Production Brigades to small groups or individual households for development. This happened on the basis of recommendations by the Production Teams, who might assist in planning and execution of reclamation, and who also decided on rent and taxes to be paid under the contract. With larger plots of land, small fruit growers' or tea growers' collectives were formed. After 1983, it seems to have been more common (there are no statistics), that the village *(cun)* government had a group of interested labourers undertake the work of terracing at a wage which varied between two and five yuan per day, depending on local income levels. Subsequently, the village government would offer the newly terraced land for lease periods of six to twenty years to interested villagers, at a public auction. The land was not always auctioned off succesfully; there are examples of newly terraced fields which have been lying fallow for several years, slowly deteriorating, because there have been no takers.

In exceptional cases, private entrepreneurs might lease a very large plot of land. Not far from Quanzhou, I visited a 33-year old private farmer who together with a classmate had contracted for a 37-ha hill in 1984. The contract obliged him to maintain the quality of water and soil, and to construct adequate embankments for the terraces and drainage facilities. His total investment, which involved the purchase and planting of seedlings, installation of an electrical pump and ducts for water from a reservoir, construction of buildings, roads and terraces, was 150,000 yuan. Almost 300 labourers had been involved in the development of his hill. Only one-third of his investment had been borrowed from the bank, with a normal interest rate of 0.72 per cent per month, to be repaid in three years. His banana trees were already productive, but the red bayberries, olive, carambola, mango and other trees would need several more years before yielding fruit. He had even planted some tea. His obvious purpose in planting this wide range of fruit was to spread the risks and maximize the use of labour. Every three months he made a labour plan, on the basis of which short-term labourers would be hired, at 2.5 to 3.5 yuan per day. This farm showed the individual willingness, under the new policies, to make large long-term investments; the farmer would need at least five more years before he recouped his original investment.

In various laws adopted in the 1980s, which bear on farmland reclamation, such as the laws on land use, environmental protection, forestry and water and soil erosion control, the government expressed its concern about long-term conservation of natural resources and devised measures to halt their destruction. Indeed, developments were alarming. The so-called 'Five Destructions' of illegal felling, illegal farmland reclamation, mining, stone quarries and building of houses and roads, were singled out by the government as main causes of erosion. However, most of the legal activities were almost as damaging. Because of soil erosion, soil layers were getting thinner, their organic matter content dropped, farmland was covered with sand (in Xianyou County, a figure of seven per cent was given), and droughts had become frequent. Reservoirs and rivers were silting up (particularly the Jinjiang, Liangxi and Jiulongjiang rivers in Southeast Fujian). Compared with 1958, by 1980 the silt content of the Minjiang had increased by 47 per cent, the Jiulongjiang by 95 per cent, the Liangxi by 130 per cent and the Jinjiang by 153 per cent (Zhao Zhaobing 1984). Fujian's area subject to water and soil erosion increased from 800,000 ha in 1963 to 1.27 million ha in 1982 and 1.4 million ha in 1985. Moreover, the forest area and timber reserves were dwindling: between 1957 and 1978, timber reserves in North Fujian decreased by 55 per cent (Nongye Weiyuanhui 1983)

The problems concern both upstream and downstream farmers, but most of all the government, which is responsible for safety against floods and for the provision of irrigation water. A sense of urgency is getting more widespread: 'Some government leaders and departments still think that water and soil erosion in Fujian is not that serious... But the ecology is worsening daily, flood and drought damages increase... In the Jiulong river basin, five out of six years are calamitous, roads are cut off, ports silt up, reservoirs become useless' (FJN 1987, 87).

In the past few years, land reclamation has come to a virtual standstill in most areas, and government departments concentrate on conservation rather than on expansion. However, in some areas the 'mountain reclamation fever' still continues. In 1987, Guangze County in the Wuyi mountains gave a 900 yuan subsidy for every reclaimed hectare of paddy fields; for newly reclaimed land a five-year exemption from taxes and obligatory sales to the state was given. Both were considered insufficient by the farmers, who preferred not to report their private reclamation at all. They had money to invest, and children to be provided with food and with future land; there were few opportunities and they had few skills outside farming (Xie Xingfa 1987).

Government regulations and supervision

The Provincial Water and Soil Conservation Bureau has only very limited staff and financial means (in 1987, the Bureau Chief indicated that at least 250 million yuan would be needed to realize all plans, but the actual amount spent, mainly by local government, fell far short of that) and exerts its influence mainly through cooperation with all related departments. This cooperation is backed up by the water and soil protection regulations adopted by Fujian Province in 1987 (which superseded the 1984 draft regulations). Some of the main rules are: (a) the rural *(xiang)* governments must appoint a special official for water and soil erosion control (WSEC) and inspection work; (b) all government departments which use land, must include a WSEC proposal in their plans, which must have obtained approval of the WSEC bureaux of the same administrative level (the fine for infringements will be five to ten yuan per square meter); (c) slopes which are steeper than 25 degrees may not be sown to agricultural crops; however, they can be used for forest, grass, fruit, tea and other tree crops (the limit of 25 degrees dates back to the 1950s; Fujian did not make use of the possibility, given to provinces under article 7 of the corresponding national law, to impose a lower limit); (d) reclamation of slopes in reservoir districts, and of slopes along irrigation canals which are steeper than ten degrees, is forbidden; (e) the approving authority for land reclamation plans is the county government, except for state farms; terraces should be built with embankments, and 'rational cultivation methods' should be used (a fine will be applied here of 300 yuan to 450 yuan per ha for infringements); (f) household fuel bases must be established, based mainly on privately contracted mountain plots; (g) it is forbidden to dig grass sods or burn mountain sides for fertilizer (fine same as above); (h) existing reclaimed slopes which do not conform to the rules must be taken out of cultivation; terraces must either be made level, or be changed over to forest or grass; (i) fines for unauthorized digging of earth are five to ten yuan per cubic metre, if in danger zones, 20 to 30 yuan (Shuitu Baochi 1987).

These rules seem strict enough for agricultural crops. However, for tea, fruit and other tree crops, which are the main cause of erosion, they may not be too effective. Also, enforcement will be difficult in all those cases, where the existing land use contracts concluded between village governments and households have to be reconsidered. Thus, the cadres of the WSEC bureaux have indicated that their main job is a reduction of damages caused by new land reclamation projects; for the existing ones, patient education and propaganda will have to be the main thing. To that end, in Fujian more than 300 WSEC model demonstration stations had been set up by the end of 1985. Also, the County Governments gave a premium of 300 yuan per ha of land which was treated for conservation (to be used for the purchase of fertilizer and seedlings), to which the village governments might add something, too.

Planning the Future: Afforestation and Tree Crops?
Opinions on future land use and erosion control are divided. There is obviously a need to replant forests, because if felling goes on at the current rate resulting in an annual deficit between consumption and repletion of 170 million cu.m., all mature forests in China will have been exhausted by 1997 (Renmin Ribao, August 6 1989). However, some forestry specialists have voiced doubts about the effectivenes of planting firs and other trees near populated areas. Peasants remove fallen needles, leaves, and branches for fuel and the soil is exhausted and erosion increases (Huang Bingwei 1987). However, China firs have a better resistance against drought and disease than most other trees, and grow faster. In the humid climate of Fujian, forests can regenerate quickly, if protected well, and Fujian still has 3.3 million ha which are suitable for afforestation. A combination of trees, shrubs and grasses would yield the best results, but would be labour-intensive.

Economists and local officials stress that land use plans must yield immediate local benefits, in order to obtain the necessary cooperation of the peasantry for soil improvement. Bamboo, bayberries, pomelos and other tree crops may combine ecological and quick economic profits (Dong Wanxiang 1986). Planners have been looking mainly at integrated farming, and trial districts have been set up where farmers reclaim barren mountains for cultivation of tree crops, use shallow flats on the sea shore to raise shrimps, and also fish off the coast. Dongwuyang is one such experimental district, where an economic planner has distinguished seven different models of development (Yu Xuemao 1988).

Conclusion and Prospects

In the mid-1980s, the willingness to experiment and to adapt measures to local conditions was an obvious positive factor in finding appropriate solutions to the dilemma of a choice between short-term profits and long-term conservation of resources. The rapid growth of income and employment, outside of crop growing, alleviated rural population pressure. Investments in tea and tree crops, undertaken in previous years, were beginning to bear fruit, and could be expected to bring substantial returns for many years to come. The price rises for timber finally made afforestation an economically viable activity, although the time span required for it to be harvested is still too long for individual farmers. The growth of foreign exports enabled Fujian to consider imports of more foodgrain, which could provide more room for agricultural specialization. However, it became increasingly difficult for the government to maintain adequate rural agrotechnical services.

Recent political and economic developments have not been very favourable. Early in 1989, the government introduced new taxes on fruit, tea, timber and other economic crops, in order to support its drive for increased grain production. Price controls were reinstated, and urban purchasing power declined in 1989, both of which affected farmers' incomes and the economic returns of previous investments in fruit and other crops. A high rate of inflation has made long-term investments less attractive. There has been a hardening attitude towards entrepreneurial farmers with high incomes, which may stifle the search for economic efficiency and the popularization of new crops. Such developments overshadow the above-mentioned positive elements of more effective and legal control over land utilization, greater awareness of environmental problems, and increased research.

In the long run, however, there are several economic and political factors which are bound to increase provincial government support for afforestation and crop specialization: (a) the increasing scarcity and high price of timber; (b) the export earnings from tea and processed fruits; (c) Fujian's ability to pay for its own foodgrain imports; (d) the costs of state subsidies of grain cultivation as against the tax income derived from commercial crops; (e) the higher employment-generating effects of commercial crops; (f) a reduction of transport costs because of an improvement in road and railroad links and of means of transportation; (g) a lack of individual willingness to invest in politically and economically risky mountain development schemes; (h) the increased damage caused by erosion, and a greater public and government awareness of its cost. Moreover, the growing economic cooperation with Taiwan will increase capital and know-how, which will, most likely, result in a better exploitation of Fujian's land resources and comparative advantages in the international context. Thus, in the future one may expect a continued opening up of mountain slopes, undertaken by local government (or at least with its support) rather than by individuals, and on a larger scale than before, organized with more advanced techniques and with a greater concern for both economic results and environmental costs.

Although the current political priority for foodgrain cultivation and the need to create employment favour reclamation of land from the sea, the present labour costs of such schemes are high, and economic returns are insufficient. However, the last wave of polder projects was 15 years ago, and the silt flats expand continuously. In another ten years or so, with new techniques of sand transport, the creation of new land may become viable again.

Notes

1. In 1952-1954, one-sixth of Jinjiang's rural population worked overseas (Fujiansheng Nongcun Diaocha, 1952). At that time, some of the overseas labourers may not have decided yet whether to maintain family links or not.
2. China Daily Business Weekly, September 24, 1989.
3. As one official remarked: 'The incorrect thought of the peasants that "closing the mountain is like closing one's mouth" was corrected in meetings. We used as slogans: "Whoever the mountains belong to, may close them. Whoever closes them, may cut grass and keep it. The mountain forests do not move away!" After these meetings contracts were signed which clearly staked out all closed off areas, pastoral areas, areas for banana trees et cetera', Jinjiang Nongmin, December 15, 1952.
4. Land is defined as being subject to water and soil erosian if its plant cover is less than 80 percent. The Chinese distinguish between light, medium and serious water and soil erosion areas, with respective soil plant cover rates of 60-80 per cent, 30-60 per cent, and below 30 per cent.
5. By 1969, one-third of Fujian's 1,800 kilometer of dikes, which protected 870,000 hectares of farmland, reached the standard requirement of a height of 50 cm above the historical highest water level (HHWL), a width at the top of three to four meters, a gentle slope and a good vegetation cover. In the 1980s, the standard has been raised to 100-120 cm above HHWL. By 1984, the total length of dikes had increased to 4,500 km (Shuiliju 1985).
6. Shuiliju (1985): This source gives a total state investment in water conservancy projects in Fujian during 1949-1984 of 1.9 billion yuan, involving 2 billion cu.m. of earth work.

References

Dai Dajin (1946): Dai Dajin, 'Fuxing Fujiansheng yuanyi shiyedi jingjikan' (An economic view on reviving the horticulture business of Fujian Province). *Fujiansheng Yinhang Jikan*, 1:3-4 (January 1946).

Dai Yifeng (1988): Dai Yifeng, 'Jindai Minjiang shangyou shanqudi shangpin shengchan' (Commercial production in the mountain areas of the Min River upper reaches in the modern period). *Xiamen Daxue Xuebao*, 1988:4.

Dianliju (1960): Fujiansheng Shuili Dianliju, *Fujiansheng shuili shuidian jiben gaikuang* (Basic situation of water conservancy and hydro-electriciy in Fujian Province). Fuzhou.

Dong Wanxiang (1986): Dong Wanxiang, 'Fujiansheng jiang shuitu liushiqu jiancheng jingli zuowuqu (Fujian Province makes its water and soil erosion areas into economic crop areas). *Zhongguo Shuitu Baochi*, 1986:9.

FJN 1985: *Fujian jingji nianjian 1985* (Fujian economic yearbook 1985). Fuzhou, 1986.

FJN 1986: *Fujian jingji nianjian 1986* (Fujian economic yearbook 1986). Fuzhou, 1987.

FJN 1987: *Fujian jingji nianjian 1987* (Fujian economic yearbook 1987). Fuzhou, 1988.

Fujian Nongkenzhi (1943?): *Fujian nonkenzhi jingying fangshi* (Management methods of land reclamation in Fujian). No place, no date.

Fujiansheng Nongcun Jiaocha (1952): Huadong Junzheng Weiyuanhui Tudi Gaige Weiyuanhui, *Fujiansheng nongcun diaocha* (Investigation of rural villages in Fujian Province). No place.

Huang Bingwei (1987): Huang Bingwei, 'Huanan podi liyong yu gailiang: zhongyaoxing yu kexingxing' (Utilization and improvement of slopes in South China: importance and feasibility), *Dili Yanjiu* 6:4 (December 1987).

Huang and Su (1989): Huang Zhanggui and Su Liangtai, 'Nonghu jilei ruogan wenti chutao' (A preliminary investigation into some problems of accumulation in peasant households). *Fazhan Yanjiu*, 1989:1.

Lai Jiapan (1940): Lai Jiapan, *Nan'anxian jianshe gaikuang* (Situation of construction in Nan'an County). Nan'an.

Lai Shishuang and Lai Shiqing, 'Fujiansheng nongcun shengyu laolidi xianzhuang ji zhuanyi tujing' (Present situation and channels of transfer of the superfluous labour force in Fujian Province). *Fazhan Yanjiu*, 1988:9.

Lian Yuqing (1986): Lian Yuqing, 'Fujian haian fengsha weihaidi zhili' (Control of the damage by sand dunes along the Fujian coast). *Zhongguo Shuitu Baochi*, 1986:9.

Lin Gengsheng (1982): Lin Gengsheng, 'Gudai cong hailu yinjin Fujiandi zhiwu' (Plants imported into Fujian from overseas in the ancient period). *Haijiaoshi Yanjiu*, 1982:4.

Ministry of Commerce (1988): *Zhongguo shangye nianjian 1988* (Commercial yearbook of China 1988). Beijing.

Ministry of Finance (1957): *Basheng nongcun jingji dianxing diaocha* (A model investigation of the village economy in eight provinces). Beijing.

Ministry of Forestry (1987): *Zhongguo linye nianjian 1949-1986* (Forestry yearbook of China 1949-1986). Beijing.

Nongye Gaikuang (1942): *Fujiansheng gexianqu nongye gaikuang* (Agricultural conditions in all counties and districts in Fujian Province). Fuzhou.

Nongye Weiyuanhui (1983): Fujiansheng Nongye Weiyuanhui (ed.), *Fujiansheng shandi ziyuan heli kaifa liyong xueshu lunwen xuanbian* (Selected scholarly articles on rational exploitation and use of mountain resources in Fujian Province), Fuzhou.

Shuiliju (1985): Fujiansheng Shuili Shuidian Ting Shuiliju, *Fujian shuili shizhi ziliao* (Historical materials on water conservation in Fujian). No. 5, October 1985.

Shuitu Baochi (1987): Fujiansheng Shuitu Baochi Weiyuanhui, *Fujiansheng shuitu baochi tiaoli* (Fujian provincial regulations on water and soil erosion control). No place, no date.

Su Qiutao (1983): Su Qiutao, 'Jin bashi nian Quanzhou nongyedi gaijin gongzuo' (Agricultural advancement work in Quanzhou in the past eighty years). *Quanzhou Wenshi Ziliao*, vol. 11.

Su Zongwen (1937): Su Zongwen, *Fujiansheng banli tudi zhenbaozhi jingguo* (The process of management of land reporting in Fujian Province). Reprinted in the *Minguo ershi niandai Zhongguo Dalu tudi wenti ziliao* series, no. 40, 20183-20446.

Vermeer (1977): E. B. Vermeer, *Water Conservancy and Irrigation in China: Social, Economic and Agrotechnical Aspects*. Leiden.

Wang Qigui (1946): Wang Qigui, 'Fujian zhi kenwu yu zhanhou kenzhi jingying' (Reclamation affairs of Fujian and post-war undertakings of reclamation and cultivation). *Fujiansheng Yinhang Jikan*, 1:3-4 (January 1946).

Wu Zeng (1937): Wu Zeng (ed.), *Fanshu zayong* (Miscellaneous Praise For The Potato). No place, 1937 ed. of Qing original.

Xie Xingfa (1987): Xie Xingfa, 'Encourage rational reclamation, stop blind and wasteful opening up of land'. *Fujian Jingji Yanjiu*, 1987:7.

Yongchun (1984): *Yongchun fengwu* (Customs and matters of Yongchun). Yongchun.

Yu Xuemao (1988): Yu Xuemao, 'Fujiansheng nongye shengtai xitong mianlindi wenti yu duice' (Problems facing the ecological system of agriculture in Fujian Province, and remedies). *Fazhan Yanjiu*, 1988:11.

Zhang Linchi (1986): Zhang Linchi, *Dangdai Zhongguodi nongken shiye* (State farm and land reclamation undertakings in present China). Beijing.

Zhao Zhaobing (1965): Zhao Zhaobing, in *Dili Xuebao* 31:3.

Zhao Zhaobing (1984): Zhao Zhaobing, 'Fujian shandidi ziran tedian jiqi kaifa liyongdi chubu shexiang' (Natural characteristics of Fujian's mountain land and preliminary suggestions for its development and use). *Dili Xuebao* 39:4 (December 1984).

Zhen Guojin (1987): Zhen Guojin, in *Fujian Luntan*, 1987:11.

Zhen Mingzhang (1943): Zhen Mingzhang, *Fujian liangshi wenti* (grain problems of Fujian). Fuzhou.

Zhen Taoying (1946): Zhen Taoying, 'Fujianshengdi liangmi wenti' (Rice problems in Fujian Province). *Fujiansheng Yinhang Jikan* ,1:3-4 (January 1946), 213-226.

Zhen Xicheng (1936?): Zhen Xicheng, *Fuqing, Huian Tongan sanxian huangdi diaocha* (An investigation into wasteland in the three counties of Fuqing, Huian and Tongan). No place, no date.

Zhou Jinfei (1987): Zhou Jinfei et al., 'Fujiansheng nonghu xiaofei he jilei' (Consumption and accumulation of rural households in Fujian Province). *Fujian Luntan*, 1987:8.

Irrigation Management at Collective Sector Level:
A Note on Decentralisation in the PRC

Thiagarajan Manoharan

From the time of the semi-legendary Emperor Yu, the Great Engineer, the people of China are renowned for their skill in water management. In contemporary China a fascinating aspect of the many-faceted water resource management is the collective effort mobilised for it and the means adopted. Since the separation of the commune from the administration, and the near universal adoption of the household responsibility system, many decisions regarding irrigation water management have been decentralised to the collective sector administration (former commune area administration: at town, township and below).

Decentralisation can be viewed from various inter-related perspectives. Currently, in the PRC, the water management units are exhorted to be self-reliant with respect to the financial resources for operation and management, based on the criterion that the area which benefits should raise the resources required; in the state-local fiscal relations, reforms have been introduced to demarcate clearly collective sector's fiscal resources; a part of its self-raised, self-managed funds, the levy on rural enterprises' profits, is to be devoted to irrigation. The impersonal and automatic operation of economic levers is a form of decentralisation: in the PRC, presently such instances are the full costing of water supply and the conversion of state grants, as for instance for farmland construction, to loans. In decentralisation of management a system of responsibility contracts plays a significant role; contracts are viewed in this note not from the legal angle; given the overall plan, the parties set mutually agreed details, with clear allocation of duties and rights, penalty payments for default and sharing of gains from increased efficiency.

Decentralisation is subject to overall planning: rural irrigation work is planned at the higher, county, level; water allocation to the farms is subject to overall plan. Also, some features of the former communes, like 'labour accumulation' and integrated use of funds for simultaneous development of industry and agriculture, have been retained, but with a large latitude for variations according to local circumstances.

A study of irrigation management has to include many dimensions: socio-economic planning, engineering, environment, development administration, legal framework etc; all these aspects have to be viewed in the context of scarcity of water as projected in long-term requirements. This modest note focusses only on irrigation water delivery in the context of the economic responsibility system. Some basic data and information are hard to come by: for instance, country-wide data on collective sector's fiscal operations and on 'labour accumulation'; sufficiently illustrative judicial decisions on contracts. Some broad indications of a qualitative nature are presented below on the aspects of decentralisation.

Management

Irrigation District

Irrigation planning and management, by the state and the collective sector, at the most decentralised level, is through 'irrigation district' (*guan qu*) [1], as under the former commune system [2, 3]. The organisational structure of the irrigation district is responsible for the construction, management and maintenance of irrigation waterworks and water environment, norms and modes of water allocation, including integrated, equitable and efficient water use, water fees, scientific experiment and research in local irrigation practices and technological level of the staff [4].

Irrigation districts vary with respect to the command area in them and the major part of the irrigated area seems to be under small (and medium-sized) districts, as can be inferred roughly from the available data, given in Table 1.

Table 1. Irrigation districts; their irrigated area

Irrigation district: *Total area*	*Number*	*Effective irrigated area (mill. ha)*
1983:		
Over 20,010 hectares	143	7.87
667 - 20,010 hectares	5,145	12.95
Total	5,288	20.82
1987:		
Over 33,000 hectares	70	6.01
7,000 - 33,000 hectares	550	6.81
1,000 - 7,000 hectares	4,723	8.32
Total	5,343	21.14

Source: 'Shuiku Guanqu Weizhi Shiyitu', *Zhongguo Shuili*, No. 9, 1984. pp 45-46. Guojia Tongjiju Nongcun Shehuijingji Tongjisi bian: *Zhongguo Nongcun Tongji Nianjian* 1988. Beijing. 1989. p 243.

Irrigation districts, in particular the large and medium sized, are formed on the basis of natural resource endowment and climatic conditions, source of water supply and minimisation of supply cost, cropping pattern and level of technology [6]. They transcend administrative boundaries *within* a province. Where they lie within more than one administrative area their management is vested at higher level water resource management at higher administrative level or with the highest beneficiary among the water resource management offices. In case where it is organised on the basis of a large reservoir or large main canals, with spread-out channels, the management is divided but coordinated at the large reservoir/main canal.

Irrigation districts within the boundaries of the collective administration are to be managed at the collective level; but the procedures laid down for state-operated irrigation districts are to be followed. Irrigation districts cannot be altered without the approval of state administration.

At the apex of management of the irrigation district is the irrigation district congress; it comprises leading professional water managers and, as representatives of the users, representatives of state administration and leading Party cadres. Its meetings are convened once a year by the Party to decide on the major policy and administrative issues in the management of the irrigation district and its decisions are subject to the supervision and approval of higher level state administration. While it is not in session its decisions on day to day operations are implemented by the irrigation district management committee appointed by the congress and with a predominance of professional managers; they are basically coordinating unit of the water conservancy bureau (state administration). Under the committee work smaller committees established for main, branch and sub-branch canals. At the collective level similar canal management structure prevails. At the village level the management committee's counterpart is a single peasant water manager, a farmer chosen from the village by the collective secton administration.

People's participation in irrigation management, along with state professionals, is constantly emphasized in the PRC. It is exemplified by farmers who form a part of the staff of the management units and who, at the same time, are engaged in agricultural production. An instance is Jing Huiqu irrigation district in Shanxi province: in the fourteen water management main stations there were 148 professionals and in the substations, as compared to 4136 professionals, there were 1142 peasant technicians [4]. The professional staff are to act as the backbone and are enjoined constantly to enhance and upgrade the skill of the peasant technicians. The overall managerial organisations of the irrigation districts are entrusted with the task also of upgrading throughout the district the level of irrigation and allied technology.

The separation of the Party from government administration, the declared official policy, is still under evolution and the progress so far in this direction is admittedly slow. Even where such separation is taking place the Party's leadership role, as emphasized in a Party policy pronouncement in October 1987, is still: "..to ensure in their local areas the implementation of directives from government at higher level and from the State Council, *to propose policy decisions on important local problems, to recommend outstanding cadres to local state organs and to coordinate activities of various local organisations.*" (Italics supplied) [7]. Traditionally the Party's role in water resource management has been strong and it continues to be decisive in the irrigation district congress, in policy planning and implementation, in resolving disputes among different water users and among different levels of administration, in mobilisation of manpower and other resources for waterworks construction, in appointment of leading cadres etc.

Enterprise Orientation
Concomitant with the production responsibility system in agriculture, though not necessarily

its consequence, are some policy measures introduced in 1985: the water management units are to be run as business enterprises; irrigation projects at the county level and below are to be, to the maximum possible, dependent on the resources they can raise; efficiency in construction and operation is to be ensured through a system of economic responsibility, with built-in rewards and punishments.

Water Users Congress

Under a guideline [8] issued by the Ministry of Water Conservancy and Electric Power the irrigation district congress is to be composed entirely of elected representatives of water users, the actual beneficiary households. The congress is to elect a board of directors, which will appoint the executive head of the irrigation district on a performance-based tenure. The head is to be empowered to organise the leading groups and to appoint and supervise senior staff. At each unit of management a system of financial responsibility is to be enforced, with a gradual withdrawal of subsidies. The management and staff are to be brought under a system of floating wages and productivity-linked wages, with bonus awards. Workers who had been hired before 1966 are to be retired, with adequate living allowances. No progress has been reported so far on in the direction of conversion into users' congress.

Management Contracts

Towards transforming the management units into self-financing enterprises a system of responsibility contract has been introduced [9]. Specialised households, cooperative economic groups or less formalised household groups and even single households as well as the management staff or local administrative units can enter into contracts which specify management responsibilities, rights and duties; the contracts are entered into with the government at the concerned level. The main sources of income for the management units run as enterprises are the water fees and the income from subsidiary farming activities. Considering the requirement that the subsidiary activities should not interfere with efficiency in water management the successful instances cited of such integrated activities are mostly small or medium-sized irrigation management units.

Along with the system of management contracts, a system of administrative reforms is being tried as in Shanxi province [10]. Administrative divisions are broken up and water conservancy and water and soil conservation service centres are being established taking the river systems, canal systems, drainage areas and well areas as units; the centres are established by the administration but are to function as autonomous units. There is a binding system of contracts : county water conservancy bureaus with the centres, the centres with the households contracting for specialised tasks, the specialised households with the households they serve. Under these contracts the centre builds and manages a project or manages or offers technical services to the project built by the collective or offers technical guidance to the project built and managed by specialised contracting household.

At the collective level [11], an instance of the nature of the water management contract can be given from Liaoning province. The contract entered into by the specialised household provides 'four fixes, two guarantees, rewards and punishments (*siding, liang baozheng, jiangcheng*)': fixed number of staff, coordinated operation, fixed wages and fixed costs with guarantees of timely and assured water supply and maintenance and repair of water works;

the reward or punishment for performance under the contract is a twenty per cent addition or subtraction from the wages.

Construction Contract

A system of economic responsibility contract for basic construction projects was introduced in 1983 [12]. In the following two years 85.6 per cent of water conservancy projects directly under all the provinces, regions and cities have adopted such reform and in some provinces like Yunnan, Jilin and Heilongjiang the adoption has been total, according to official statistics [13]. Such contracts are concluded by entities at various levels: within the ministry, between higher and lower level management units; between the ministry and construction unit; between the construction unit and the survey and design unit. In the case of labour intensive low technological level of construction, as in the collective sector, the higher level construction units, while remaining as the backbone, can enter into contracts with construction units in the collective sector.

At the collective level, the construction specifications, including pollution control, in the contract are laid down by the county administration and its water conservancy bureau undertakes to supply the construction materials and, in the case of large projects, supplementary funding. Any failure in this respect is to result in administrative punishment of the official; in the case of any negligence on the part of the construction unit, there is to be a deduction in wages by ten per cent. The reward for fulfilling the contract is distribution of bonus to the workers of one to two per cent of the funding provided by the administration. Construction materials saved are to be retained by the construction unit, provided they are used in future construction of water works.

Since 1984 there has been repeated official urging of the adoption of bidding for contracts in basic construction projects, with widest participation, without any restriction based on administrative or ministerial boundaries or on the nature of the units, whether state or collective or individual [14]. However by the end of 1985 only 7.3 per cent of the water conservancy projects under the provinces, autonomous regions and municipalities have implemented public bidding [13]. The requisite, well-known, institutional arrangements are in place [15,16] and there is a growing awareness of the need for strengthening them. Construction units which win the bid have to enter into construction contracts.

The operation of the system in the PRC, however, has some special characteristics [17, 18]. Local administration is an active participant in fixing tender specifications and procedures. Such participation can ensure that the area's material base is fully utilised and can facilitate the arrangements regarding labour employed from outside the area; it could also lead, as many commentators in the PRC point out, to restriction on competition from outside the area. Two ways of enlarging the extent of competition and minimising the weight of local administrative influence that are under consideration are to further encourage vertical cooperation among the construction units at varying levels to put in joint bids and to entrust the bidding arrangements to an autonomous Engineering and Consultancy Company. In judging the quotations, the bid-inviting authorities allow only five to ten per cent downward variation in the cost estimated by them; this limited float is considered by the commentators in the PRC as an advantage compared to capitalistic economies where, according to them, collusive practices restrict competition in bidding.

For judging the quotations costing norms are being fixed [19]. But a basic issue continues to remain: the availability of material inputs in construction, in time and in requisite amount and at prices used in fixing norms for the cost of the project; instances are cited of construction firms having to pay thirty per cent more, and even higher, than the cost estimates when they have to resort to the 'free market'.

Funding: Operation and Maintenance Expenses

Official policy calls for self-financing by the water management units of their organisation and maintenance expenditure (including that on 'simple reproduction' based on provisions for depreciation and major repairs). The principal means towards that end are levy of water fees and establishment of commodity production enterprises.

Water Fees

Water fees regulations [20] provide for financial autonomy at the most decentralised level of water resource management, the irrigation district. Subsystems in the irrigation district like collectively-owned water projects or projects which contract for management as enterprises (like reservoirs) may decide their water fee standards and formulate their own collection methods in the light of the norms laid down by the irrigation districts; they can also levy a surcharge.

Prior to the reforms of the water fee system in the provinces around 1983 and the 1985 regulation, the water fee standards were not changed since 1965; according to Li Baining, Vice-minister, the Ministry of Water Conservancy and Electric Power, '...water fees were set too low and some places collected effectively no water fees.'[21]

The 1985 regulation stipulates that all water projects will have to be paid for the water they supply be it for industry, agriculture and daily use in cities and towns and for electricity generation; also for underground water supply, drainage water and industrial reusable water. Stoppage of water supply in case of non-payment and penalties for delayed payment is provided for. To ensure payment and to assure water supply, in some areas the system of pre-paid water coupons issued before the start of the irrigation season prevails [26]. Payment of water fees in kind is permissible.

Water fees vary according to the purposes for which water is utilised. Water fees for grain crops are to be based on the cost of water supply while those for cash crops and livestock breeding may be slightly higher than supply cost. Seasonal variations in water fees are allowed as also total exemption or nominal charges at high-water season or in case of utilisation of water not covered by the water allocation system. The fees for farmland irrigation, excepting drainage water, are according to provincial regulations, the lowest [23, 24]. Generally the rates are in ascending order on water for irrigation, industrial and urban household use and electricity generation. The Xinjiang regulation provides for grading of water fees according to the reliability of water supply from the irrigation system, starting with the most-assured and well-developed. Where the management units, eg., reservoir or main canal, are self-reliant accounting units they are allowed to levy a surcharge. Also, towards the resettlement of persons displaced by reservoir construction and by flood-prevention measures the levying of supplements to water fees is provided for [27].

Water fees are to be levied according to the volume of water supplied under the plan for its allocation. Volumetric pricing is the officially desired objective; among the factors inhibiting its wide-spread adoption are the mode of irrigation eg., field-to-field flooding and the need for greater availability of low-priced automatic measuring devices. In the absence of such devices, hydrological measuring standards are to be used. In practice, as indicated by the numerous albeit short accounts available, water fees are charged basically according to the area irrigated, with a supplement based on volume where feasible as in the case of pump wells and reservoirs.

Costing of water supply aims at the recovery, in full, of the costs of operation and maintenance (O & M) through the levy of water fees. In the PRC, the O & M costs are to include the costs of 'simple reproduction' and for maintaining the capital stock; provisions for depreciation and major repairs are to be included in the O & M costs. Detailed official regulations[1] on costing have been issued along with official exhortations on the importance of auditing and accounting of project expenditure in water conservation and management, in line with such requirement in all sectors of the economy.

The regulations provide for: (a) a distinction, in the case of investment (valued at original cost) between the state projects and collective projects. In the case of collective projects it includes collective financial investment, and local materials but excludes collective labour input valuation as capital investment; (b) inclusion of investment in pre-project work, a component generally underestimated or neglected; (c) operating expenses to include not only staff and other expenditure but also that on housing and other social benefits, generally underestimated before, as well as on training and research experimental station; (d) ways of allocating the fixed investment costs in multi-purpose projects among the various purposes and, in the capacity of the reservoirs, among flood control, storage and stagnant water; (e) computation of depreciation rates and provisions for major repairs seperately, thus avoiding the past experience when major repairs were undertaken beyond the cost of new installation; (f) correction to the cost of supply from main channels according to the effectiveness of irrigation coefficient; (g) interest to be charged on the fixed and variable cost of water supply at between four and six per cent (in water-scarce areas, six per cent).

Data available, on a country-wide basis, on water fees in 1983 [33] indicate that out of the total financial resources of the irrigation districts only half was from water fees.[2] The water fee per *mu* (of 0.84 yuan) was an increase of 45 per cent over that in 1980. However the rate, judged by its proportion of 1.9 per cent to cost of agricultural production can be viewed as still low.[3] Comparable figures after the 1985 regulation are not yet available; there are various reports of increased rates and improved collection [35-38]. Progress towards full costing can be expected to be slow [39]. Among the contributory factors are the autonomy for collectively managed units to set their own water fees, for the adaptation of the fees to local conditions like water resource endowment and for fixing the fees in the light of overall economic policy towards lightening the burden on the farmers.[4]

Official pronouncements in the PRC recognise that pricing of water supply is a useful supplement to but not a substitute for efficient management. There are many technical and economic requirements for efficient pricing, with its allocative advantages, that are not fully present now in the PRC: to mention a few, full costing at prices which reflect the scarcity of factors of production; adequate metering of water deliveries; adequate control structures for withholding of water supply for non-payment. Generally, in the PRC as in other developing countries, while efficiency in water use can be induced through water fees, other factors like efficient allocation of water supply and planning and adoption of appropriate intensity of water application are equally if not more important. In the PRC the objectives of levying water fees are to promote careful use of water through the 'visibility of direct charges', through escalation of fees for intakes above planned norm and through reduction of fees where households contract for economy in water intake [40] and to assist in mobilising resources for self-financing of water management units [41].

Auxiliary Income

Towards self-sufficiency in funding the water management units are expected to rely, in addition to water fees, on income generated through multiple production activities. In fact the official policy calls upon them to expand such activities, without lesseninig their efficiency in water management operations [42].

The subsidiary production activities form part of the management contracts the water management units conclude with the supervisory administrative authorities, including the undertaking to become financially self-sufficient self-management units. No local administrative or other units are permitted to indiscriminately transfer resources or promote egalitarianism (*yi ping er diao*) among the units in pursuing such production activities as autonomous enterprises. As fiscal incentives, the income from such operations is to be exempt from commodity and value-added taxes for two or three years.

The auxiliary activities cover a wide range: from crop production, fishery, livestock and pig breeding, planting of trees and primary processing to tourism, manufacturing and extension of technical services [43-49]. Initially on a small scale, they are gradually evolving into large-scale operations, integrating production with marketing, with lateral links across administrative and geographical boundaries; such links, in the case of fisheries, help avoid the free-rider phenomenon (fish breeding in one area and fish catch in another area). An indirect benefit is the formation of a skilled labour force in the water management units which is available, under technical service contracts, to other production units in the project area.

A direct impact of such income-generating auxiliary activities is on the wages of the administrative staff of the water management units. The part-time peasant technicians among the administrative staff are allocated economic plots (*jingji tian*), to be decided by the collectives in the light of local conditions, or machinery for primary processing [50]. All the accounts available refer to the much-needed increase in income, housing and social welfare services thus brought about for the staff.

In 1983 the income from auxiliary activities accounted, in the whole country, for 13 per cent of the total income of the irrigation districts [33]. Comparable country-wide figures are not available to assess the impact of the vigorous official promotion of such activities since then. It is reported that in eight provinces and in cities like Shanghai the supplementary activities have contributed substantially to balancing the expenditure of the management units, excepting major repairs and depreciation [51].

O & M Expenditure: Self-Financing

In 1983 the income of the irrigation districts, country-wide, from water fees and subsidiary activities accounted for 63 per cent of the total, indicating the extent of reliance on other sources of budgetary support. Comparable figures for later period are not available. An indication of such continuing dependence can be gathered from a report for the whole country on state-run water management units: in the three years since 1981 the extent of their self-reliance for current expenditure (*richang jingfei*) increased from 40 to only 50 per cent [51]. Progress is being made towards self-financing: the diverse reports from various parts of the country provide scattered but unmistakable evidence. However there is continuing need for for financial support to the water management units for their operational and maintenance expenditure.

Funding: Self-raised

Investment at the collective sector level is, as is well-known, significant in irrigation construction, both in terms of material and labour input, as is illustrated in Table 2. Of the labour input, the major part is accounted for by the labour input at the collective sector level, as shown by Table 3. The levels in 1980, given in the tables, are considered a benchmark, as indicated by the frequent urgings, from the highest policy level, on the collective administration to strive to achieve [52]. Comparative figures for current years are not available [53]. In view of the reiterated policy emphasis, that those who benefit must mobilise the resources, some indications of a qualitative nature are presented below.

Table 2. Outlay in five Large Irrigation Projects: Jiangsu Province, 1980
(Hundred million yuan)

Total outlay	State outlay	Collective (commune) outlay	Outlay on labour input
144	36	38	70
	25.0%	26.4%	48.6%

Source: Lin Tianfu [29], p. 345. State and collective outlays are on material inputs.

Table 3. Labourers Engaged in Basic Farmland Construction, Shanxi Province, Muyang County, (1967-1979) (Per cent based on cumulative figures)

Agricultural labour as a proportion of total labour force	39.1%
Distribution of agricultural labour input by level:	
Production brigade	74.6%
Commune	10.1%
County	15.3%
(Total)	(100%)

Source: Lin Tianfu [29], p 345.

Tax Revenues

Collective sector has been allotted, under a regulation in 1985 [54, 55], a number of low revenue-yielding taxes.[5] It shares with the state the income-tax on collectively-owned enterprises [56]. It levies a surcharge on the state agricultural tax [57].

Some special characteristics of state-local financial relations in the PRC deserve to be noted here in view of their impact on collective sector's resources for, among others, rural infrastructure development: (a) In the PRC the state alone can enact tax laws. *All* tax collection is exclusively carried out by the local officials, appointed by local governments, resulting in tax exemptions in the interests of local development; (b) Local governments (provincial, collective sector) cannot borrow, but enterprises owned by them can, from the banking sector; (c) The state tax revenues the collective administration collects are shared by them with the provincial government which sets the ratio on the basis of need-based equality amongst the counties. Negotiations and bargaining play an important role.

State Grants

The PRC does not have a system of formula grants. In addition to *ad hoc* grants there are two sources, important with respect to farmland construction including irrigation: (a) The revolving fund for rural development [58] financed by the state budget has been extending since 1981 interest-free loans for rural development through specialised banks, including for infrastructural projects like irrigation construction. Where repayable conditions exist the grants previously given are to be converted to loans; (b) The proceeds from a recent tax on farmland converted to non-farming purposes [59] are to be equally divided between the state and localities and are specifically earmarked for the revolving fund for rual development. Exemptions from payment of this tax include land for resettlement of people displaced during irrigation construction and natural calamities and land directly used in construction of irrigation works.

Self-Raised Funds in the Collective-Sector

Self-raised funds at the collective sector are outside the state budget; they are generally referred to as *jiti tiliu*. The administration at the collective level has autonomy with respect to their collection and utilisation. There are no officially fixed guidelines except that they should not be arbitrarily fixed or increased.

Under the 1985 regulation, collective sector administration imposes levies for its governmental administrative expenses, fees for the social services it provides like education and health and for any public utility it runs. The number of such levies, their rates and the amount collected vary from one administration to another. Relevant budgetary details are not available.

Following the abolition of the commune system, with its unified system of collective accumulation and distribution of collective income, official policy statements have called for support of agriculture from the industrial sector at the collective level [60, 61]. The source of funding is the after-tax (including state income-tax on them) profits of the collectively-owned township and village enterprises (CTVEs); profits of enterprises set up by voluntary cooperative economic groups and of private enterprises.

At the initial stage the contributions directly supported the collective welfare fund and the collective administrative expenditure; they also subsidised the input costs of the farmer, the price differentials between the free-market sales and state-purchase of foodgrains and equalisation of the wage differentials between the industrial and farm sectors, at the collective level. At official urging, followed by the practices in comparatively more developed provinces, the contributions are now being utilised towards farmland construction, including construction and repair of farm level irrigation facilities, thus changing over from 'supporting agriculture through industry' *(yigong bu nong)* to 'constructing the village with (help from) industry' *(yigong jian cun)* [62-64].

There are no overall guidelines on the amount of such contributions from the rural enterprises nor on its allocation amongst the various forms of support to the farming sector. Some scattered data, broadly indicative, are available [65] for some provinces on the financial contribution of the CTVEs to the farm sector; they show variations not necessarily reflecting the comparative strength of the CTVEs in those provinces. Practices differ. There is a large degree of variation in the extent of vitality of the CTVEs and a large proportion of them, themselves, are in need of financial support: instances are reported of the CTVEs resorting to bank borrowing to meet the target levy.

Labour Accumulation

Mobilisation and organisation of labour *(laodong touzi)* for water conservancy projects in the PRC, and the comparatively large labour input even in its large and medium-sized projects, have fascinated students of contemporary China. Currently the mandatory practices regarding labour input in basic rural construction, which continued under the early production responsibility contracts even after the abolition of the commune system, are being reverted to, after some experience with hiring labour under labour contracts in the rural sector.

The Commune System

Under the Commune System, the responsibility for water construction work and water management was divided according to the immediate beneficiary, production team, production brigade and commune. The construction work was undertaken by the team or where the water work was spread, by the brigade. Where funding was necessary for materials or professional expertise was necessary it was provided for from the collective accumulation fund of the commune; in addition the beneficiary had to mobilise local materials and labour input, uncompensated by cash payment. Where in a joint undertaking between two production teams one of them fell short of its mandatory labour input the settlement between the two was decided by the brigade or by the commune which also decided the ownership (user) rights of teams and brigades.

At the production team or brigade level the input required was naturally, for the most part, labour. The mandatory labour input required was allocated to the production team generally on the basis of the land under it: for instance according to the land under cultivation or total land with, say, four *mu* counted as one *mu* of cultivated land [66].[6] Where the household was not in a position to meet the mandatory labour input target, it could make mutual arrangement with other households or make a compensatory payment in cash to the production team, as fixed by the Party in consultation with the commune. Similar arrangements prevailed between production teams and between the team and the brigade.

The Party regulations [67, 68] on the commune had fixed overall guidelines on the proportion of collective accumulation funds to be spent on basic rural construction (three to five per cent) and the mandatory labour days for it (minimum of three per cent of labour days in a year). The term, mandatory labour, is somewhat of a misnomer: the labour put in for collective accumulation was valued in work points applicable for the team as a whole and hence the element of compulsion to work in construction activities was not significant; where the labour input in construction was in excess of the quota fixed for the production team it was compensated for in cash by the brigade or the commune, available for distribution within the production team; to prevent inter-team income disparities the monetary evaluation of the excess or deficit workpoint was undertaken by the Party Committee at the (higher) county level in consultation with the commune authorities. Thus, under the system the difficulties in monetary resource mobilisation in a rural context were avoided and collective decision was made on the choice of labour allocation between current production and accumulation for future in terms of rural infrastructure.

The Production Responsibility System
During the period immediately following the announcement of the policy of separation of the administration from the commune, the land responsibility contracts specified the labour input the contracting households had to provide for collective farmland construction. The organisation and deployment of such labour input followed the practices under the commune system, with the administration at various levels replacing the commune three-tier system and with the Party units continuing to decide important policy issues. The labour input was truly mandatory as there was no longer the system of payment by work points.

With the near universal adoption of the individual household responsibility system in the farm sector, the contracting household's contribution to farmland construction, among others, was limited to only monetary payments to the collective accumulation fund, as fixed under the contract. Basic farmland construction, including irrigation waterworks, began to be undertaken by the collective administration with hired wage labour. There are no regulations regarding contracts in rural labour market.

Labour force in the rural area is constituted not only by farmers who are seasonally unemployed or whose plot of land is not adequate to provide subsistence or itinerant labourers but also by those who have left the land but not the village; while the former could be drawn upon for minor irrigation work, construction work calls for labour force of a more permanent nature. In fast growing areas, as in the Eastern coast, rural enterprises and housing construction provide alternative avenues of employment, raising the wages for labourer in basic construction [69]. Thus the employment of wage labour in basic farmland construction was faced with falling fund allocation and raising wage level.

With the official call in the beginning of 1986, and reiterated in 1988, for labour accumulation in farmland construction and with the guidelines issued in 1988 [70, 71], beginnings have been made in mandatory labour for that purpose. Relevant compulsory provision is included in the production responsibility contract or separately in mandatory work contract (*shigong baogan zerenzhi*). The 1988 guidelines follow the practices under the commune system as outlined above, with two changes: the decision is left to local authorities according to local conditions and requirements; where the collective administration has the financial resources it can employ paid labour. Ten to twenty days' labour in a year, according to local requirements, is laid down [72-76].

An Overall View

Budgetary data on the collective sector are neither available on own revenues, tax-revenue allocation from county level, grants (and their conversion into loans) etc., nor on expenditures, current and capital, categorywise, or on 'labour accumulation' The absence of such data inhibits any analysis of the taxable capacity at the collective sector level and its utilisation, for instance, for basic rural construction. Some indication of the overall trend in collective accumulation, on which rural basic construction including irrigation is based—is given below in Table 4. As another pointer, the trend in the allocation of CTVEs' profits for rural basic construction is presented in Table 5.

Table 4. Rural Income; its disposal

	1978	*1980*	*1984*	*1986*	*1987*
Income (hundred million yuan)					
Gross income	1881.3	2464.5	4891.0	6881.9	8408.0
Prodn. exp.	748.0	963.7	1790.0	3090.7	4035.8
Net income	1133.3	1500.8	3101.0	3791.2	4372.2
Disposal (as per cent of gross income)					
State tax payment	3.2	2.7	2.8	3.3	3.2
Payment to collective	10.0	9.0	4.6	4.3	4.7
Personal disposable income	47.0	49.2	56.0	47.5	44.1

Source: *Zhongguo Nongcun Tongji Nianjian 1988*, p 175. 8

Table 5. CTVEs' Net Profits; Major Allocations

	1978	*1980*	*1984*	*1986*	*1987*
Net profit	88.1	118.4	128.7	161.0	187.8
Net profit utilised	68.2	94.6	99.6	n.a.	n.a.
Allocation					
Capital maintenance	30.9	47.0	61.0	80.3	100.0
Farm machinery purchase	11.5	9.1			
Rural basic constructn.	11.8	9.4		6.9	8.5
Poor prodn. teams	3.1	4.2	*6.4		
Collective welfare	4.0	6.8	15.7	14.5	18.0

Source: *Zhongguo Nongcun Tongji Nianjian 1988*. p 176.
Note: * denotes the sum of all three for 1984.

The trend emerging from Tables 4 and 5 indicates a significantly slow growth in collective accumulation with adverse effects on basic rural construction. The proportion of CTVEs' profits allocated also shows a declining trend. Since 1989 the expansion of CTVEs at their past rate is beset with uncertainty.

Irrigation Water Allocation System
Decentralisation of irrigation water management notwithstanding, allocation of irrigation water is subject to plan. Formal criteria are laid down at the level of province/large reservoir. The allocation procedures are the same as under the commune system. Under the near universal adoption of household responsibility system how efficiency in distribution and equity in allocation are maintained is considered below.

Allocation System [4]
In the distribution of water for irrigation in a planned way, specific water requirements for each of the major crops are worked out and communicated to all management offices down to county level. The dominant determinant in water distribution plan is the crop-water requirement, as compared to other developing countries in Asia where the area of land holding or each cultivating household having a right to equal amount of water is often used as criteria.

Water available for irrigation is to be utilised in an integrated manner within the irrigation district: (a) In canal-based irrigation districts with other sources, water from canal, surface storage and groundwater, is to be used proportionately and where canal supply is not adequate, surface storage and groundwater should be drawn upon. Where canal water is in excess, it should be stored; (b) In reservoir-based irrigation district, the priority in use is: ponds first, particularly those unused, then reservoir; high level water for high level fields and low level water for low level fields; (c) Where both canal and well irrigation prevail, well is to be drawn upon for nearby plot and canal for distant plot, canal water to soak the field and well-water for irrigation, canal water as the mainstay and well-water as supplement, well water for urgent need and canal water for development.

In water allocation, priority is to be given to high level plots over low level plots, distant plots over nearby plots, plots downstream over plots near the canal source, plots with economically valuable crops over others, small plots collectively managed as large units over individual small plots.

Where the main canal flow is reduced, a planned rotational system among the sublateral canals, with a proportionate reduction in the frequency of irrigation, is to be followed.

Surface irrigation methods fall into four main groups: check basin irrigation (*getian yanguan*), mainly for paddy rice; flood irrigation (*manguan*) which is discouraged as wasteful, with encouragement for storing flood water; furrow irrigation (*gou guan*) for crops like maize, cotton; and border irrigation (*qiguan*) for cereal crops, herbs and vegetables.

Irrigation methods, particularly the last two above, require land-levelling. The framework, legal and administrative, for land-levelling exists. Under the 1986 Land Management Law, administration at every level is authorised to take steps in land management to protect and enhance land productivity [77, 78].

Performance Targets

Detailed performance targets are fixed. They are of relevance also with respect to the management contracts referred to above. They include proportion of planned irrigated area achieved, proportion of planned volume of water supplied, coefficient of efficiency of canal water flow, coefficient of irrigation efficiency, volume of canal waterflow supplied to the field, proportion of outflow to inflow at each station and the increase in production achieved as compared to plan target.

Land Contracts

Efficiency and equity, however defined, in irrigation water distribution will be determined by the nature of land distribution among the households and the fragmentation of land holdings. In this context the current near universal *baogan daohu* system is briefly reviewed. Relevant data and information are based on the findings of an official national survey [79] in 1984-1985 of a sample of 272 villages, 37,422 households and 93 townships and 71 counties in all provinces except Xizang Zizhiqu. No comparable nationwide study is available for later years.

Equity

Equity in land distribution (strictly expressed, land use rights) is a necessary, though not a sufficient, condition for equity in irrigation water distribution. Though there is a diversity of forms, there are four main criteria used in the contracts, as indicated below; also given is the percentage, in their total of 10,481, of the (former) production teams which have adopted such criteria: (a) Population criterion: each household receives an equal share of the land for contracting: 70.1 per cent; (b) Labour force criterion: everyone in the rural labour force gets an equal share: 7.3 per cent; (c) Proportion of labour force to population: applied to each household: 21.3 per cent; (d) Ability: based on technological level and farm managerial capacity: 0.4 per cent.

In practice equity was ensured with the allotment of foodgrain fields (*kouliang tian*) on the basis of population and responsibility fields (*zeren tian*) on the basis of the other criteria; a variation in this system has been recently introduced in Sichuan province as noted below.

Demographic changes and changes in occupational structure can strain the system [80]. Some pilot projects have been undertaken to allow for demographic changes but they have not been widely adopted [81]. The official policy is stability with minor adjustments in land contracts (*da wending, xiao tiaozheng*). The small, uneconomic size of the plots has recently brought changes in official attitudes and they are relevant with respect to equity as well as efficiency in water distribution.

In the distribution of land and the fragmentation of holdings, the relative productivity of land, the extent of nearness to irrigation source etc are taken into account by the collective administration; when inequities still persist, concessions are given while fixing collective levies and mandatory grain delivery [82]. Recently scientific gradation of land, before the conclusion of land contracts, is being reported [83].

Equity and Efficiency

Efficiency in irrigation water delivery increases the less fragmented the holdings are. The country-wide average for the land area contracted for cultivation is 8.5 *mu* per household, fragmented into 9.7 plots with an average area per plot of 0.86 *mu*. There are of course wider variations, with greater fragmentation, within the country [84]. Various practices are being adopted to increase the size of the uneconomic holdings.

Transfer of land contracts, according to official policy. has to be through the collective which in turn redistributes the land under contract. The person who receives the land-use right has to compensate the original holder for the improvements the latter has made in the land, at the same time inheriting the responsibilities in the original contract. The amount of compensation, usually in terms of grains, is left to mutual negotiations between the two parties.

The households which surrender the contract to the collective are those who have shifted to non-agricultural operations or whose manpower has been reduced due to demographic changes or those who find their land allocated disadvantageously placed for discharging the mandatory obligations. The land thus redistributed has gone mainly towards readjustment due to demographic changes in the household and as compared to the officially permissible contract period of 15 years there are reports that such redistributions take place in three years so that adjustments will be on a small-scale.

The scale of such collective redistribution is small. For the country as a whole, in 1984-1985, the proportion of households to the total who surrendered land was 2.7 per cent and the proportion of cultivable land surrendered was 0.7 per cent; such proportions in the case of households receiving land were 4.5 per cent and 1.3 per cent. Some slight discrepancies in the coverage of the survey notwithstanding, it does not seem that such collective redistribution has been significant with respect to increasing the size of holdings. Reports from Sichuan province also confirm this conclusion [85]. Unofficial, illegal, transactions in landrights are on the increase and publicly recognised [86, 87]. The unofficial renting-in of land is a significant phenomenon as signalled by various reports at the provincial level and considering the uneconomic size of the plots and the traditional hunger for land the rent exacted could be exorbitant, as seen from the auction prices under experiment in Sichuan province. However, for purposes of this note, it is not evident from the reports whether it is the uneconomic farmers who rent-in and whether it is from farmers who have left the land but not the village; specialised households, renting-in or renting-out, can not give rise to this phenomenon on a significant scale as their number is, according to the stricter statistical measurement currently adopted, much smaller than the estimates a few years back.

The 'two field' system [88-90], spreading in Sichuan province with official blessing, is aimed at ensuring equity while enlarging the size of the holding. Half the cultivable land in the village or land based on a fixed target per person is distributed as grain field (*kouliang tian*). The rest is put up for auction (*zuren tian*). Land rights pertaining to auctioned land are transferable while those in grain fields are not. In the beginning, the administration held auction for all the land or for land for mechanisation of farm operations or the villagers themselves organised the auctions. But currently the most prevalant variant is the 'two field' system.

Under the 'two field' system the period of contract for grain fields is ten to 15 years while the distribution of auction land depends on manpower changes in the village. Grain fields pay only agricultural tax and water fees while the auction land, in addition, has to contribute to the collective fund and the various collective fees. The auction prices are high and in some areas they can be 40 to 60 yuan per *mu*. To distinguish from the traditional deservedly-hated rent system, a part of the auction price earnings (10 to 20 per cent) is directly ploughed back into rural basic construction work, including irrigation.

The experience with the 'two field' system as seen in the three counties in Sichuan in 1986, drawn upon above, does not indicate any significant impact on accumulation of land towards enlarging the size of the holding. The grain field is usually of 0.4 to 0.5 mu while there is observed an overall restriction that no person in the village should have a holding less than 0.8 mu, thus significantly cutting into the land available for auctions. An overall study of 12 counties in Sichuan indicates that in 1986 the proportion of cultivable land transferred to the total was only 1.34 per cent [91].

Unified farming practices in small plots can alleviate the problems arising from their size. This was directly achieved under the earlier system of production team. In 1984-1985, of the 10481 original production teams, only 7.7 per cent continued to operate in the former unified way. Specialised villages (*zhuanye cun*) come under these systems and, as the numerous accounts about them indicate, such villages specialise mostly in processing, animal husbandry and rural transport.

The official rural policy announced in 1987 [61] encourages various types of cooperation in voluntary cooperative economic groups of which numerous instances are being reported; among them are area-based groups basically concerned with land resource management. They are at present in a formative stage and aim basically at combining the advantages of individual household responsibility system with the features of the earlier responsibility system (*lianchan chengbao zerenzhi*).

Among the various instances that can be cited, one [92] from Jiangsu province, Jianhu county, is a good illustration. The village group agrees on: (1) production for contracted delivery and for market sale and their division among households; (2) the purchase of inputs and their distribution among the plots for maximal output, with subsidy for low productivity plots towards meeting contract delivery; (3) payments to the collective administration and collective labour accumulation; (4) maintaining soil fertility, with household targets for green manure and composting.

Evolution of the system into higher stages of cooperation [93, 94] faces issues relating to the valuation of member's inputs, particularly land-use rights, modes of allocation of profits, management arrangements and voting rights. No nationwide data are available on the nature and number of such cooperatives and the extent of area/households covered.

Legal Framework
The comprehensive 1988 Water Law [95], specifically lays down, in section 12, that no unit or person can divert, store or use water at the expense of the public's or other person's interest and, in section 31, that in the runoff of stored water or in allocation of water attention should be paid to both higher and lower reaches and to their left and right. Commentators in the PRC underline that, under the Law, water allocation is not left free nor is it prescribed

in detail as in some countries but, subject to specified overall criteria, local adaptations are allowed [96]. While demarcating the responsibility for construction and protection of waterworks the Law also specifies payment of compensation where cultivable land is taken over. Disputes are to be settled through mutual discussions or by mediation at every stage of the litigation process; if these fail arbitration by the administration is to be resorted to. The Law also provides for appeal to the People's Court if either of the parties disagrees with the administrative decision [97].

Worthy of note, also, are the recent regulations [98] concerning land management, like that on improving land registration records and on the work of land gradation and classification.

A notable feature of the judicial process in the PRC is the reliance on mediation at every stage and the prior consideration given to mediation before judicial adjudication. There is no system of case law. Compilations of judicial decisions are made and circulate as internal documents; they are for information and are not cited as legal precedents. Even in the sparse reports available on court decisions the legal basis for the decisions is generally not given. Lawyers in the PRC are state functionaries; while advising the clients he is expected to cooperate with the official process and abide by the award of the arbitrator; at any stage he can on his own terminate his role as an attorney. Overshadowing the judicial process is the fact that the members of the judiciary, though nominally elected by the corresponding-level People's Congresses, form part of the *nomenklatura* system.

Cadres' accountability under law [99, 100] is slow to evolve; some systematic effort has been made under the 1989 Administrative Law (Litigation Procedures) which is to come into effect on 1 October 1990. Generally the courts, in adjudicating cases involving administrative organs, do not consider whether the administrative organs conform with the powers given to them under the law. They actively encourage the parties to resort to higher level administrative arbitration or to the state notarial organisations. Evaluation of cadres' performance in public and the 'letter and visit' system are meant to ensure cadres' responsiveness to the public; they work but admittedly imperfectly.

As can be inferred from the recent annual work reports of the People's Supreme Court, at lower levels of the judiciary the level of legal understanding has to be upgraded, the higher levels courts have still to provide leagal leadership to the lower levels, the living standards have to be improved and 'bureaucratism' prevails (i.e., refusal to register legal complaints and hear cases, law's delay, lack of adequate implementation of judicial decisions).

Though there are passing references in the journals to land and water rights disputes precise information is not available. A notable exception is a nationally publicised case,[7] referred to as *Nongmin Gao Xianfu* [101].

Some Tentative Observations

An overall non-technical performance criterion of water delivery for irrigation since the introduction of the economic responsibility system is the area irrigated and the water delivered to the farmers. Available, limited, statistics indicate that during the period 1983-1986 the trend has been stationary with minor variations, as indicated in Table 6.

The factors accounting for the decline in effective irrigated area were surveyed countrywide for 1984, the only such survey available: of the total decline 35 per cent was accounted for by obsolete motor-pumped wells, 16 per cent by inadequacy in or absence over a long period of water delivery, 14 per cent by water works installations damaged or obsolete, 5 per cent by encroachments on land for waterworks and the rest due to miscellaneous causes [102]. Hence the repeated official calls for priority for the renovation and upgrading of the existing structures rapidly built in the past, protection of the waterworks area from unauthorised conversion to housing, farming and routes for public transportation, and breaches for diversion for unplanned water utilisation.

Decentralisation of financial responsibility, through water fees and auxiliary farming activities, has made progress. However state grants are needed; an important source of grants, the state tax on cultivable land, is still to be effectively implemented. Economic levers, like conversion of grants to loans, are still to operate effectively. With the declining trend in collective sector accumulation, mandatory 'labour accumulation' and levy on CTVEs, features of the commune system, are resorted to, but with local variations permitted.

Decentralisation in management, along with increased efficiency, is to be fostered by a system of responsibility contracts, for construction and for management, and of public bidding. Apart from the legal aspects, the statistics available indicate a low rate of adoption. Considering the high proportion of small-sized irrigation districts and the important role attached to peasant technicians, with a single waterman at the village level, there is need for upgrading the technical skill, as evidenced by the frequent official exhortations.

Table 6. Irrigated area (million ha)

	1986	*1985*	*1984*	*1983*
Area under cultivation(*gengdi*)	96.23	97.82	98.78	99.07
Effective irrigated area (*you xiao guangai mianji*)	47.87	47.93	48.40	48.55
Actual area irrigated	39.94	38.67	39.93	39.38
Water supply for agriculture (billion cubic metres)		364.3	353.7	

Note: Effective irrigated area is currently defined as the area under cultivation which has a defined source of irrigation water, whose plots are comparatively well-levelled, where there already exists a conveyance system and where, *over a period of a 'few years'*, irrigation can be carried out. See Yan Sen zhubian, *Nongye Tongji*, Zhongguo Tongji Chubanshe. Beijing. 1985, 76-79.

Source: Various issues of *Zhongguo Shuili*. Irrigation statistics are subject to periodic revision.

It is the generally accepted view that where water flow is adequate water allocation could be left to the authorities but users' associations can play a useful role in the middle and lower reaches. Users' associations are officially a long-term goal and some sporadic reports indicate that in some small-scale irrigation projects, built and financed by cooperative economic groups of farmers, they are beginning to be established. In the meantime it is the leading cadres who make the decisions.

A detailed system of rules and regulations exists for water allocation and the published accounts naturally reflect their successful working. A formal legal procedure has been laid down in detail for the resolution of water disputes. Equity in water allocation is facilated by equitable land allocation but in a situation where the population/land ratio is unfavourable small-sized plots dominate and various cooperative measures for upgrading the economic viability of the farmer's landholding are being tried.

Notes

Numbers in the text and in the notes, encased in square brackets, identify sources according to the list of references.

1. For an explanation of the latest accounting practices see [28]. For the perceptions in the PRC of the techniques in investment analysis of water resources projects see [29], chapter 9, pp. 268-295. Some case studies of project evaluation in irrigation, utilising both the concepts of period of recoupment and the rate of return but neglecting indirect costs and indirect benefits, are available: see [30, 31, 32]. Many of the regulations currently issued on costing of water supply have not yet been made publicly available and no attempt is made in this note at detailed assessment. The references made here are intended to indicate that water supply is not considered a free good and that the objective of the official regulations is full costing.

2. The data are given in terms of water supply from small outlets in the canal (*an qudao mao shuiliang*) and thus can be taken as including collectively-owned units.

3. Water fees in 1983 as a national average, 0.84 yuan per *mu*; costs of production in 1983 as an average per *mu* of six major crops, 43.73 yuan, as given in [34].

4. For instance see [24]: 'The water fees are not to exceed, at the most, five per cent of the annual value of agricultural production'; see [23]: 'In fixing the water fees the economic capacity to pay of the benefitting unit and of the masses (*canzhao shouyi danwei he qunzhong de jingji zedan nengli*) are to be consulted'. Also see [20], article 2, section 4.

5. For details see Urban Maintenance and Construction Tax (Guowu Yuan, *Chengshi Weihu Jianshe Shui Zanxing Tiaoli*, 8 February 1985); Livestock Sales Tax (Guowu Yuan, *Shengchu Jiaoyi Zanxing Tiaoli*, 13 December 1982); Market Transaction Tax (Caizheng Bu, *Guanyu Jishi Jiaoyi Shuide Zanxing Guiding*, 16 April 1962); Slaughter Tax (Zhengwu Yuan, *Tuzai Shui Zanxing Tiaoli*, 19 December 1950); Real Estate Tax (Guowu Yuan, *Zhonghua Renmin Gongheguo Fangchan Shui Zanxing Tiaoli*, 15 September 1986); Vehicle and Boat Tax (Guowu Yuan, *Zhonghua Renmin Gongheguo Che Chuan Shiyong Shui Zanxing Tiaoli*, 15 September 1986).

6. This refers to the practices in 1979 and provides details of settlement in cash among production teams.

7. The case involves some rural households (including three Party members) putting up structures impeding water flow and flood control. The account of the judicial processes indicates that they are not without impact and, unusual in the PRC, the laws invoked are cited: at first the appeal of the households against the administration to the Party, and the Party, through the 'letter and visit system', investigating and educating the households on the social consequences; the households approaching the Village People's Committee and the Committee's refusal to interfere with higher-level decision; the local, provincial and national press taking up the cause of the households; the appeal to the People's Economic Court for compensation and the final decision by the Provincial People's Court in favour of the local administration, without compensation to the households, for dismantling the structures.

References

(In Chinese)

1. Shuili Bu (1981): *Guanqu guanli zanxing banfa*. 7 November 1981.
2. Hunansheng Gemingweiyuanhui Shuilidianliju, *Zhaoshan Guanqu*. Beijing: Shuilidianli Chubanshe, 1978 {1-22.}
3. Shandongsheng Gemingweiyuanhui Shuiliju, Shandongsheng Linbaoxian Gemingweiyuanhui, *Yeyuan Shuiku Guanqu*. Beijing: Shuilidianli Chubanshe, 1979. {74-86.}
4. Shuilidianli Bu Nongtianshuilisi, *Guanqu jihua yongshui banfa he jingyan xuanbian*. Beijing: Shuilidianli Chubanshe, 1984.
5. International Commission on Irrigation and Drainage: *Guangai Paishui Jishu Mingci Biaozhun Fuhao*. Jingjibu Shuiziyuan Tongyi Guihuaweiyuanhui Yiyin. March 1962. (Standard reference for irrigation terminology).
6. *Zhongguo nongye baike quanshu. Shuilijuan*. 2 vol. Beijing: Nongye Chubanshe, 1987. {(section, *Guangai guihua*,vol 1, pp 214-215).}
7. Zhao Ziyang, *Yanzhe you Zhongguo tesede shehui zhuyi daolu qianjin (zai Zhongguo Gongchangdang di-shisanci Quanguo Daibiao Dahui shang de baogao*. 25 October 1987).
8. Ministry of Water Conservancy and Electric Power, 'Opinions on the Reform of Business Management Structure of State-Operated Irrigation Districts'. *Nongtian Shuili yu Xiaoshuidian*. No. 5, May 1985. English translation in JPRS-CAG-86-001, 8 January 1986.
9. Guowu Yuan Bangongting zhuanfa, *Shuilidianli Bu Guanyu Gaige Shuili Gongcheng Guanli Tizhi he Kaizhan Zonghe Jingying Wenti de Baogao de Tongzhi*, 8 May 1985; *Shuilidianli Bu Guanyu Jiaqiang Nongtian Shuili Sheshi Guanli Gongzuo Baogao de Tongzhi*. 17 October 1985.
10. *Nongye Jingji Wenti*, No 1, 1984, pp 44-46, p 13. Song Lusheng, Shanxisheng Jingdongnandiqu Xingshu Shuiliju, 'Nongtian Shuili, Shuitu Baochi Fuwu Zhongxinde Xingshi he Tedian'.
11. *Zhongguo Shuili*, No 5, 1983, pp 30-33. Liaoningsheng Shuliju Diaochazu, 'Guanyu Shuili Guanli Zeren-zhide Diaocha Baogao'.
12. Guojia Jihua Weiyuanhui, Laodong Renshibu, Zhongguo Renmin Jianshe Yinhang, *Jiben Jianshe Xiangmu Baogan Jingji Zerenshi Shixing Banfa*, 3 March 1983.
13. *Zhongguo Nongye Nianjian 1986*. p 90. Section on 'Shuili Jiben Jianshe Shixing Chengbao Zerenshi'.
14. *Renmin Ribao*, 2 June 1984, p 1. Zhao Ziyang, 'Zhengfu Gongzuo Baogao'.
15. Guowu Yuan, *Jianshe Gongcheng Zhaobiao Toubiao Zanxing Guiding*, 8 November 1984.
16. Chengxiang Jianshe Huanjing Baohu Bu, *Jianzhu Anzhuang Gongcheng Zhaobiao Toubiao Shixing Banfa*, 7 June 1983.
17. *Zhongguo Shuili*, No 4, 1985, pp 10-11. Ma Zhihong, 'Shixing Zhaobiao Chengbaozhi shi Jiben Jianshe Tizhi Gaige de Yige Tupokou'.
18. *Zhongguo Shuili*, No 7, 1985, pp 14-15. Chen Bingliang, 'Jianli Juyou Zhongguo Tese de Zhaobiao Chengbaozhi'.
19. *Jianzhu Jingji*, No 7, 1985, pp 19-22. Tang Ligui, 'Zhoubiao Chengbao Danxiang Gongcheng Yusuan Chengben de Jisuan Banfa'.
20. Guowu Yuan, *Shuili Gongcheng Shuifei Heding, Jishou he Guanli Banfa*, 22 July 1985.
21. *Zhongguo Shuili*, No 9, 1984, p 5. 'Jiefang Sixiang Yongyu Gaige - Li Baining Fubuzhang Da Benkan-zhi Wen'.
22. *Zhongguo Shuili*, No 2, 1985, p 9. Li Decheng, Guangdongsheng Shuidianting, 'Gaige Xianyou Shuili Gongcheng de Jinying Guanli'.
23. *Liaoningsheng Shuili Gongcheng Shuifei Zhengshou Shiyong Guanli Banfa*, 1 August 1983.
24. *Xinjiang Weiwuer Zizhiqu Shuili Gongcheng Shuifei Zhengshou Shiyong Guanli Banfa*, 25 April 1983.
25. *Zhongguo Shuili*, No 2, 1983, pp 27-29. Gu Zemin, Shanxisheng Shuiziyuan Guanli Weiyuanhui Bangongshi, 'Shanxisheng Shuifei Gaige Gongzuo Qude Jinzhan'.
26. *Zhongguo Shuili*, No 2, 1983, pp 27-29. Ni Datian, Zhuo Peijie, 'Hexi Zoulang Guanqu Shixing Shuibiao-zhi'.
27. Guowu Yuan, *Guanyu Zhuajin Chuli Shuiche Yimin Wenti de Baogao*, 29 July 1986.

28. *Zhongguo Shuili*, No 4, 1986, pp 13-15. Shuilidianlibu Shuiliguanlisi Zonghechu, 'Guanyu Shuili Gong-cheng Gongshui Shuifei Cesuan zhong Ruogan Wenti de Jieshi he Jianyi'.

29. Liu Tianfu deng bian, *Nongye Touzi Jingji Xiaguo Yanjiu*. Nongye Chubanshe. Beijing 1985.

30. *Nongye Jishu Jingji*, No 4, 1983, pp 38-42. Lin Yunfa, 'Qianmu Diguan Shidian Jingji Xiaoyi Chuxi'.

31. *Nongye Jishu Jingji*, No 9, 1983, pp 16-20. Guan Qingtao, Li Weiwu, 'Nongtian Guangai de Jingji Xiaoyi Fenxi'.

32. *Nongye Jishu Jingji*, No 2, 1983, pp 21-26. Miao Fuchun, Fang Lingdi, 'Xuhai Diqu Shuili Touzi Jingji Xiaoguo Qianxi'.

33. *Zhongguo Shuili*, No 4, 1985, p 29. Shuidianbu Jihuasi Tongjichu, '30 wanyishang Guanqu 1983 nian Gongshui ji Shoufei Qingkuang'.

34. Guojia Tongjisi, *Zhongguo Nongcun Tongji Nianjian 1985*. Zhongguo Tongji Chubanshe. Beijing. 1986.

35. *Nongmin Ribao*, 3 October 1985, p 1. 'Luoyang Ge Guanqu Gaige Shuifei Zhidu Xiaoyi'.

36. *Zhongguo Shuili*, No 8, 1986, pp 12-13. Huang Wei, 'Women de Shuifei Tupole Baiwanyuan Daguan'.

37. *Zhongguo Shuili*, No 4, 1986, p 17. Chen Ankang, 'Jieshao Jizhong Nongtian Shuifei Jishen Banfa'.

38. *Zhongguo Shuili*, No 8, 1986, p 13. Liu Changling, 'Zhuwei Shuiku Zhengshou Shuifei de Jingyan'.

39. *Zhongguo Shuili*, No 4, 1986, p 16. Zhou Zhixian, Hubeisheng Yichengxian Shuiliju, 'Shuifei Gaige yu Nongmin Zedan'.

40. *Zhongguo Shuili*, No 8, 1986, p 11. Wang Jinshui, Li Yousheng, 'Gaige Gei Guanqu Dailai Huoli'.

41. *Zhongguo Shuili*, No 10, 1986, pp 9-10. Lujiangxian Renmin Zhengfu, 'Gaige Guanshui Banfa Tigao Guangai Xiaoyi'.

42. Guowu Yuan Bangongting zhuanfa, *Shuilidianlibu Guanyu Gaige Shuili Gongcheng Guanli Tizhi he Kaizhan Zonghe Jingying Wenti de Baogao de Tongzhi*, 2 May 1985.

43. *Zhongguo Nongye Nianjian 1985*. Section: *Shuili Gongcheng Zonghe Jingying Xiaoyi*. pp 431-433.

44. *Nongmin Ribao*, 29 January 1986, p 2. 'Zhengtian Shuiku Duozhong Jingying Xinxin Xiang Rong'.

45. *Zhongguo Shuili*, No 11, 1986, p 33. Chen Yaqi, 'Ningxia Shuili Xitong Zonghe Jingying Yipiao'.

46. *Zhongguo Shuili*, No 10, 1986, p 34. Yang Fuxi, Zhang Haifa, 'Huangheanshang de Yige Mingzhu'.

47. *Zhongguo Shuili*, No 9, 1986, p 30. 'Yishuiweizhi Zonghe Jingying Shuinonggongshang Lianhe Fazhan'.

48. *Zhongguo Shuili*, No 3, 1986, p 36. 'Liuyu Jigou Zonghe Jingying Kaishi Qibu'.

49. *Zhongguo Shuili*, No 2, 1986, p 34. Liu Shilian, 'Chongtouzhen Shuilizhan Zoushang Qiyehua Daolu'.

50. *Zhongguo Shuili*, No 12, 1986, pp 18-20. Cheng Mingfan, Henansheng Mixian Shuiliju, 'Xiaoxing Shuili Gongcheng zai Shangpin Jingji Xingshixia de Jingying yu Guanli'.

51. *Zhongguo Shuili*, No 12, 1985, pp 6-9. Li Boning, 'Yige Xinxing Shiye de Jueqi'.

52. Guowu Yuan, *Guanyu Dali Kaizhan Nongtian Shuili Jiben Jianshe de Jueding*, 15 October 1989, section 5.

53. Guojia Tongjiju Guiding Zichan Touzi Tongjisi bian, *Zhongguo Guiding Zichan Touzi Tongji Ziliao 1950-1985*. Zhongguo Tongji Chubanshe. Beijing. 1987. p 369; p 425.

54. Guowu Yuan, *Guanyu Shixing 'Huafen Shuizhong, Heding Shouzhi, Fenji Baogan' Caizheng Guanli Tizhi de Guiding*, 21 March 1985.

55. Caizheng Bu, *Xiang(zhen) Caizheng Guanli Shixing Banfa*, 12 April 1985.

56. Guowu Yuan, *Zhonghua Renmin Gongheguo Jiti Qiye Suodeshui Zanxing Tiaoli*, 11 April 1985.

57. *Zhonghua Renmin Gongheguo Nongye Shui Tiaoli*, 3 June 1958.

58. Caizheng Bu, *Zhongyang Caizheng Zhinong Zhouzhuanjin Shiyong Guanli de Jixiang Zanxing Guiding*, 12 May 1985. Caizheng Bu, *Guanyu Chengdian de Caizheng Zhinong Zhouzhuanjin Chuli de Guiding*, 27 June 1986. Caizheng Bu, *Guanyu Zhinong Zijin Jiancha Zhong Youguan Caiwu Chuli Wenti de Zanxing Guiding*, 5 February 1987.

59. Guowu Yuan, *Zhonghua Renmin Gongheguo Gengdi Zhanyongshui Zanxing Tiaoli*, 1 April 1987. Caizheng Bu, *Guanyu Gengdi Zhanyongshui Juti Zhengce Guiding*, 8 August 1987. Caizheng Bu, Zhongguo Renmin Jianshe Yinhang, Zhongguo Gongshang Yinhang, Nongye Yinhang, *Guanyu Yinhang Koujiao Gengdi Zhanyongshui Tuoqian Shuikuan*, 7 July 1988. Caizheng Bu, Guojia Tudi Guanliju, *Guanyu Quebao dui Feinongye Jianshe Yongdi Zhengshou Gengdi Zhanyongshui*, 7 July 1988.

60. Zhonggong Zhongyang, Guowu Yuan, *Guanyu 1986 Nongcun Gongzuo de Buzhu*, 1 January 1986. Section 3.

61. Zhonggong Zhongyang Zhengzhiju, *Ba Nongcun Gaige Yinxiang Shenru*, 22 January 1987. Section 7.

62. *Nongmin Ribao*, 6 March 1986, p 1. 'Dangqian Nongcun 'Yigongbunong' you Naxie Xin Xingshi?'

63. *Nongye Jingji Wenti*, No 2, 1986, pp 9-13. Sun Han, 'Nongye Shidu Guimo Jingying he Shixing 'Yigongbunong' de Taolun'.

64. *Nongcun Gongzuo Tongxun*, No 5, 1986, p 28. Feng Yunlong, ' 'Yigongbunong' Yingyou Zhanlue Yanguang'.

65. *Wenshi Zazhi*, No 4, 1987, pp 53-60, p 40. Haozhi, Wuqiang, ' 'Yigongbunong' de Keguan Jichu yu Youxiao Tujing de Taolun'.

66. *Zhongguo Shuili*, No 4, 1983, p 23. Sichuansheng Hechuanxian Shuidianju, 'Hechuanxian Shixing Toulao Chouzi Xin Banfa Jianshe Shuiku'.

67. Zhong Yang, *Nongcun Renmin Gongshe Gongzuo Tiaoli (shixing caoan)*, 18 December 1978, articles 18-20, 42. Zhong Yang, *Nongcun Renmin Gongshe Gongzuo Tiaoli (xuizheng caoan)*, 11 October 1962, articles 4, 35. Zhong Yang, *Guanyu Gaibian Nongcun Renmin Gongshe Hexuan Danwei Wenti*, 23 February 1962. Zhong Yang, *Guanyu Nongcun Renmin Gongshe Fenpei Wenti*, 3 December 1971.

68. Caizheng Bu, Nongye Bu, *Zhiyuan Nongmin Gongshe Touzi Shiyong Guanli Zanxing Guiding*, 21 May 1979.

69. *Nongye Jishu Jingji*, No 1, 1987, pp 29-31. Chen Sheng, Jiangsushengwei Nongcun Gongzuobu, 'Laodong Jilei zai Nongye Touzi zhongde Diwei jiqi Bianhua Qishi'.

70. Guowu Yuan pizhun *Shuili Bu Guanyu Yikao Qunzhong Hezuo Xingxiu Nongcun Shuili de Shitiao Yijian*, 2 November 1988.

71. Zhonggong Zhongyang, Guowu Yuan, *Guanyu 1986 Nongcun Gongzuo de Buzhu*, 1 January 1986, section 3. Zhonggong Zhongyang, Guowu Yuan, *Guanyu Duoqu Mingnian Nongye Fenggu de Guiding*, 25 November 1988.

72. *Zhongguo Shuili*, No 12, 1986, p 10. 'Hunansheng dui Dong Nongcun Shuili Jianshe Gongzuo de Buzhu'.

73. *Zhongguo Shuili*, No 12, 1986, pp 11-12. Zhonggong Muyangxianwei Nonggongbu, 'Yanjiu Xin Qingkuang Hejue Xin Wenti Tansuo Xin Banfa'.

74. *Zhongguo Shuili*, No 11, 1986, pp 9-10. Wu Haian, 'Anhuaxian Caiyong Duozhong Laodong Jilei Xingshi Xingban Nongtian Shuili'.

75. *Zhongguo Shuili*, No 5, 1988, pp 15-16. Li Sen, 'Wajue Nongcun Neibu Qianli Yikao Qunzhong Zhenxing Shuili'.

76. *Zhongguo Shuili*, No 2, 1989, pp 18-19. Wu Zhenyou, 'Gaige Touzi Banfa Tuixing Laodong Jilei Gong Zhidu'.

77. *Zhonghua Renmin Gongheguo Tudi Guanli Fa*, 25 June 1986, article 3, section 20.

78. *Sichuansheng Tudi Guanli Shishi Banfa*, 2 July 1987, article 2, section 11.

79. Zhongyang Shujichu Nongcun Zhengce Yanjiushi, Guowu Yuan Nongcun Fazhan Yanjiu Zhongxin, 'Nongcun Gaige de Xianzhuang yu Qushi - Quanguo Nongcun Shehui Jingji Dianxing Diaocha Baogao'. 1986.

80. *Zhongguo Nongye Nianjian* 1982. pp 263-264. Zhongguo Nongcun Fazhan Wenti Yanjiuzu, 'Anwei Chuxiandiqu Yanjiuzu, 'Shuangbao Daohu' hou de Fazhan Qushi'.

81. *Nongcun Kuaiji*, No 11, 1984, pp 30-32. 'Yuce Renlao Bianhua Gaohao Tudi Diaocha - Fuxian Sidao de Dadui Shixing 'Renlao Yuce Chengbao Fa' de Diaocha'.

82. Lin Zhili zhubian, *Lianchan Chengbaozhi Jianghua*. Jingji Kexue Chubanshe. Beijing. 1983. pp 66-68.

83. *Lilun Yuekan*, No 3, 1988, pp 43-45. Zhang Ziyi, 'Wanshan Tudi Chengbaozhi de Yi Xiang Zhongyao Cuoshi'.

84. *Nongye Jingji Wenti*, No 6, 1988, pp 34-37. Xue Shexu, 'Woguo Nongye Touzi Gongji Buzhu de Zhuyao Yuanyin'.

85. *Nongcun Jingji*, No 6, 1988, pp 13-14, p 30. Lin Kaifeng, Jiang Zhiwei, 'Nongcun Tudi Chengbao de Wenti yu Zhengce'.

86. *Nongmin Ribao*, 16 January 1986, p 1. 'Yanjin Maimai Tudi'.

87. Guowu Yuan, *Guanyu Zhizhi Maimai, Zuren Tudi de Tongzhi*, 19 November 1983.
88. *Nongcun Jingji*, No 10, 1987, pp 10-12. 'Shifangxian Shixing Tudi 'Liangtianzhi' de Diaocha yu Sikao'.
89. *Nongcun Jingji*, No 12, 1988, pp 12-13. Zhang Maoxin, 'Cong Juntianzhi dao Liangtianzhi - Yilai Zitong-liangxian Tudi Chengbaozhi de Diaocha'.
90. *Nongcun Jingji*, No 11, 1988, pp 21-23. Chen Shuchun, Jie Shurui, 'Qiantian Nongcun Tudi Shidu Guimo Jingying Wenti'.
91. *Tianfu Xinlun*, No 2, 1988, 92-96. Lin Kaifeng, Ren Po, Jiang Zhiwei, 'Sichuansheng Tudi Jingying Guimo Guanzhuang ji 'qi.wu', 'ba.wu' Qijian de Fazhan Qushi he Ying Caiqu de Zhengce'.
92. *Nongcun Jingji*, No 6, 1988, p 36. Cao Kecheng, 'Jianding 'Silian' Tudi Chengbao Hetong Banfa Hao'.
93. Guowu Yuan Bangongding Diaoyanshi, *Guanyu Nongcun Shenhua Gaige de Diaocha*, 7 December 1988, section 3.
94. *Zhonggong Zhejiangshengwei Dangjiao Xuebao*, No 2, 1988, pp 49-53.
95. *Zhonghua Renmin Gongheguo Shuifa*, 21 January 1988.
96. *Zhongguo Shuili*, No 7, 1988, pp 34-36, p 32. Li Yongyue, 'Lun Xiandai Shuifa Zhongde Yongshuiquan'.
97. *Zhongguo Shuili*, No 8, 1989, pp 33-35. Ye Xun, 'Xuexi >Xingzheng Susong Fa< Tigao Yifa Xingzheng Shuiping'.
98. *Nongcun Gongzuo Tongxun*, No 1, 1988, pp 34-35. 'Guanyu Jiaqiang Diji Guanli Gongzuo de Tongzhi'.
99. Zhang Tianxing, Zuigao Renmin Fayuan Yuanzhang, *Zuigao Renmin Fayuan Gongzuo Baogao*, 1 April 1988; 6 April 1987.
100. Yang Yizhan, Zuigao Renmin Jianchayuan Jianchazhang, *Zuigao Renmin Jianchayuan Gongzuo Baogao*, 1 April 1988; 6 April 1987.
101. *Zhongguo Shuili*, No 5, 1989, pp 26-28; No 6, 1989, pp 31-33; No 7, 1989, pp 30-31, p 29 (in three parts). Wu Hehu, ' 'Nongmin Gao Xianfu' Baisu Shimo'.
102. *Zhongguo Shili*, No 7, 1985, p 23.

(in English)

103. Gustafsson, Jan-Erik, *Water Resources Development in the People's Republic of China*. Royal Institute of Technology. Stockholm. 1984.
104. Gustafsson, Jan-Erik, 'A Tentative Overview of Water Management in China', ECARDC, 18-20 November 1989.
105. Nickum, J.E. (edited with an introduction by), *Water Management Organization in the People's Republic of China*. M.E. Sharpe, Inc. New York. 1981.
106. Nickum, J.E., *Irrigation Management in China*. World Bank Staff Working Paper No.545. Washington. 1982.
107. Stone, B., 'Appendix A. The Use of Agricultural Statistics: Some National Aggregate Examples and Current State of the Art' in Randolph Barker and Radha Sinha with Beth Rose, *The Chinese Agricultural Economy*. Westview Press. Boulder. 1982.
108. Vermeer, E.B., *Water Conservancy and Irrigation in China: Social, Economic and Agrotechnical Aspects*. University of Leiden Press. The Hague. 1977.
109. Wittfogel, K.A., *Oriental Despotism: A Comparative Study of Total Power*. Yale University Press. 1964.

APPENDIX

Life-Quality Index of China

Walter H. Aschmoneit

The following pages cannot be called poetry; they are simple and plain, factual and solid answers to a few questions: Which places are the poorest in China, not only in economical terms but also in organizational capacity for development? What is the socio-economic profile of a given county or city in China? How do the counties and cities compare?

It is a manual for those active in development assistance and in sociological and economic research. It will be fully useful only when China finds its own path back to 'perestroika' (*kaifang* = opening, *jiegou gaige* = structural reform) and democratic political reforms.

As a field representative of three European non-governmental organizations (Oxfam, United Kingdom; NOVIB, Holland; Deutsche Welthungerhilfe, Federal Republic of Germany) I had to find out which are the poorest places in China. Government institutions at that time were reluctant to hand out general information. Only on a case to case basis funding agencies were told that this or that county is very poor. Some were really poor, others however were not. In order to have a basis for an objective judgement I developed the life-quality index based on official Chinese statistics.

This analysis has first been tested in a workshop in Beijing on April 4, 1989, and the response was quite positive. I improved the third draft on the basis of the suggestions given to me by the participants of this workshop.

Many people - Chinese and non-Chinese colleagues and friends - helped me gather the material, to design the formula, to compute the data, to draw a first map. The beginning was quite difficult; Mr. Eugen Wehrli brought me on the track and in many discussions particularly with Ms. R. Kuhlmann the concept became gradually clearer. The final editing has been possible with the help of Professor Johannes Küchler (Technical University of Berlin) and Mr. W. Straub (Cartography). I am thanking all.

1. Meaning: Criteria for Development Assistance

The answer given by the statistics is referring to the question 'where are the places in China which are most in need of assistance?' The question 'are there poor places in China?' has been answered in the affirmative. My concern when working in China as the first resident project coordinator for Western NGO's has been: Where are the places to go when selecting new project sites? The Chinese administrators had some answers to this question: It was always a poor county assigned to them for special care by the State Council; in relative terms these places were certainly not well-off, but after some time of looking around it was obvious they did not belong to the group of the very poor administrative units.

Many times I asked this question to a number of different partners in the Chinese administration. Some did not care much about it; for them the foreign exchange earnings were vital - after all it was their institutional task in the administrative set-up. With others

I found contact soon and exchanged information, ideas and concepts. Still the Chinese researchers - brilliant as any place else - did not dare to share the comprehensive statistics and detailed information they had: the bureaucrats still practiced the policy of the cultural revolution: any figure given to a foreigner might later be a state crime. So I had no choice but to follow one of the few lasting principles of Mao Zedong: *Zili gengshen* or: Rely on your own strength!

The source for such an analysis was not classified at all: The *Population Atlas of China* was published in 1987; its data are based on the third vast census of the People's Republic of China in 1982. The first national census was undertaken in 1953, the second in 1964 (see *Population Atlas of China*, 158).

2. Contents: Cultural, Health and Economic Parameters

The Life-Quality-Index is a relative value; in absolute terms it is meaningless. Only by comparing the respective administrative units is this index of a certain meaning. The Life-Quality-Index of rural China complements the rating of administrative units according to the purely economic figure of per-capita-income. The Life-Quality-Index is an aggregate figure composed of the values of

- gross value of industrial and agricultural output per capita
- employment rate
- rate of industrial workers by total employed population
- rate of illiteracy and half-illiteracy
- rate of middle school graduates
- rate of university graduates
- infant mortality rate
- death rate.

Beyond the *economic* data the Life-Quality-Index indicates the *organizational capacity* of the administrative unit to tackle its problems: The better the educational and health systems are organized, the easier problems of comprehensive development may be solved. Or, seeing the other side of the coin: integrated projects are most needed in the places listed below.

3. Data

The data in the population census of 1982 are quite comprehensive. However, a number of questions cannot be answered by the type of data given: There are no figures on national minorities in the counties and urban districts. Also figures which allow us to grasp the status of women are not published in this context. Another serious deficiency in this Population Atlas concerns the data on child mortality in Tibet; they have simply been left out. I had to estimate a figure and after long discussions with a number of experts I chose the figure of 150 per 10,000. This figure is also based on the findings of Trevor Page who made a survey in Tibet in 1988. It is also based on the figures on child mortality in the counties neighbouring the Autonomous Region of Tibet. Despite all these deficiencies I think it is hard to find equally comprehensive data for any other Third World country.

4. Selection: All 2,378 Basic Administrative Units

In this map all administrative units (urban + rural = 2,378 units of basic county level administration) are included in the calculation; a sample page of the printout is reproduced at the end this appendix.

In a first circulation of a print-out (third draft) presented at a NGO-workshop on the Geography of Poverty in China (Beijing, 4 April 1989) I included the rural counties (*xian*) only. For several reasons I now include the urban administrative units as well: Firstly, the rating of the rural counties does not change even if related to a calculation basis including the figures of all administrative units. Second, urban units are included and can be related to rural counties; it can be seen that some cities are also among the bracket of the poorest units.

5. Choice of Parameters: Categories and Units

The Population Atlas lists 17 types of figures:

Category	*Unit*
Population	Person
* Value of industrial and agricultural product per capita in 1982	Yuan
* Population density	Persons/km²
* Gender relation	Males per 100 females
* Median age	Year
* Persons from 0 to 14 years of age	per cent to total population
* Persons of 65 years and older	per cent to to total population
* Women between 15 and 49	per cent to total population
* Birth rate of 1981	Per thousand
+ Death rate in 1981	Per thousand
+ Infant mortality	Per thousand
+ University graduates	Persons per 1,000 population
+ Middle school graduates	Persons per 1,000 population
+ Illiteracy and half-illiteracy	Percentage to total population of 12 years of age and older
* Employment in agriculture, forestry, animal husbandry and fishery	Percentage to total employed labour force
+ Employment in industry	per cent to total employed labour force
+ Employment rate	per cent of employed persons to total population

+   selected for Life-Quality-Index
*   included in listing-columns

6. Weight of Parameters

Among the above 17 parameters given in the Atlas, eight can be considered sufficiently unequivocal as indicators of better or worse physical and cultural life conditions. In order to emphasize the parameters which are very clearly related to *basic needs and fundamental conditions*, one of the parameters in the three groups—economy, culture and health—will be given double weight. The parameters marked (*2) will be counted twice; the figures will either be added (+) as positive values or subtracted as (−) negative values.

Economy:
GVIAO/capita	(+) (*2)
employment in industry	(+) (*1)
employment rate by total population	(+) (*1)

Culture:
rate of illiteracy/half-illiteracy	(−) (*2)
middle school graduates	(+) (*1)
university graduates	(+) (*1)

Health:
child-mortality rate	(−) (*2)
death-rate	(−) (*1)

7. Calculation Method of the "Life-Quality-Index"

7.1. Common denominator: Apples + Eggs?
Currency units (Renminbi), unemployed people, industrial workers, university and middle school graduation certificates, illiterate people, dead babies and other persons cannot be added up to one meaningful figure. But the *Relative deviation from the average* in each category can be added up. This is an abstract category which serves as the common denominator.

7.2. Loaded Average
The average of statistical data (GVIAO per capita, child mortality ...) is taking the population factor into account. The nominal average would be the sum of all 2,387 units' averages divided by the number of units (2,387). The loaded average is found by multiplying the administrative unit's average with the respective county population, adding these 2,387 figures and dividing the sum by the total population of rural China: 1,003,888,739 persons in 1982.

7.3. Definitions
p = population of an administrative unit
p = population of China (= sum of 2,387 units).

Values of a given administrative unit   *Weight of parameters*

x = administrative's unit figure	
x1 = value of GVIAO/capita	n1
x2 = value of employment in industry	n2
x3 = value of employment rate by total population	n3
x4 = value of rate of illiteracy/half-illiteracy	n4
x5 = value of middle school graduates	n5
x6 = value of university graduates	n6
x7 = value of child-mortality rate	n7
x8 = value of death-rate	n8

x = loaded average   c(x) = deviation

The sum of the eight (resp. 11: three basic values being counted twice) figures is the *life-quality index* of the administrative unit. Sorted according to this index the range is from −21,905 to +86,353, zero being average.

7.4. Formulas and Presentation

Using the formula for deviation will always result in positive values; the administrative unit exactly on the total average line will have the value 1; those below the average will have the value < 1; and those above the average have the value > 1. In order to clearly demonstrate that an administrative unit is below average line, it will become a minus-value by simply subtracting 1: this formula is purely for presentation.

Loaded average   Deviation   Presentation

$$\bar{x} = \frac{\sum (x*p)}{\frac{2387}{p}} \qquad\qquad d(x) = \frac{x}{\bar{x}} \qquad\qquad D(x) = \frac{x}{\bar{x}} - 1$$

LQ-Index

$$LQ = \sum_{i=8}^{8} n_i D(x_i)$$

8. Classification in Groups: Map (made by W. Straub)

Group	Value	Number of administrative units
1	> 12	85
2	12	112
3	12 - 6	53
4	6 - 4	64
5	2 - 0	253
6	0 - (-2)	542
7	(-2) - (-4)	625
8	(-4) - (-6)	261
9	(-6) - (-8)	150
10	(-8) - (-12)	130
11	(-12) - (-16)	92
12	< (-16)	11

9. Abbreviations

AB	Autonomous Banner
AC	Autonomous County
AD	Administrative District
AP	Autonomous Prefecture
AR	Autonomous Region
B	Banner
Co.	County
Ci.	City
D	District
FB	Front Banner
FR	Forestry Region
IAD	Industrial-Agricultural District
JB	Joint Banner
L	League
LB	Left Banner
LWFB	Left Wing Front Banner
LWMB	Left Wing Middle Banner
LWRB	Left Wing Rear Banner
MB	Middle Banner
MMAC	Multi-Minority Autonomous County
RB	Rear Banner
RTB	Right Banner
RWFB	Right Wing Front Banner
RWMB	Right Wing Middle Banner
RWRB	Right Wing Rear Banner

SZ   Special Zone
O   County before 15 April 1988
O#   County opened on 15 April 1988
=*   County opened on 5 August 1988
O=   County opened on 23 October 1988.

References

Anonymous, 1981, *The Administrative Divisions of the People's Republic of China 1980*, Cartographic Publishing House, Beijing.

Anonymous, 1988, *Zhonghua Renmin Gongheguo Xingzhengqu Huatuce* (Maps of the Administrative Divisions of the People's Republic of China), Zhongguo Ditu Chubanshe, Cartographic Publishing House, Beijing.

Administrative Office for Foreigners of the Beijing Security Bureau, Publishing and Printing Department) (ed.), 1988, *Dui waiguo ren lüxing kaifang diqu, The Open Places Announced by the Government of the People's Republic*, Beijing, 15.4.1988.

Chen Chao, Wang Xiguang, 1986, *Zhonguo Xian Shi Zhengqu Ziliao Shouce (Handbook for China's County and City Administration)*, Beijing, 339 p.

Li Chengrui et al. (ed.), 1987, *Population Atlas of China*, Beijing, 223 p.

Li Chengrui et al. (ed.), n.d. 1988, *A Census of a Billion People. Papers for International Seminar on China's 1982 Population Census (Population Census Office under the State Council, Department of Population Statistics of the State Statistical Bureau, People's Republic of China*, Beijing, 704 p.

State Bureau of Foreign Experts, PRC (ed.), 1988, *The Foreign Expert's Handbook - A Guide to Living and Working in China*, Beijing, New World Press, 313 p.

Page, Trevor, 1988, *Appraisal Mission: WFP-Assisted Project China 3357. Integrated Agricultural Development Lhasa River Valley, Tibet Autonomous Region, Technical Notes on Agricultural Sociology*, Beijing.

Xinhua News Agency, 1988, *Wo guo you you 38 ge shi xian dui waiguo ren kaifang (Our country has again opened 38 cities and counties to foreigners)*, in Renmin Ribao, 5.8.1988.

RUNNING HEADER

LIST#	RURAL/URBAN UNIT	PREFECTURE	PROVINCE	LQ_IND	GV_LIST	X/OPEN	GVIAO/C	EMPLOY	IND_LA	ILLIT	MID_SC	UNI_G	INF_M	DEATH	POPULATION	P/KM²	GENDER	RUR_LA	BIRTHR	MED_AG	AGE65	UR_RU

LIST#: Listing of the administrative units in order of the life-quality (ascending)
COUNTY/URBAN UNIT: Name of unit in Hanyü Pinyin.
    PREFECTURE: Name of prefecture in Hanyü Pinyin.
        PROVINCE: Name of province in Hanyü Pinyin.
            LQ_IND: Life quality Index on the basis of eight economic, cultural and health data.
                GV_LIS: Listing of units according to the per-capita GVIAO.
                    X/OPEN: Units open to foreigners are marked with "0"; closed units with "x" (open in 1988 only: #,=|).

Components of the Life-Quality-Index:

                GVIAO/C: Per capita Gross Value of Industrial and Agricultural Output per capita of the county.
                    EMPLOY: Employment rate of the unit.
                        IND_LA: Employed Labour in industry in relation to total employed population.
                            ILLIT: Rate of Illiteracy including Semi-Illiteracy.
                                MID_SC: Middle-School Graduates.
                                    UNI_G: University Graduates.
                                        INF_M: Infant Mortality Rate.
                                            DEATH: Deathrate

Not Components, Data for Comparison

                POPULATION: Population of the unit.
                    P/KM²: Persons per KM²
                        GENDER: Gender Relations
                            RUR_LA: Rural Labour Force by total employed population.
                                BIRTHR: Birthrate.
                                    MED_AGE: Median Age
                                        AGE65: Persons aged 65 and above
                                            RU_UR: Listing of rural and urban units.

RUNNING FOOTER WITH LOADED AVERAGES

LIST#	RURAL/URBAN UNIT	PREFECTURE	PROVINCE	LQ_IND	GV_LIST	X/OPEN	GVIAO/C	EMPLOY	IND_LA	ILLIT	MID_SC	UNI_G	INF_M	DEATH	POPULATION	P/KM²	GENDER	RUR_LA	BIRTHR	MED_AG	AGE65	UR_RU
####	CHINA'S AVERAGE			0			491	51,4	9,8	34,7	1608	17	33,7	6,5	402880	353,8	105,2	82,6	21,6	21,9	4,9	##

Listing structure of the Life-Quality Index

LIST#	RURAL ADMIN. UNIT	PREFECTURE	PROVINCE	LQ_IND	GV_LIST	X/OPEN
1	Darlag Co.	Golog Tibet. Aut. Pr.	Qinghai	-21,90517	1790	x
2	Gadê Co.	Golog Tibet. Aut. Pr.	Qinghai	-19,90913	971	x
3	Shache Co.	Kashi Pr.	Xinjiang	-18,65783	984	O#
4	Jigzhi Co.	Golog Tibet. Aut. Pr.	Qinghai	-17,98303	1826	x
5	Jiashi Co.	Kashi Pr.	Xinjiang	-17,78959	128	x
6	Yengisar Co.	Kashi Pr.	Xinjiang	-17,75077	313	x
7	Coqên Co.	Ngari Pr.	Tibet	-16,37539	1222	x
8	Daocheng Co.	Garzê Zang Aut.Pr.	Sichuan	-16,35678	719	x
9	Markam Co.	Qamdo Pr.	Tibet	-16,17149	292	x
10	Lhari Co.	Nagqu Pr.	Tibet	-16,06770	1095	x
11	Butuo Co.	Liangshan Yi Aut.Pr.	Sichuan	-16,01473	365	x
12	Jomda Co.	Qamdo Pr.	Tibet	-15,94922	296	x
13	Jinyang Co.	Liangshan Yi Aut.Pr.	Sichuan	-15,93442	168	x
14	Gê'gyai Co.	Ngari Pr.	Tibet	-15,93255	1176	x
15	Baxoi Co.	Qamdo Pr.	Tibet	-15,90360	293	x
16	Litang Co.	Garzê Zang Aut.Pr.	Sichuan	-15,89218	1239	x
17	Banbar Co.	Qamdo Pr.	Tibet	-15,88759	282	x
18	Yopurga Co.	Kashi Pr.	Xinjiang	-15,87943	851	x
19	Akqi Co.	Kizilsu Kirgiz Aut. Pr.	Xinjiang	-15,86131	329	x
20	Fugong Co.	Nujiang Lisu Aut.Pr.	Yunnan	-15,84066	48	x
21	Gonjo Co.	Qamdo Pr.	Tibet	-15,62402	291	x
22	Nyainrong Co.	Nagqu Pr.	Tibet	-15,61976	1458	x
23	Chindu Co.	Yushu Tibet. Aut. Pr.	Qinghai	-15,57624	1477	x
24	Zhag'yab Co.	Qamdo Pr.	Tibet	-15,52171	295	x
25	Nyêmo Co.	Lhasa Ci.	Tibet	-15,48630	67	x
26	Zogang Co.	Qamdo Pr.	Tibet	-15,48348	301	x
27	Lhorong Co.	Qamdo Pr.	Tibet	-15,45959	127	x
28	Zhaojue Co.	Liangshan Yi Aut.Pr.	Sichuan	-15,43928	305	x
29	Maizhokunggar Co.	Lhasa Ci.	Tibet	-15,39947	586	x
30	Damxung Co.	Lhasa Ci.	Tibet	-15,29845	1345	x
31	Namling Co.	Xigazê Pr.	Tibet	-15,29596	601	x
32	Sog Co.	Nagqu Pr.	Tibet	-15,25449	360	x
33	Baiyu Co.	Garzê Zang Aut.Pr.	Sichuan	-15,21853	720	x
34	Mêdog Co.	Lhasa Ci.	Tibet	-15,14115	85	x
35	Xaitongmoin Co.	Xigazê Pr.	Tibet	-15,09012	807	x
36	Lhünzhub Co.	Lhasa Ci.	Tibet	-15,02123	4	x
37	Bainang Co.	Xigazê Pr.	Tibet	-15,00911	746	x
38	Dêngqên Co.	Qamdo Pr.	Tibet	-15,00617	332	x
39	Biru Co.	Nagqu Pr.	Tibet	-14,95834	400	x
40	Riwoqe Co.	Qamdo Pr.	Tibet	-14,95227	376	x
****	CHINA'S AVERAGE			0		

Sample printout of the Life-Quality Index

GVIAO/C	EMPLOY	IND_LA	ILLIT	MID_SC	UNI_G	INF_M	DEATH	POPULATION	P/KM²	GENDER	RUR_LA	BIRTHR	MED_AG	AGE65	UR_RU
621	45,1	2,9	76,8	365	24	244	25,5	19445	1,0	98,2	84,7	41,8	17,9	3,5	1
378	42,5	2,0	77,2	347	23	216	19,2	19367	3,0	95,4	88,5	36,3	17,9	4,3	2
379	55,5	4,8	47,9	926	13	228	21,4	450857	55,0	104,7	89,0	43,2	22,9	5,5	3
642	42,6	1,4	66,7	532	36	215	18,0	14435	2,0	96,2	82,7	40,8	18,3	4,8	4
207	53,3	1,1	51,4	670	10	205	17,9	218442	31,0	106,4	94,1	42,6	21,2	6,2	5
259	50,7	2,9	41,6	852	12	214	20,1	153587	45,0	105,0	90,3	47,1	20,7	5,8	6
429	58,1	0,0	90,1	113	9	150	17,2	7965	0,3	98,5	92,7	31,1	24,0	7,0	7
336	54,9	1,5	77,7	402	21	166	17,1	23075	4,0	97,2	86,8	32,3	20,6	4,3	8
255	56,5	0,6	88,7	104	6	150	13,3	60340	5,0	94,3	95,2	27,7	22,6	5,2	9
403	51,9	0,7	85,2	144	2	150	15,4	16678	1,0	98,5	89,4	34,9	21,3	5,6	10
272	51,7	2,2	72,9	381	15	154	19,6	119510	70,0	102,3	91,9	48,6	18,0	3,2	11
255	49,0	1,1	83,6	203	7	150	13,7	52506	4,0	94,7	93,8	30,6	21,0	6,0	12
226	51,0	1,0	73,9	386	12	143	21,4	110199	73,0	104,2	93,0	43,1	18,0	3,9	13
419	58,2	0,0	86,8	181	7	150	15,5	8213	0,2	101,8	92,5	38,8	20,9	5,0	14
255	57,0	0,4	81,4	158	9	150	15,1	28986	2,0	94,2	93,3	32,4	22,7	5,2	15
432	49,4	1,4	79,3	391	19	159	16,8	40767	3,0	93,7	87,7	33,5	21,7	4,2	16
252	58,7	0,5	80,5	203	13	150	16,3	22192	3,0	92,9	94,5	34,2	21,6	5,1	17
358	54,2	1,3	41,9	1009	16	198	17,0	94150	31,0	106,6	92,0	41,6	22,7	6,7	18
263	41,1	3,1	32,2	1178	46	217	15,7	22456	2,0	101,3	79,4	46,5	18,1	3,9	19
165	50,9	1,2	72,9	605	12	141	21,9	45943	25,0	102,3	90,9	44,0	17,5	3,6	20
255	65,0	0,3	86,4	368	4	150	12,3	35914	6,0	94,8	96,6	29,2	24,6	6,2	21
494	53,3	0,2	88,1	128	12	150	14,2	19541	2,0	93,8	93,8	33,3	20,3	4,6	22
499	44,1	1,1	75,0	312	15	165	13,5	32130	2,0	92,0	89,1	35,3	17,3	3,7	23
255	57,7	0,4	84,9	207	8	150	11,4	43733	5,0	91,8	96,0	26,8	23,4	6,3	24
178	56,5	0,7	81,4	116	8	150	11,0	22978	7,0	91,0	94,0	34,5	21,0	4,1	25
256	57,4	0,4	87,9	123	7	150	9,5	32779	3,0	93,9	94,1	30,9	21,4	4,6	26
207	55,4	0,5	80,1	206	10	150	12,2	28643	4,0	92,4	94,1	35,4	21,2	5,4	27
257	52,4	2,3	66,2	279	23	149	21,3	189771	72,0	102,1	90,5	47,9	18,1	3,1	28
312	54,4	0,2	79,5	145	9	150	13,1	32878	6,0	93,9	94,7	36,3	20,1	3,8	29
462	51,3	0,2	86,6	102	3	150	10,6	27661	3,0	97,1	90,6	39,7	21,1	6,0	30
314	54,5	0,1	88,6	74	5	150	8,0	50621	6,0	92,8	97,3	35,0	20,7	4,7	31
271	53,5	0,0	80,7	170	10	150	11,1	23240	4,0	97,1	94,1	34,2	21,9	6,7	32
336	52,8	3,4	77,9	300	26	155	15,1	34717	4,0	96,5	89,0	31,9	23,5	5,2	33
188	54,8	6,1	85,0	65	0	150	8,2	7642	0,2	100,3	81,6	21,5	22,3	4,9	34
350	57,9	1,4	81,0	86	8	150	11,7	29947	2,0	95,2	94,9	34,9	21,8	4,3	35
104	43,4	3,2	72,0	114	14	150	10,9	42488	10,0	92,9	89,6	32,0	19,8	4,4	36
341	54,6	0,4	89,0	57	9	150	7,1	30965	13,0	100,1	96,3	34,1	19,8	4,0	37
264	53,4	0,4	82,5	164	5	150	8,1	42585	4,0	96,1	95,2	28,4	21,2	5,6	38
278	52,1	1,6	82,2	144	16	150	10,0	30622	3,0	94,1	91,6	34,9	21,5	6,5	39
274	52,0	0,9	75,9	219	8	150	11,2	27546	5,0	98,8	92,6	32,0	20,4	6,7	40
807	52,1	15,5	32,1	1772	44	31,6	6,4	422157	691,1	105,6	74,3	20,9	22,5	4,9	****

Calculation Table for Averages

Category of Data	Loaded Average	Maximum	Minimum	Nom. Average	Max to Min
Life-Quality-Index	(0.00000000363)	86.353	(21.905)	(1.819)	108.258
GVIAO/per capita	807.21857	28,475.000	70.000	657.913	28,405.000
Indust. Lab / Total Lab.	15.47088	76.900	0.000	12.949	76.900
Employment / Pop.	52.12685	463.300	30.000	51.077	433.300
Illiteracy + Half-Ill.	32.07607	90.100	2.700	35.353	87.400
Middle School Grad.	1,772.95555	4,227.000	0.000	1,631.044	4,227.000
University Grad	43.66033	583.000	0.000	34.015	583.000
Child Mortality (Tibet:150 assumed)	31.58051	319.000	6.000	42.362	313.000
Death Rate	6.35780	25.500	1.300	6.854	24.200

For Comparison (not included in LQ-Index)	Loaded Average	Maximum	Minimum	Nom. Average	Max to Min
Population	4.91856	6,320,829.000	3,836.000	422,156.000	6,316,993.000
Persons at/above the age of 65	105.60176	42.000	0.200	4.710	41.800
Gender-Relations	691.12236	153.800	82.700	105.814	71.100
Persons per sq-km	74.32822	28,357.000	0.100	367.211	28,356.900
Rural Labour	22.51887	97.300	0.000	76.609	
Median Age (Average)	20.93627	31.200	15.600	21.842	
Birth Rate		48.600	9.200	22.743	

Figures in brackets must be read as negative (-) values. Since the operations calculating the values for loaded averages have been including up to the 9th position (x.xxxxxxxx) the loaded average of Life Quality is not exactly zero.

Calculation table for averages

CONTRIBUTORS

Walter Aschmoneit, formerly lecturer at Osnabrück University, is project coordinator (Asia) for Terre des Hommes, Paris and has done research on the modern history of Indochina and China.

Claude Aubert is director of research at the Institut de la Recherche Agronomique, Economies et Sociologies Rurales, Paris. He is the author, with Cheng Ying, of *Les Greniers de Nancang; Chronique d'un village Taiwanais*, Paris 1984.

Flemming Christiansen is lecturer in East Asian Politics, Department of Government, Manchester University. He is co-author of *Die demokratische Bewegung in China*, München 1981 and has published on rural change in China (1978-1989), land questions, private enterprise and related subjects.

Delia Davin is lecturer in East Asian Studies at the University of Leeds. She has written extensively on women, gender and population problems in China. With W.J.F. Jenner, she edited and co-translated *Chinese Lives, an Oral History of Contemporary China*. Pantheon 1987; Macmillan 1988; and Penguin 1989.

Jørgen Delman is a research fellow with the Institute of East Asian Studies, University of Aarhus, Denmark. He worked at the FAO Representation in China as a project administrator in the 1980s. His current field of research is agricultural extension in China.

Athar Hussain is director of the China Research Programme at the London School of Economics. He is the joint editor of *The Chinese Economic Reforms* (London 1983) and *Transforming China's Economy in the Eighties* (London 1988).

Johannes Küchler is professor at the faculty of environmental planning and design (Landschaftsentwicklung) of the Technische Universität Berlin and has done field research in Southeast Asia and China.

Thiagarajan Manoharan is currently senior researcher at the Centre for East and Southeast Asian Studies, University of Copenhagen. He has written on legal matters, rural organizational structure and basic party units and decentralized development.

Ole Odgaard is a postgraduate scholar at the Centre for East and Southeast Asian Studies, University of Copenhagen. He has published a book and several articles on various aspects of the economic and political reforms in post-Mao China.

Vivienne Shue teaches Chinese politics and chairs the Department of Government at Cornell University. She is the author of *Peasant China in Transition: The Dynamics of Development toward Socialism* (Berkeley 1980), and of *The Reach of the State: Sketches of the Chinese Body Politic* (Stanford 1988).

Eduard B. Vermeer teaches economy and history of China at Leiden University. His publications include, *Development of Milk Production in China in the 1980s* (Wageningen 1985), *Economic Development in Provincial China* (CUP 1988), *Trade, War and Religion along the China Coast* (Leiden 1990), and *The Value of Pei-wen as Sources of Local History* (forthcoming). He has served as a consultant in several cooperative projects with the Chinese government.

Clemens Stubbe Østergaard is associate professor in political science and co-director of East Asian Studies at the University of Aarhus, Denmark. He has published and edited a number of books and articles on Chinese politics and society.

INDEX